DISCARDED LIBRARY
CAL POLY HUMBOLDT

Applied
Business
Communication

Applied
Business
Communication

robert c. cornwell
darwin w. manship

Boise State University

wcb WM. C. BROWN
COMPANY PUBLISHERS
2460 Kerper Boulevard, Dubuque, Iowa 52001

Copyright © 1978 by Wm. C. Brown Company Publishers

Library of Congress Catalog Card Number 77-87357

ISBN 0-697-08025-0

All rights reserved. No part of this publication may be
reproduced, stored in a retrieval system, or transmitted, in
any form or by any means, electronic, mechanical, photocopying,
recording or otherwise, without prior written permission of the
publisher.

Printed in the United States of America

Contents

Preface

Applied Business Communication was written to promote the acquiring of successful writing skills by college students who are preparing for the business of life. More specifically, the book is intended to serve those students who are majoring in business subjects.

The need for ability to express ideas clearly is apparent in many business fields. Promotability—even employability—is often determined by the ability to express oneself clearly. The reaction of students and teachers to this need for clarity of expression is, however, often quite different from that of business executives. Some students resent the prospect of being taught the fundamentals of writing, saying that precision is not necessary since the reader can usually "figure out" what is meant. Another of their objections is that the individual's writing style has already been formed and is not likely to change. The result of these differing reactions is that colleges and universities graduate students who do not meet employability levels.

In the past, teachers handled the problem in a variety of ways. One method was to assume that the problem did not really exist. Other methods included the giving of token coverage to fundamentals and allowing students to solve any writing deficiencies by their own methods.

This text differs from others in that it responds to the real writing needs of the student. The basics are neither glossed over nor dismissed, but are instead presented as the necessary foundation for the development of writing skills. The foundation then serves as a stepping stone toward the actual production of effective letters and reports.

Because of the constantly growing need for improving communication skills, the market has been supplied with many kinds of business communication textbooks. However, the authors of this book, after five years of research and experimentation involving students at two universities and one college, have not only recognized a need for an approach to business communication that was not found in any of the available textbooks, but also fulfilled that need. So, rather than learning what other books are NOT, read on to learn what *Applied Business Communication* IS.

Applied Business Communication was written for today's college students. These students want the practical. They would be quick to recognize the verbosities and the impracticalities of the material presented in many of the previous textbooks. We found, typically, a real need for a better understanding of basic writing principles. Some textbooks omit this area, others give it a polite mention in passing, and some relegate it to a position of unimportance by stating a few rules of grammar in an appendix. *Applied Business Communication* presents these writing principles as a portion of the text to furnish a foundation for writing. However, at least two aspects of this presentation are different. First, *Applied Business Communication* presents only those principles that have been found through extensive research to be *practical*. Second, the book shows how to apply each of these principles as a means toward achieving effective communication, using a variety of letters and reports representing realistic business situations as examples. Today's business students are not turned off by this practical, sound approach to good writing.

An additional step that ensures the appropriateness of this book for today's student is seen in the level of readability. We have described the Gunning Fog Index within the text. Application of this index to passages selected at random from the text shows a readability level ranging from 9.7 to 13.2 with a mean of 11.3. This is lower than the readability level of most of the other business communication textbooks. Most of the writing is in the active voice; the words are simple and concrete, and the sentences are short, to make sure that students will be able to gain the real meaning of the writing. While the material has been written so that it will neither tax the students' ability to comprehend nor insult with its simplicity, it will challenge them to put forth a good effort.

This attention to practicality and readability has resulted in a textbook that is somewhat shorter than many others. The admonition, "avoid vain repetition," has been observed. Some ideas have been repeated for emphasis and should, therefore, be of benefit to the students. The teacher who uses this textbook can more easily handle the material within the framework of the academic term. Most important, this text does not omit any of the writing principles that one would find necessary to the teaching and learning of these skills.

The text is organized into six parts. These are:

- Interpersonal and Organizational Communication (two chapters)
- The Purposes of Human Interaction (one chapter)
- The Foundation of Writing Skills (two chapters)
- The Techniques of Business Writing (six chapters)
- Oral Communication (one chapter)
- Report Writing (three chapters)

Each part is a logical step in the building of writing skills. The first part establishes a foundation for communication by explaining the process and the participants. It also describes the methods of transmitting messages (verbal and nonverbal), and small group communication in business organizations.

The second part explains the objectives of communication, and includes an introduction to the application of logic as a basis for achieving these objectives.

Part three covers the fundamentals of writing (words, sentences, and paragraphs), and gives special attention to the structure of sentences. This part explains how words function to supplement each other so as to effect a transfer of meaning from the sender to the receiver. The practicality of good grammar is also explained. It should be emphasized at this point that the teacher need not be a master teacher of grammar to teach this unit.

The essence of the textbook is in part four. The first chapter of this part explains the mechanics of writing and shows examples that point up the importance of appearance and letter format. Punctuation is also presented here as a writing tool because of the special effect that can be achieved by the skillful use of punctuation.

The student learns in the next chapter how to apply the principles of psychology to letter writing through organization and by giving careful attention to the techniques of emphasis, viewpoint, letter tone, and meaningful expressions.

In the remaining four chapters of part four, these writing principles are applied to the writing of most kinds of business letters which include letters conveying good news, bad news, routine requests, and messages designed to persuade. The student will also apply his learning to the writing of sales and collection letters. Chapter 10 covers the many kinds of letters associated with the job-getting process—the personal data sheet, the letter of application, letters of followup, and letters accepting and declining employment. This chapter also covers the interview by reason of its close association with this phase of communication.

The final chapter (11) of this part is designed to add finesse to each student's writing. The emphasis here is on logic. To our knowledge, this subject is not handled in this manner in any other textbook. The special treatment given this important topic will add measurably to the quality and effectiveness of each person's writing.

Part five applies the principles of communication to the oral presentation of business data. This includes the presenting of oral reports, the giving of instructions, and the dictating of business information. A special section covers an up-to-date look at the concept of word processing.

Finally, part six covers all aspects of report writing. This three-chapter presentation includes the following topics: Classification of Reports, The Reason for Business Reports, Identification of Business Problems, Methods of Gathering Data, Secondary and Primary Research, Interpreting Business Data, Developing the Report Outline, Applying Writing Fundamentals, Parts of the Report, and Appearance of the Report.

This thorough coverage of the elements of report writing enables the student to develop complete business reports. Here again, the emphasis is on the practical.

An appendix includes special and supplementary material on grammar, spelling, and report writing. One section offers helpful hints to both teachers and students.

The appendix also includes one "Reading." After giving considerable thought to the practicality of readings, we settled on this one because of its powerful message and its particular pertinence to writing excellence. We think most teachers will want their students to read it and apply its message.

The careful arrangement of this textbook into these parts gives it unsurpassed flexibility. For example, many teachers cover report writing as a separate course. Those teachers can easily omit part six if they so desire. Others may teach a separate course in Communication Theory, or Interpersonal Communication. They will, in all likelihood, omit a portion or all of part one. Each part has built-in flexibility that will enable the teacher to spend more or less time on it by varying the emphasis given to certain principles.

Applied Business Communication contains abundant internal learning aids. No one teacher is likely to use all the end-of-chapter exercises, cases, and writing assignments. Their inclusion recognizes the differing preference of each teacher and makes allowances for the selection of those learning aids that are best suited to the needs of each group of students. Many of the cases and writing assignments are adapted from actual business experiences and describe situations to which the students can easily relate.

The intermittent inclusion of analogies assists the student in reading and understanding the text and maintains interest in the material. The writing style also promotes those goals.

Even though many examples of letters are shown, we have tried to vary the writing style of each so that the students will not be tempted to mimic a certain style. We believe that the best approach is to teach certain principles and allow the students to apply their own writing style within those principles. For that reason, the text does not include a "recipe" for every kind of business letter. Students who use texts that follow this cookbook approach, tend to lift phrases, sentences, and entire letters out of context and adapt them to "fit" similar situations. This results in letters that are "almost right," and stereotyped language that is often considerably less than effective.

We would say, then, that *Applied Business Communication* approaches the matter of writing on an individualized basis. Even though certain writing principles are rather rigid, the flexibility of wording and creativity is, in the final analysis, limited only by the individual student. The teacher who follows this approach will enjoy the rewards of sound results.

Supplementary to this textbook, and of significant benefit to the teacher, is a unique teacher's manual. This manual goes beyond the traditional approach of supplying answers to end-of-chapter exercises, furnishing suggested test questions, and analyzing case studies.

In addition to each of those features, the manual gives helpful hints and suggestions pertaining to each of the chapters in the text. These are based on the combined experiences of the authors and reflect questions and comments received from students. We believe these tips will add measurably to the teacher's ability to teach with confidence and familiarity in each of the subject areas.

The teacher's manual also contains special exercises that the teacher may adapt for classroom exercises or additional writing assignments for the students. The manual will help the teacher to be an expert in each of the subject areas.

Applied Business Communication represents a fresh, new look at the practical approach to teaching and learning business writing.

PART 1

Interpersonal and Organizational Communication

Communication: The Process, the People, and the Organization

As you study the theory in this introductory chapter, you will:

1. develop an increased awareness of the scope and importance of communication in interpersonal and organizational settings.

2. learn why communication skill requirements have been increasing rapidly in recent years.

3. understand more thoroughly the respective roles of senders and receivers in the human transaction.

4. appreciate the importance of and need for empathy when interacting with others.

5. learn how providing employees with a knowledge of results of their work activities can generate higher morale and productivity.

6. see how communication can contribute to the motivation of workers.

7. develop an understanding of conflict in organizational behavior and learn how communication can be used to resolve this conflict.

One of the most-used words in modern-day business vernacular is *communication*. This word is most frequently used by business men and women as they discuss the need to exchange operational and nonoperational information within the structure of the organization. The operational data pertain to the specific objectives of the firm (business information), whereas the nonoperational data relate particularly to the interpersonal dimension of working together (social information).

Whatever meanings are assigned to the term *communication,* we know that it is a factor crucial to the successful operation of any form of organized activity. All of the functional phases of management processes—planning, organizing, staffing, directing, and controlling—are based on the assumption that communication will serve as a catalyst in the activity. Planning, for example, requires a substantial amount of communication with the managers and employees in all organizational units. Similarly, information relating to other management duties must be transmitted to appropriate levels of the organization.

The entire concept of Management by Objectives (MBO) is based on the assumption that there will be adequate communications throughout the organization to facilitate employer/employee goal-setting activities. In short, any type of management activity that involves people requires effective communication skills. Communication is the ingredient that makes organization possible.

The Need for Better Communication Skills

Generally, the need for communication increases in direct proportion to the number of communicators involved. The more people who participate in a joint effort, the greater will be the need for communication among them. Other factors, such as the nature of the work performed and the type of organization, will also affect this exchange among workers. The continued growth of our population base and subsequent growth of our business organizations have led to complexities of human interaction requiring a high level of communication skill.

These organizations have evolved into very complex structures for reasons other than sheer population expansion. Specialization has created a need for the transmission of data not previously required. Furthermore, the technical nature of the data has demanded that workers communicate with a higher degree of precision than ever before. Automation and computer technology have led to the development of some very sophisticated techniques for performing work, and with these developments has come the need for more interaction among workers than was previously required. Naturally, this interaction has led to an interdependence among employees.

Recordkeeping requirements of various local, state, and national governments have created an even greater need for effective communication. Regulations imposed upon business organizations in the form of tax laws, safety requirements, interstate commerce rulings, and state and federal communication mandates have all contributed to the need for more information to be processed.

Management's Response to the Need for Better Skills

Management has responded to this need for better communication skills. Businesses have spent millions of dollars and many hours in recent years upgrading these skills. Professionals in communication training have presented many workshops and seminars to business people throughout the country. Certainly those charged with the responsibility of managing business and industry cannot be accused of letting the problem slide. These efforts have been at least partially successful in that there is probably a greater awareness of the importance of communication today than ever before. This awareness, however, does not solve the problem of communication difficulties that are common to so many of us.

Perhaps the problem we encounter in our communication training is that the emphasis is too often placed on the "how to" approach. Unfortunately, there is no specific set of behavioral patterns that will permit us to overcome what we have chosen to call communication problems. We contend that it is *people* and not *things* that are at the heart of the problem. Therefore, we need to examine the characteristics of the person who is doing a particular job, rather than to examine only the job itself. This is not to say that the job is an unimportant factor in the process; what we are saying is that it is secondary to the human element.

The Communication Process

To understand the significance of communication as it pertains to interpersonal and organizational activity, we need to have a basic understanding of the communication process itself. We need to be able to answer many questions about what happens when one person tries to transfer meaning and understanding to another. We also need to know the steps involved and what needs to happen at each step to be better able to understand each other as we work together toward common goals.

Many models and diagrams have been developed for explaining the process of communication. Common to all of these explanations are such terms as *senders, information,* and *receivers.* Each of these elements in the process receives varying degrees of emphasis depending upon the focus of the particular author. For our purposes, we will create a six-step procedure to develop an understanding of what is involved in this relatively complex phenomenon (table 1.1).

The steps include: Ideating, Encoding, Transmitting, Receiving, Decoding, and Acting. The first three steps involve action on the part of the sender—the last three involve action on the part of the receiver. Before we begin our analysis of each of these steps, we should keep in mind that in our day-to-day communication activities we do not normally think of any one transmission of information as being necessarily separate from other transmissions. In other words, several communication processes or cycles will probably be taking place almost simultaneously. For example:

> Mary: "John, I want to tell you about the visitor I had yesterday."
> John: "I'd like to hear about it. Judging by the way you said it, it sounds interesting."

The Participants	The Steps	The Action	The Variables	Table 1.1
				The Communication Process
Responsibility of the Sender	Ideating	Developing the idea to be communicated	Determined by the situation, motivation, sender's background	
	Encoding	Selecting the symbols that represent the idea	Determined by sender's background, education, perception of the situation and of the receiver	
	Transmitting	Sending the symbols— verbals and nonverbals	Determined by the most appropriate medium available	
Responsibility of the Receiver	Receiving	Perceiving— listening, observing, reading	Determined by the receiver's sensory capabilities and motivation	
	Decoding	Interpreting that which was perceived— assigning meaning to inputs	Determined by the receiver's background, education, perception of the situation and of the sender	
	Acting	Doing something with that which has been perceived— speaking, gesturing, reflecting	Determined by the receiver's felt need to respond	

In this situation, two primary transmissions are taking place at almost the same time. Mary is sending a message to John, and John is sending one to Mary. For purposes of analysis we could consider each message apart from the other, but we would have to do so within the context of the total communication situation.

Let us now consider each step in the communication process as identified in table 1.1. The first step, Ideating, is simply the idea stage. It is at this point that the sender develops the idea (message) to be transferred to the receiver. No words have been spoken, no sounds have been uttered. Ideating, then, is a mental procedure wherein the message is conceived.

The Encoding step is next. This requires that the sender select the various symbols that will represent the information to be developed in the idea stage. The signs selected may be words (the most common symbols used in the modern world), or some form of kinesic behavior such as gestures or facial expressions. Also, as we will discuss further in this chapter, the *way* in which something is said (paralanguage) will have an influence on the communication.

The message (idea) is next transmitted (sent) to the intended receiver. This message can be transmitted in several ways, depending upon the situation. Methods of transmission include speaking, gesturing, and writing. Naturally, speaking face to face with the receiver has many advantages over other methods of communication. First of all, the speaker can take advantage of the nonverbal techniques that are not available otherwise. Often these nonverbal cues, such as gestures and facial expressions, can enrich the transmission by allowing the sender to add different shades of meaning to what is spoken. Also, face-to-face communication has the advantage of relatively unlimited cycles. If the message is not understood the first time it is sent, the sender can simply repeat it in a modified form. Finally, the spontaneity of face-to-face delivery can improve the quality of the communication. Conversely, the situation may require that a written record be available for future reference. Presumably, the telephone would have some advantages over the written form but fewer than would a face-to-face encounter.

After the message has been developed, encoded, and sent, the task is, for the moment, finished. At this point, the receiver takes over by perceiving the message (receiving), decoding it (interpreting), and taking some sort of action in response to it.

As the receiver hears, reads, or otherwise senses the transmission, sensory capabilities become particularly important. We perceive only according to our abilities to see, hear, touch, taste, and smell. Naturally, these abilities will vary among individuals and account for some interesting problems in communication. Perceiving is, of course, tied to decoding in that both are dependent upon past experiences of the receiver. We will discuss later in this chapter the significance of one's background as it is related to communication. Suffice it to say for now that perception is a key ingredient in effective communication, and good communicators will remember this point.

Decoding is the second major responsibility of the receiver. During this stage in the communication process, we make interpretations of the message that is received. Meanings are assigned to the various symbols transmitted by the sender. If there is a high degree of agreement between what the sender intended and what the receiver understood, then we have a reasonably accurate effect.

The last step in the communication process, Acting (taking action), gives the sender some indication of the success in getting the message to the receiver. This action step is often referred to as *feedback*. Feedback is vital to the communication process, for without it we would have no evidence of the accuracy of our transmissions. The action step of one process is, of course, the first part of a new communication; therefore, we can see how interdependent and simultaneous several transmissions are in any situation.

Perception and Reality

When we speak of perception in a communication sense, we are talking about the way one *sees* things. The things that one sees can be called *reality*. By definition, everything that *is* can be called reality. It is everything that exists in the real world. A discussion of reality is important at this time for two reasons. First, we perceive only a portion of reality. Second, we seem to be influenced more by our perception of reality than we are by reality itself. Many communication problems result from nothing more than perceptual differences between communicators.

By considering selected aspects of reality, we may be better able to understand why these perceptual differences exist.[1] The first aspect

1. For an in-depth analysis of these characteristics of reality, see Raymond V. Lesikar, *Business Communication: Theory and Application*, rev. ed. (Homewood, Ill.: Richard D. Irwin, Inc., 1972).

that we should examine is the unending nature of reality. The infinity of reality can overwhelm our sensory capacities. We are not able to perceive everything there is about any given thing in reality. Because of this inability, we attend to only certain things that attract our attention. Perhaps a good example of this is an executed football play. With twenty-two players and six officials all going in different directions at essentially the same time, and with a mass of spectators viewing the scene, each from a somewhat different vantage point, there is little wonder that the same play is seen differently by each person. This situation is especially true when we recognize that personal biases also tend to distort our perception of things. Whether we mean to or not, we often see only what we want to see.

In addition to the infinity of reality, we must also realize that no two things in the world are exactly alike. This condition is called the uniqueness of reality. The differences may be so slight that they are insignificant, but they may also be the cause of communication problems. For example, the tendency for us to categorize others has led to many difficulties—some with serious consequences. We should point out that while not all stereotyping or classifying is undesirable, it often is fraught with problems. The basis for attitudes about different races is a classic example of inappropriate stereotyping.

A third aspect of reality is that of change. All things in the real world change; reality is dynamic. Of course, the changes vary in degree and intensity, but they do occur. This information is important to us as communicators because we tend to make decisions about reality that are based in part on our previous experiences with it. Obviously, if things are no longer as they once were, a static viewpoint will lead only to a further misperception of the present event. An important point to note at this time is that animate objects (people, for example) change more quickly than do inanimate objects (buildings, roadways, statues, etc.). It becomes obvious, then, that we must be aware of the danger of perceiving others from a static viewpoint.

We can see, now, how important accurate perception is to the communication process. We should recognize that, while each step in the basic process is important, encoding, receiving, and decoding are crucial to effective communication. The sender of a message must encode according to the perceptual capabilities of the receiver, and the receiver must decode with a similar concern for the sender.

The Importance of Empathy

One of the frailties of human beings that is often the cause of communication problems is the tendency to perceive a situation by using a personal frame of reference exclusively. Stated another way, we tend to look at things only to the extent that they affect us. Seldom do we try to understand why another person may see the same situation differently.

To be successful communicators, we must be able to remove the personal bias from the situation by developing the *you viewpoint* rather than the *me viewpoint*. Projecting oneself into the role of the other person is called *empathy*, and it is a critical prerequisite for better understanding among people. Applied to our steps in the communication process, this *you viewpoint* becomes the *receiver viewpoint*. As we will see in later chapters, the receiver viewpoint is a basic requirement of effective written communication.

Other Communication Strategies

Up to this point, we have been concerned with some of the more general considerations of communication and how important the topic is to the successful operation of the enterprise. Because communication is so much a part of all phases of business activity, we can benefit from an understanding of its impact in specific areas of concern.

Communication and Knowledge of Results

Human behavior is obviously very complex and many variables influence what a person does and how that person does it. Since good managers seek to learn ways to increase productivity and employee satisfaction, an awareness of the importance of feedback is essential. The term *knowledge of results* refers to the information that is fed back to employees who perform tasks within the organization. Research suggests to us that workers generally improve their rate of productivity and efficiency when they are told the results of their previous efforts.[2]

2. R. Henry Migliore, "Improving Worker Productivity Through Communicating Knowledge of Work Results," *Human Resource Management*, (Ann Arbor, Mich.: University of Michigan, Graduate School of Business, Summer 1970), pp. 26-32.

Information of this nature can be communicated to employees by holding regularly scheduled meetings to discuss matters relative to the work being done, problems common to all workers, trends in the business, etc. Written communications can be sent to the workers telling them of production results and providing other information pertinent to their jobs. Bulletin boards can be used as "communication centers" where all employees can obtain specific figures and facts about the work they have done and are doing. Too often a company will spend all its efforts looking ahead to what *will* be done when they might benefit as much or more by looking back at what *has been* done.

Communication and Motivation

Providing employees with information about the work they have done is important to future productivity efforts because workers seem to be better motivated as a result. Motivation can also be provided by allowing employees to participate in the goal-setting activities usually performed exclusively by management.

Generally, top management will establish the goals of the organization and communicate them downward to the appropriate department and its management group. Supervisors are then given the information; they, in turn, pass it on to the employees who perform the specific functions. Often the employee on the bottom of the communication chain is so far removed from the goal-setting activity that it is difficult, if not impossible, to identify with it. Yet, management expects every employee to see the mutuality of goals and interests. Little wonder that employees have a problem in seeing how their goals coincide with those of the organization! Attempts to bridge the gap in this context have been made through job enrichment, job enlargement, and mutual goal setting such as that suggested by the procedure referred to earlier in the chapter as MBO.

Communication and Resolution of Conflict

Many managers believe that their primary responsibility is to perform the basic management functions in such a way that they are free to deal with matters which arise out of conflict. Methods of resolving conflict vary with the type of leadership offered, the nature of the problem, the organizational and time constraints, and the individuals involved. While no one procedure will always serve to satisfy every problem involving conflict, the method that seems to be most effective is the one that allows participants to present their position and case. This method is often called problem solving or confrontation. Burke[3] has studied the various methods of resolving organizational conflict and has identified them as Withdrawal, Smoothing, Compromise, Forcing, and Confrontation. Each of these methods is used to some degree and each results in a different degree of satisfaction and effectiveness. Naturally, communication is a key ingredient in resolving operational problems to the extent that predetermined goals and objectives can be obtained. Good managers, then, will strive to establish the proper communication climate that will permit the free and open exchange of ideas and feelings.

Summary

A key word in organizational environments today is *communication*. This factor is an important ingredient for the successful interaction of people who work together. Though communication means different things to different people, businesses have recognized its importance and have taken positive steps to improve skills in this area. While not all efforts to improve communication skills within organizations have brought immediate results, there has developed an increased awareness of its importance.

Essential to the improvement of communication skills is an understanding of the basic process of transferring meaning from one person to another. The critical steps in the process are Ideating, Encoding, Transmitting, Receiving, Decoding, and Acting. Knowledge of what each of these steps involves is important to both the sender and the receiver of a message.

Because the Receiving Step in the communication process requires that we perceive a portion of reality, we must understand the relationship between *perception* and *reality*. This understanding, of course, involves a knowledge of the characteristics of infinity, dynamics (change), and uniqueness. Pervading all aspects of communi-

3. Ronald J. Burke, "Methods of Resolving Superior-subordinate Conflict," *Readings in Interpersonal and Organizational Communication* (Boston: Holbrook Press, 1973), pp. 218-37.

cation, naturally, is the need to empathize with others in the human transaction.

Communication strategies include providing workers with a knowledge of their results, understanding how communication facilitates motivation, and knowing how to use communication to resolve conflict.

1. Develop a meaningful definition of the term *communication.* Compare your definition with those of other members of the class. Modify your approach, if necessary, to have a more meaningful and understandable definition of the term.

2. Do you think management, in general, has an adequate understanding of what effective communication really involves? Why?

3. Explain the statement that many communication problems result from nothing more than perception differences between communicators.

4. Which steps in the communication process as described in this chapter could possibly be factors that cause communication problems? Discuss each one.

5. Which steps in the communication process are probably *most likely* to be the cause of communication problems? Support your choice.

6. What is a synonym for encoding? for decoding?

7. Do you think we are influenced more by our perception of reality than we are by reality itself? Explain your answer.

8. Why is it never possible to perceive reality as it really is?

9. Do you think people who have a more accurate perception of reality are more successful than others? Why?

10. Do you think it would be easier to change the perceptions of young people than it would be to change those of older people? Why?

11. Why do you suppose it is important that workers have a knowledge of the results of their efforts? Why would knowing what they have done in the past work periods have an effect on future performance?

12. Explain how communication influences the level of motivation in workers.

13. How is the type of leadership related to methods of conflict resolution?

14. How could time act as a constraint in the context of conflict resolution methods?

15. Do you think it is ever possible to have organizational activity without some type of conflict? Is all conflict in organizations necessarily bad? In what instances would it not be bad?

16. Some theorists suggest that an international or universal language be developed that would allow all people throughout the world to communicate with one another. Do you think this *unilanguage* would lead to better understanding among nations? Do you think we would then be able to overcome communication problems that are due to cultural differences, or do you think cultural differences go beyond the language problem? Explain!

17. Do you think it is necessary to have both a sender and a receiver in order to have communication? Why?
18. Do you think it is possible to communicate with an inanimate (nonliving) object? Why or why not?
19. Why is empathy such a significant factor in effective communication?
20. Why is it that two people who observe the same event may give conflicting views about what they have seen and/or heard?
21. Select and read an article on any aspect of communication from a current business periodical. Develop a one-page, typewritten abstract of the article and include the necessary source information (author, title of article, title of publication, date, and page numbers). Write a one-page evaluation and analysis of the article showing how the subject matter relates to the communication theory presented in chapter 1.

Behavioral Considerations in Business

2

A study of information in this chapter will allow the reader to:

1. identify many of the nonverbal cues that are transmitted and be able to relate them to the transfer of meaning and understanding in human relationships.

2. learn the barriers to effective listening and corrective measures that can be taken to improve this skill.

3. better understand the important role that small group communication plays in the modern business firm.

Through the study of psychology and human relations, we have learned that human beings have many predictable patterns of action and reaction. Most of these behavior patterns exist regardless of whether the individual is fulfilling the role of a member of a household, a citizen in the community, or a worker on the job. While it is not the objective of this book to examine all aspects of behavior, we can learn much about performance on the job if we can understand certain things about why an individual responds to events in an organizational environment. This chapter, then, considers nonverbal communication, listening skills, and small group communication in an effort to increase our knowledge and understanding of the human dimension.

Nonverbal Communication

Within the broad spectrum of communication we have several modes available to us that permit the transmission of messages. This book, of course, focuses on writing as a basic mode. Another method is nonverbal behavior. Interesting and important relationships exist between written and nonverbal communication.

By way of background, we should know that a considerable amount of information is transmitted in nonverbal form. Harrison[1] reported that we communicate as much as 65 percent of the social meaning of a message through this "silent message" channel.

Attitude is another word for social meaning, and it refers to the way we feel about a person, an object, or a situation. Our attitude has a tendency to show through these silent messages.

1. Randall Harrison, "Nonverbal Communication: Explorations into Time, Space, Action, and Object," in *Dimensions in Communication: Readings,* 2d ed., James H. Campbell and Hal W. Hepler, ed. (Belmont, Calif.: Wadsworth Publishing Company, 1970), p. 256.

Everyone communicates by using such messages, and most of us do it without even being aware that it is happening. Furthermore, we apparently do not need to be trained to communicate nonverbally; we seem to do it automatically. Generally, we study nonverbal communication by classifying behavior into three distinct but related topics: proxemics, kinesics, and paralanguage.

Proxemics pertains to space and how we use it to communicate. Generally, we enjoy being physically close to things that we consider to be positive, and physically distant from those things that we consider to be negative. The ultimate expression of liking in this context, of course, is the act of touching. The handshake, a form of touching, is a good example of how attitudes toward others can be revealed. The variations in handshakes may tell a great deal about how one feels about another person, although it is possible to shake hands with another person without revealing much at all in the way of attitude. The conventional handshake with a firm, but not excessive, grip may do little more than meet the social requirement of our culture. However, variations in this basic handshake may be easily detected. An excessively firm handshake may communicate something about the aggressiveness of the person involved, or it may say something about the extent of joy over the meeting itself. Please note, though, that we must interpret any nonverbal behavior within the context of its immediate situation. The same nonverbal cue can mean two entirely different things, depending upon the circumstances surrounding the event.

An abbreviated handshake (quick release) could have several meanings. If it is a particularly short handshake, we could interpret it to mean that the one who terminated the contact is desirous of increasing the "distance" between the two. The lengthy handshake could mean anything from an expression of liking to a lack of knowing what the proper holding time should be.

More subtle ways exist wherein we communicate attitudes that are also included under the heading of proxemics. Have you ever noticed *how* a listener sits in a chair in relation to the subject being discussed? Generally one will sit forward while listening to and/or discussing a favorable or positive point. Often, when the listener moves away (to the back of the chair), this movement indicates a rejection of the idea under consideration.

Where we sit in a classroom, when given a choice, communicates something also. A student who always chooses to sit toward the back of the room may do so to avoid getting involved with class discussions, or being called upon by the teacher. It may also be that the student prefers to sleep or do homework for another class. On the other hand, one may sit up front for just the opposite reasons—or perhaps one may be hard-of-hearing or have impaired vision and be unable to see the chalkboard from the back of the room. Notice where you sit when given a choice. Do you sit near the same person whenever possible? If so, is this act saying something about your attitude toward that person?

A significant relationship seems to exist between space and power. Usually the more power (status) one has, the more space one is allocated. This evidence may be seen in the size of the house, the car, and certainly the office in the business organization. Have you observed that, as individuals move up in the organization, they usually need less space to perform the work they do, and that they receive more space in which to do it? We simply expect that those with the most power will be given the most space. This relationship between space and power is an example of a nonverbal cue.

Personal space and our use of it is also a factor in communication. Each of us has a need for personal space and this zone may be anywhere between eighteen and twenty-five inches from the individual. A failure to respect this personal "bubble" can lead to interpersonal communication problems.

Remember when someone stood too close to you while engaging in a conversation? Were you inclined to retreat to a more comfortable distance? Maybe those who are not aware of this personal space requirement are at a distinct disadvantage. Certainly such a person would be at a disadvantage in communicating with others.

Often we stake claim to certain physical areas within our own homes, at work, or in play areas. In the home, we may claim a specific chair in the living room, and at the dinner table we often feel ownership of a certain seat. We become uncomfortable if another person invades our territory.

Kinesics pertains to the study of body motions. Again, many attitudes are transmitted through this nonverbal form. This study of motion is more commonly known as *body language*, a term that is very descriptive. The three most visible aspects of body language are facial expressions, gestures, and posture.

Because we direct our attention mostly to a speaker's face, facial expressions play a significant role in supplementing the words we use.

Movements of various parts of the face (nose, eyes, lips, cheeks, etc.) add shades of meaning to the spoken message. Often we can determine very easily how a person feels about the subject being discussed simply by watching the facial expressions. When there is a conflict between what a person speaks and what the expressions say, we tend to believe the nonverbal message. Incidentally, the phrase *poker face* describes the lack of any expression.

Gestures such as those made with the arms and hands can mean many things. We can use our arms and hands to emphasize a point. By placing the palms of our hands toward us we can imply that we are receptive to the idea being discussed. Conversely, we can indicate our disagreement with the idea by placing the palms outward. Even the simple act of waving to another person can carry any one of several meanings depending on how the waving motions are made.

The history of the western United States is replete with examples of nonverbal communications between the Indians and the settlers. Until interpreters came on the scene, all of the communication between the two groups was composed of sign language. Consider the many different signs you use in your day-to-day activities to communicate meaning to others. The posture we assume also communicates attitudes. Squared shoulders, protruded chest, spread feet, and hands on hips may all suggest power. Stooped shoulders, hands together, and head bowed often imply the absence of power. A relaxed body position may communicate power and command. When two persons are communicating in a face-to-face exchange, the astute observer may be able to determine which of the two possesses the most power. In most instances, the more powerful one will be in the more relaxed position. Psychologists have suggested that one who perceives himself as being in command of a situation will feel it unnecessary to be especially alert, tense, or defensive. Such displays of power, or lack of power, are quickly seen in situations where there are obvious superior/subordinate differences as defined by the organizational structure. In other words, bosses tend to display positions of power and workers tend to display positions of compliance.

Paralanguage pertains to *how* something is said rather than to *what* is said. We can detect several shades of meaning merely by listening for such things as the speed of delivery, the gutteral sounds that accompany the words, and the pitch and volume of the voice.

We associate a high rate of delivery with anger, excitement, or anxiety, whereas we interpret the slow rate to mean boredom, pensiveness, or even reluctance. The high-pitched voice can reveal a positive or negative attitude depending upon the situation. Similarly, volume can relate to pleasantness or unpleasantness, depending upon the context in which it is used.

Nonverbal Communication and the Letter

While it may be easier to associate nonverbal cues with face-to-face transactions, it is important that we see how our written communications are affected by nonverbal elements. Appearance, tone, and emphasis are all elements of our writing that can communicate in nonverbal ways.

The appearance of our letters will certainly tell our readers something about us. We should, therefore, make certain that the body of the letter is properly placed, that we use a good quality paper, and that our typing is neat and erasures clean. Such things as the design of a letterhead and the color of ink used can affect the overall impression our communications make.

Another important nonverbal factor that affects written communication is time. If we are late in corresponding with someone about a business or personal matter, it may be interpreted to mean that the situation has a low priority in relation to other work that must be done. This delay can be a serious matter if the receiver of our message has given it a higher priority than we have. It is important, therefore, that we be as prompt as possible in developing our written communications.

Listening

Humans are gregarious creatures; they like to be around others, and enjoy communicating with them. An important part of this interaction is that of listening to others. In fact, a considerable part of our waking hours is spent listening. Of all the perceptive skills we possess, we have become more dependent upon listening to obtain information than upon any other. Apparently, it is thought that this skill is learned automatically because little, if any, training is ever provided in this area of human communication. Only a few educational institutions offer formalized instruction that pertains exclusively, or even primarily, to the subject of listening.

If we spend so much of our time listening to others, it will help us to know more about how to listen, how to identify the barriers to effective listening, and how to overcome them.

Have you noticed how, when two persons are engaged in a discussion, one seems to be preparing a rebuttal to what the other is saying rather than listening to what is being said? Is it any wonder that much of what is said is never heard and that much of what is heard is so often forgotten? Have you ever been involved in a discussion where one person seemed to be taking "mental excursions" to some far-off place rather than listening to what was being said? Or, have you ever seen someone so angry that it was impossible to hear anything that was being said, either by the angry person or by any one else involved?

These are all situations that are plagued with communication problems derived from poor listening habits. In order to understand fully the basis of the problem we need to understand something about human nature. These human elements represent barriers to effective listening.

Self-Interest

We know that we tend to perceive things (reality) as they relate to our own personal situation. Because of this perception, we tend to direct our attention only to information that is in accordance with our own needs and desires. Often, when listening to others, we are exposed to information that has little if any direct bearing on us; more likely, this information will be of primary concern to the person speaking. (Certainly this is the case when *we* are doing the speaking.) When we tune out information that does not correspond to our own needs, we, in effect, do not listen. Self-interest, then, causes us to screen or filter the information that is sent to us.

Personal Distractions

Physical and psychological distractions cause us to miss a certain amount of information. If we are experiencing physical pain, for example, our attention may well be distracted from the point the speaker is trying to establish. Or, we may stray from listening to the speaker because of some recent unpleasantness. Similarly, extraneous noise can distract us.

Speaker Delivery

Have you ever been caught up by a speaker's style of delivery rather than by what was being said? A listener can easily become more involved in the delivery than in the message. If a person constantly turns the ring on the finger while speaking, this action distracts the listener. Other forms of speaker behavior which tends to distract listeners include playing with objects such as pens or pencils, tugging at clothing, walking back and forth in a particular pattern, uttering excessive uh's and ah's between phrases, and making unusual or untimely facial expressions. Good listeners will not allow themselves to become distracted by such nonlistening activities.

Tendency to Evaluate

As human beings, we tend to evaluate what we hear. This tendency is vitally important to logical analysis, but it can also be detrimental to effective listening if it is done prematurely. Too often we evaluate only a part of what is being said. We do not wait to hear all that is to be said about a particular point. While we are busy evaluating part of the information, we are missing other key elements as they are being presented.

Presets

Perhaps the most threatening of all barriers to effective listening are presets. Presets are attitudes we have about something that cause us to shut out new information that could possibly change our opinions. We become so close-minded that we actually refuse to consider another point of view. The speaker has little chance of successfully communicating ideas if we will not hear them.

Corrective Measures

Even though it may be difficult for us to change behavior that has been developing for many years, we can improve our listening skills by giving attention to a few corrective measures. Naturally, one would have to want to become a better listener in order to improve this skill. Assuming an appropriate level of motivation to become a better listener, then, what can one do to facilitate this process?

1. Cultivate an interest in the subject being discussed. Even though the subject may not appeal directly to our immediate concerns, we will probably benefit to some extent from the information being provided. Certainly, if we lack interest in what is being said, we will have a difficult time maintaining an adequate level of concentration. In listening to our speaker, we should try to determine how the information may be related to our needs. We will probably find that we have something to gain by listening.

2. Minimize to the extent possible any distractions that may inhibit the listening process. While there are some distractions that cannot be controlled, many can be reduced or avoided completely. Often we can adjust the environmental factors such as noise, temperatures, and human traffic patterns that are undesirable. Set aside an appropriate amount of time to listen. If we are working under time constraints, we may be thinking about our next appointment or task when we should be listening to our speaker. We should be comfortable within the time frame.

3. Evaluate what the speaker is saying rather than the particular method of delivery. Concentrate on content rather than upon technique. Remember that it is *what* a person is saying that is important and not *how* it is being said. Later, as we discuss the skill of speaking, we will consider how to present our ideas so they will be listened to by others. For now, of course, we are concerned with the skill of listening.

4. Refrain from premature evaluation. We seem to evaluate information in terms of our immediate knowledge base. True, this evaluation provides the framework for our decision-making processes. The problem as it relates to listening, however, is that we are too quick to judge the information we receive. Hasty evaluation can lead to a reduction in concentration and, as a result, we do not hear everything a speaker is saying. We would be better off to delay our evaluation of the input until the speaker has presented a complete idea.

5. Have an open mind about the subject being discussed. A closed mind shuts out new information which interferes with our present mind set. If we have a closed mind about something, chances are we will not really hear what is being said. There is, of course, a fear that new or additional information may cause us to reevaluate our own position, and this can be very unsettling for us. Reexamine

presently held attitudes and beliefs to determine whether they remain tenable and make adjustments where necessary.

6. Listen for meaning. This final suggestion will increase listening efficiency. For any number of reasons, we are often reluctant to express our true feelings. We use the indirect approach to communicate our ideas; in so doing, we actually say things other than what we mean. Motivation for this behavior may come from a desire to spare the feelings of another, a fear of listener reaction, a lack of knowing what accurately expresses our true feelings, or any of several other reasons. As listeners, we may be able to distinguish between what a person is saying and what that person means. In other words, look and listen for the "double edge" of the message. Better understanding will result from such perception.

Small Group Communication in Business Organizations

Much of the communication that takes place in organizations occurs in what has come to be called the small group. A knowledge of how communication in this format differs from that in others is important to nearly everyone who is gainfully employed. Since employees must work together toward the achievement of common goals, we can expect that small group interaction would be a familiar communication format.

These employees generally represent several departments within the firm and necessarily possess a variety of skills. Examples of these skills are accounting, finance, taxation, personnel administration, advertising and public relations, administrative services, and corporate planning. (See fig. 2.1.) The functions of management (planning, organizing, staffing, etc.) are naturally assumed to be present in all of these specialties. Not all businesses, of course, will have a need for all of these areas of expertise; however, they are skills common to many. Because of this great variety of skill and the resultant specialization of employees, we find that workers must share their knowledge in order to solve problems common to all.

The small group meeting can be a most efficient device for solving various types of operational problems, but it can also represent a very costly and nonproductive way of using time if not conducted properly. What, then, are some of the variables that influence the effectiveness

Figure 2.1
The small group meeting

of the small group communication activity? And, more important to us as prospective members of a group, what can we do to prepare ourselves for effective participation at this level?

Purpose

Before any group activity can succeed, members of that group must know what purpose is being served. A lack of purpose can lead to confusion of the membership and a loss of productive effort. All members of a group must know from the outset the reason for the collective effort. Knowing the purpose will give a sense of direction to each individual and will provide the basis for member motivation. Information Processing, Fact Finding, and Decision Making are three categories of purpose that deserve special attention because they represent so much of the small group efforts that are expended in business situations.

Information Processing involves the dissemination of data. The group leader and/or members can provide the input for this type of activity. The primary purpose of this type of meeting is to share information with all other participants. The group leader, who may be a member of top management, might be meeting with department chairpersons to communicate data about the organization. Or, the various chairpersons may be imparting information about their respective departmental activities. The objective in this instance may be to share information that will be of value to those who must coordinate their departmental operations (production, quality control, sales, promotional plans, etc.). Similarly, special subcommittees within the group may need to report their findings to the other members of the larger group. Regardless of who provides the data, the purpose will be that of processing information.

Fact-finding meetings are those designed to obtain information not available in any existing usable form. This type of meeting will attempt to generate information by combining the research skills of the various members. Often, as with some information-processing meetings, subcommittees will need to be formed that can gather information and report back to the general membership.

The purpose of the decision-making group is to evaluate various inputs and to make decisions. These decisions may be based on consensus or determined by parliamentary procedure. Whichever method is employed, the objective will be to make a decision that can be implemented by the larger organizational unit. Generally, the decision-making groups are composed of individuals who have the power to make decisions within the chain of command of the formal structure.

Membership

While many variables determine the actual success of a group's efforts, none may be as basic as the individuals who make up that group. Group composition has been studied from several points of view, and a few generalizations have come to be accepted by most observers of collective behavior.

One commonly accepted facet of group membership is that each member should possess a minimum knowledge base relative to the subjects to be discussed. No member can make a significant, positive contribution without possessing some knowledge of the subject. Normally, a group member will possess this necessary knowledge base by virtue of his or her position within the organization. For example, an individual who works in payroll will probably be aware of certain payroll matters that can be shared with other members of the group who may have only limited contact with that area.

Group members should be available for participation in group meetings. This point may appear to be too obvious, but in actual practice it is often overlooked. If an individual, for whatever reasons, cannot make all, or nearly all of the meetings, this person and the group may be better advised to find a suitable alternate. Continuity of group membership and actual participation is vital to the success of the total effort.

Individual motivation is another variable that must be present in each group member. This motivation can stem from any number of sources, but it must be present if the group is to succeed. While the group leader can do much to motivate others, individuals must desire to accomplish the group's goals.

Good listening skills are important to group members. Much information will be presented and processed during the meetings, and each member will need to be particularly attentive. These skills are sorely tested in the group meeting because most members will do more listening than speaking. For too many participants this relationship between listening and speaking time has to be brought into balance.

Leadership

If the membership of a group is considered the most basic variable of all, leadership must be viewed as the most vital to the ultimate success of those participants. For without effective leadership, a group will not function properly. The motivation provided others by the leader, the extent of planning, the degree of organization, and the particular leadership style all influence what happens when individuals work in unison toward a common goal. Whether the group leader is elected from the group membership or appointed by virtue of his or her position in the formal organization, this person must be able to move the group toward the accomplishment of specific goals. In some situations a dogmatic leadership style may accomplish certain tasks, while in others a more permissive climate will generate far better results. Certainly, regardless of the particular leadership style that evolves, the leader has the responsibility for planning and organizing the meetings, for motivating individuals to participate, for addressing specific agenda items, and for keeping the group moving toward predetermined goals.

Physical Environment

Although perhaps not as critical as other variables, the physical environment can affect the success of the group. We should make every attempt to obtain a meeting place that will accommodate comfortably all members of the unit. Tables and chairs should be arranged so that each member will be able to have face-to-face communication with all other members. Whenever members cannot see all others, subgroups tend to form, or individuals tend to address only those who are immediately visible.

Proper room temperature and ventilation should exist for maximum performance of group members. Hot, stuffy rooms can inhibit individuals and lead to unproductive meetings. When time and circumstances permit, group members may benefit from being allowed to move around occasionally. And, of course, if the meeting is particularly lengthy, group leaders should provide for planned breaks and rest periods.

Summary

Several behavioral characteristics affect productive efforts in the work environment. Included among these characteristics are nonverbal communications, listening skills, and small group confrontations.

Nonverbal communication is often more significant than we realize. Many attitudes are transmitted in nonverbal form and messages are often sent inadvertently. Effective communicators have learned to read these cues and to consider their impact on the total transaction between the sender and receiver. Nonverbal meaning can occur in at least three major categories—Proxemics, Kinesics, and Paralanguage.

Good listening habits are vital to good communicating. Much of our time is spent listening to others, and few of us are as efficient as we should be in performing this skill. Barriers to effective listening include self-interest, personal distractions, speaker delivery, our tendency to evaluate prematurely, and presets. We can overcome these barriers which have been reinforced over our years of experience only by a concerted effort directed toward their resolution.

Small group communication has come to play an extremely important role in business communication. We have a need to share expertise that we have developed through specialization. In short, we have become dependent upon others in the organizational structure to help us achieve our goals. Groups have been classified according to purpose: Information Processing, Fact Finding, and Decision Making. Important variables in group communication include membership, leadership, and physical environment.

As we move now to the following chapters that deal more specifically with written communication, we must carry with us the significance of communication theory as presented in these first two introductory chapters.

Chapter Exercises

1. Discuss how it is possible for one to send and receive nonverbal communications without ever having been trained to do so.
2. In what ways can written messages communicate nonverbally?
3. If there is a conflict between what one is speaking and what one is communicating in nonverbal form, which transmission will the receiver probably believe? Why?
4. Discuss what is meant by the statement that nonverbal communication clues must be interpreted within the context of a given situation.
5. What is another word for *social meaning* and what does it mean?
6. Differentiate between proxemics, kinesics, and paralanguage.
7. Which cultures in our world seem to communicate nonverbally to a greater extent than others?
8. Discuss how it happens that nonverbal clues will not be interpreted in the same way in different cultures. How do you suppose these clues came to differ among cultures?
9. Discuss how *self-interest* can be detrimental to effective listening.
10. If a speaker's particular method of delivery distracts us, how can we overcome this barrier?
11. Discuss what is meant by *premature evaluation* in the context of listening behavior.
12. Why is it important that we listen for meaning? What is this corrective measure really implying?
13. Why is it important that we learn about the unique aspects of small group communication?
14. Why has the small group become such an important phenomenon in business organizations? Do you see it as becoming more important or less important as organizations develop?
15. Discuss how membership of a particular group can affect the performance of that group.
16. How can leadership affect the performance of the group and the quality of the decision that derive from it?
17. What factors of the physical environment can influence group performance?
18. Have your instructor read aloud an article on organizational conflict. Determine the degree of listening efficiency based on instructions provided by the instructor.

Case No. 1:   The Misplaced Towel

The local health spa provides the traditional services and facilities for its members. The exercise rooms are located in the front part of the building because most members prefer to complete this portion of their workout before entering the "wet area."

Standard procedure requires that each user carry his towel with him as he moves from the dressing rooms to the wet areas. This procedure allows each person the immediate use of his towel upon leaving the baths, and it assures him that his towel will not "walk off" by itself. Several towel hooks are located throughout the facility for the convenience of the members; however, there is usually a shortage of hooks which causes many people to put their towels on the floor or in any other available space.

Dick Connor always placed his towel around the neck of the sculptured Zeus of Greek mythology. Dick's regular trips to the spa were at 4:30 p.m. on Tuesdays, Thursdays, and Saturdays. Recently, however, because of a change in work schedule, he went to the spa at a different hour, followed his usual custom of draping his towel around the neck of his old friend Zeus, and proceeded to the whirlpool.

Shortly, a little old man appeared for his workout in the whirlpool area and was obviously alarmed to see that another towel was occupying his personal territory. He quickly removed the other towel, threw it on the floor in disgust, and put his own towel in its rightful place. He then went about his business mumbling something about the fact that no one seemed to respect the rights of others anymore.

Questions for Discussion:

1. How does this case relate to the concept of personal space and territoriality?
2. Discuss why we feel this need for personal territory. Do you think everybody has this need?
3. Can you think of territorial rights you have claimed? Have you ever felt threatened when someone else invaded your area?

Case No. 2: "Have A Seat. We'll Be Out To Serve You In A Minute."

A sign in a local pizza parlor reads, "Have a seat. We'll be out to serve you in a minute."

Questions for Discussion:

1. Considering that there are only two major areas in the parlor—the kitchen and the dining room—do you think that by using the phrase ". . . *out* to serve you . . ." management is revealing its

attitude about the relative importance of the dining room as compared to the kitchen area?

2. Would the phrase "... *in* to serve you ..." communicate a different attitude?

3. Describe a situation you have seen or experienced wherein the particular wording of a statement communicated a special attitude or meaning.

Case No. 3:   The Uninviting Store Front

Merfert and Nelson Clothing, Inc., had been in business for nearly fourteen years and had developed a fairly stable following of satisfied customers. In addition to the regulars, Merfert and Nelson did a significant amount of business with customers who happened to stop in after seeing a display in the windows, and with those who were simply walking by on their way down the street.

Because the store building itself was quite old, the owners decided to remodel the facility and put in new fixtures and a new store front. The old front was replaced with new double-paned glass, and the ancient see-through door was removed in favor of a solid oak entrance with impressive hand carvings.

Shortly after the major remodeling had been completed, the owners noticed a substantial reduction in sales to their walk-in customers. Considering the fact that the sales force, store policies, and procedures remained the same, they decided that the new closed look of the entrance was the thing that was causing the drop in sales.

Questions for Discussion:

1. Do you thing such reasoning on the part of the owners was logical? Explain your views.

2. Do you think factors such as closed doors can influence the way a situation is perceived with respect to the communication environment? Explain your opinion.

3. Can you think of other factors which may have communicated ideas to explain the decrease in business?

Case No. 4:   The Abrasive Employee

Assume that you are the manager of a particular department in a fairly large business organization. You are responsible for the supervision of twenty workers, each of whom, because of the nature of the work, functions independently of everyone else. Little team work is required and the only interaction needed is that between you and each individual.

One of the employees under your supervision is especially capable of doing quality work, but he cannot resist evaluating and assisting others in the department. Members of the department have begun to ask you to talk to this worker and get him to leave them alone. They do not want or need his "help" and many of them are getting very irritated by his constant intrusions. The situation has become so sensitive that you, as manager, must take some kind of action. What specific steps would you propose to resolve the problem?

Procedure: Ask your instructor how to proceed with this problem.

Suggested Readings

Applbaum, Ronald L.; Jenson, Owen O.; and Carroll, Richard. *Speech Communication—A Basic Anthology.* New York: Macmillan Publishing Co., 1975.

Bormann, Ernest G., and Bormann, Nancy C. *Effective Small Group Communication.* Minneapolis: Burgess Publishing Co., 1972.

Campbell, James H., and Hepler, Hal W. *Dimensions in Communication: Readings.* Belmont, Calif.: Wadsworth Publishing Co., 1970.

Cathcart, Robert S., and Samovar, Larry A. *Small Group Communication: A Reader.* 2d ed. Dubuque, Iowa: Wm. C. Brown Company Publishers, 1970.

DeVito, Joseph A. *Communication—Concepts and Processes.* Englewood Cliffs, N.J.: Prentice-Hall, 1971.

Gieselman, Robert C., ed. *Readings in Business Communication.* Champaign, Ill.: Stipes Publishing Co., 1974.

Goldhaber, Gerald M. *Organizational Communication.* Dubuque, Iowa: Wm. C. Brown Company Publishers, 1974.

Hall, Edward T. *The Silent Language.* Garden City, N.Y.: Doubleday and Company, 1959.

Haney, William V. *Communication and Organizational Behavior.* Homewood, Ill.: Richard D. Irwin, Inc., 1973.

Huseman, Richard C.; Logue, Cal M.; and Freshley, Dwight L. *Readings in Interpersonal and Organizational Communications,* 3rd ed. Boston: Holbrook Press, 1973.

Jacobson, Wally D. *Power and Interpersonal Relations.* Belmont, Calif.: Wadsworth Publishing Co., 1972.

Keltner, John W. *Elements of Interpersonal Communication.* Belmont, Calif.: Wadsworth Publishing Co., 1973.

Lewis, Phillip V. *Organizational Communications: The Essence of Effective Management.* Columbus, Ohio: Grid, Inc., 1975.

Malcolm, Andrew. *The Tyranny of the Group.* Totowa, N.J.: Littlefield, Adams & Co., 1973.

Mehrabian, Albert. *Silent Messages.* Belmont, Calif.: Wadsworth Publishing Co., 1971.

Pei, Mario. *The Story of Language.* New York: J. B. Lippincott Co., 1965.

Phillips, Gerald M. *Communication and the Small Group,* 2d ed. New York: Bobbs-Merrill Co., 1973.

Rogers, Carl R. *On Becoming a Person.* Boston: Houghton Mifflin Co., 1961.

Rogers, Everett M., and Agarwala, Rekha-Rogers. *Communication in Organizations*. New York: Free Press, 1976.

Schneider, Arnold E.; Lahiff, James M.; and Hatfield, John D. *Organizational Communication*. New York: McGraw-Hill Book Co., 1975.

Shaw, Marvin E. *Group Dynamics: The Psychology of Small Group Behavior*. New York: McGraw-Hill Book Co., 1971.

Thayer, Lee. *Communication and Communication Systems*. Homewood, Ill.: Richard D. Irwin, Inc., 1968.

The Purposes
of Human Interaction

PART 2

The Objectives of Communication

3

As we study the information in this chapter about the objectives of communication, we will be able to:

1. distinguish between primary and secondary objectives.

2. learn how the elements of correctness, clarity, conciseness, completeness, and concreteness contribute to the overall effectiveness of our messages.

3. understand that every business message should be developed with an awareness of the importance of the goodwill factor.

4. determine how reader viewpoint, empathy, sincerity, and tact are primary requisites to effective expression.

Every communication, regardless of its form, has at least two objectives. The primary objective is to convey a particular message within the context of the immediate situation. For example, the statement "Meet me at my office no later than 3:15 P.M." is intended to provide information about when and where a meeting is to be held. The objective of this communication could be any one of several possibilities. Examples of possible objectives in this encounter include:

"We are meeting because I want to help you."
"We are meeting in my office because I want to control the encounter."
"The meeting must start before it gets too late."
"I agree with you that the subject of the meeting is important."
"I respect your feelings in this matter and I want to help."

Of course, we could list many other possible objectives, depending upon the circumstances of the situation. The point is that there will almost always be a "double edge" to a message and the good writer will be aware of this possibility.

Often, because of the circumstances surrounding the communication, the sender of the message will either consciously or subconsciously subordinate the primary purpose to one of lesser importance. When the primary purpose is subordinated to one of lesser importance, clear and accurate communications can become difficult to achieve. The receiver may not know just what it is the sender is trying to communicate, and the wrong response will result in a failure to achieve the primary goal. This failure can result in confusing communications as well as in wasted time and money. All persons in the communication process, therefore, should know what the primary and secondary objectives are.

In our business writing, we can clearly define and identify

these important elements. The primary goal should be simply *to convey the message* inherent in the business situation. The goal could be to confirm an order, to set prices, to allow a discount, to thank someone for services rendered, or any number of such reasons. The secondary goal or objective of the business letter should be *to promote goodwill*. Because we are interested in developing our business as a continuing enterprise, it will be to our advantage to establish and maintain good relations with our many associates.

The Primary Objective—Conveying the Message

The primary objective of communications—conveying a message—can best be achieved by attending to the elements of correctness, clarity, conciseness, completeness, and concreteness. If these elements are not present in the writing, confusion and ambiguity may result. The writer should first have the message well in mind and this may be possible only after gathering information and determining precisely what the message should convey. With a goal in mind, the writer is ready to give attention to those elements which help to achieve that goal.

Correctness

The statement, "Good writing is correct writing, but correct writing is not necessarily good writing," has much substance. One of the essentials of good writing is correctness, for meaning is achieved, in part, through the relationship that words have to each other in the sentence. We must be certain, then, that the words we use are the correct ones and that they are placed in correct order. As seen in a later chapter, many rules of grammar can aid in determining which are the correct words and where are the correct places to put them. For the moment, and for purposes of illustration, consider these examples:

> As one of Smith's preferred customers, we would like to inform you of our special discount sale.

According to the word order in this example, *we* are the customers being referred to. The word *we* is the first one to appear after the introductory phrase and is, therefore, the one that is being described or modified. This word order is not only confusing but also incorrect. To be correct, the statement should read:

As one of Smith's preferred customers, you are invited. . .

In this corrected version of the communication, there should be no question as to who the preferred customer is. Now consider the following group of words:

Because we have not received your balance of $76.

By definition, a sentence is a complete thought. This definition implies both a subject and a predicate. In this example, we do not have a complete thought; we have a sentence fragment. Sentence fragments are neither correct nor complete and, therefore, seldom have a place in business communications. Now read the next example.

We are happy to except your payments by check.

In this example, *except* is an incorrect word. *Accept* should be used to communicate the idea intended by this sentence. Wrong word choice is another form of incorrectness and will serve only to diminish the effectiveness of the writing. Obviously, a good vocabulary is important to good writing.

We need to distinguish between certain words if our writing is to be considered correct. The following list contains only a few of the many words that are frequently misused. Learn the difference between each set presented and you will be able to avoid a common form of incorrectness.

affect/effect

Affect is a verb meaning *to influence*. "How will this decision affect net profits?"
Effect is a noun meaning *result*. "What effect will this decision have on net profits?"
Effect can also function as a verb. When so used, it means *to bring about*. "We will effect the change immediately."
(Note: *Affect* is always a verb—*effect* can be a verb or a noun.)

anxious/eager	*Anxious* is an adjective meaning *troubled* or *possessing anxiety or fear.* "He is anxious about the test results." (He fears that he did not do well on the test.) *Eager* is an adjective connoting an intense desire. It has a positive meaning whereas *anxious* has a negative meaning. "She is eager to begin her vacation." (Note: These two words have been so frequently interchanged that many dictionaries now list one as an acceptable synonym for the other.)
adapt/adopt	*Adapt* is a verb meaning *to fit for a new or different use.* "We will adapt to the new policies." The word implies adjustment or change. *Adopt* is a verb meaning *to accept or take up something.* "Starting next week we will adopt the new rules."
all right/alright/ all-right	*All right* means *satisfactory.* "Her work is all right." *Alright* is generally considered substandard and should not be used. *All-right* is a slang expression meaning *dependable or honest.* "John is an all-right person."
accept/except	*Accept* is a verb meaning *to receive something.* "I will accept the position if it is offered to me." *Except* is a preposition implying the exclusion or omission of something. "He never mentioned it except jokingly."
advice/advise	*Advice* is a noun meaning *suggestion or counsel.* "They gave us good advice on the purchase of our house." *Advise* is a verb meaning *to recommend* or to inform. "Please advise us which form you think is best." "Advise them of their rights."

amount/number	Use *amount* to refer to things that are judged on the basis of weight or sums. "The amount of revenue collected during the sale was substantial." Use *number* to refer to items that can actually be counted. "The number of complaints had decreased over the past two years."
balance/ remainder	Use these words interchangeably only when referring to bookkeeping or accounting matters. "The remainder (or rest) of the boxes are in the basement."
can/may	Use *can* when referring to the ability to perform. "You can do a good job when you put forth the effort." Use *may* when expressing permission. "You may take your vacation next week as requested."
compare to/ compare with	Use *compare to* when you wish to liken two things or when you wish to put them into the same category. "She compared her job to his." (Noting the similarities) Use *compare with* when you wish to examine or show differences. "She compared her job with his." (Noting the differences)
differ from/ differ with	Use *differ from* when referring to things; use *differ with* when referring to people. "These bolts of cloth differ from those received in last week's shipment." "These two groups differ with each other on several points."
different from/ different than	Use *different from* and you will probably never be wrong.
disinterested/ uninterested	Use *disinterested* to communicate a neutral position. "The committee secured a disinterested person to arbitrate with the union." Use *uninterested* to communicate a lack of interest in the subject. "He is just uninter-

	ested in the subject matter and will not study it."
farther/further	Use *farther* when referring to physical distances and *further* for everything else. "Reno is farther west than is San Diego." "Let's discuss this further tomorrow."
imply/infer	Speakers and writers *imply* while listeners and readers *infer*. "The mayor implied that he was opposed to the new legislation." "Perhaps we just inferred that because we did not hear his entire speech."
in/into	Use *in* when referring to location and *into* when referring to action. "She is in town today." "He fell into the stream."
its/it's	*Its* is possessive. *It's* is a contraction for *it is*. "The ambulance approached with its lights flashing." "It's going to be a warm day."
loan/lend	*Loan* is a noun often used in a financial context. "The loan was approved." *Lend* is a verb. "Lend me your book."
shall/will	These two words may now be used interchangeably. *Will* is used more frequently than *shall*. *Shall* is perhaps a bit more formal and emphatic. "We shall defend these rights at all cost."
self-addressed	Because an envelope cannot address itself, it cannot be *self-addressed*. Use ". . . enclosed, addressed envelope."
toward/towards	*Toward* is correct for conventional usage. *Towards* is not necessarily incorrect but is used primarily in England. Use preferred spelling in all cases.

Remember that careful selection of words will help you to achieve correctness. Reference to a good dictionary or thesaurus will help you to make the right word choice.

Correct writing is also void of redundancies. A *redundancy* is a word or phrase that is not necessary because it merely repeats what has already been said or implied. In information theory, it is the extent to which a signal repeats the same message. While this kind of repetition may reduce the probability of error, it can and does limit the effective capacity of the channel of transmission. We should, therefore, keep our communications as short as possible without making them seem abrupt or incomplete.

The examples of redundancies that follow are familiar to most of us:

1. As you may or may not know — *May* implies *may not.*
2. Congregate around — *Congregate* implies *around.*
3. Close proximity — *Close* means *proximate.*
4. Bright future ahead of him — The future *is* ahead.
5. Totally annihilate — *Totally* is implied.
6. Basic fundamentals — Basic *is* fundamental.
7. Consensus of opinion — Consensus *is* opinion.
8. Take immediate action at once — *Immediate* means *at once.*
9. Future potential — *Potential* implies *future.*
10. It's raining outside — Hopefully not inside.
11. Surrounded on all sides — *Surrounded* means *all sides.*
12. Modern, up-to-date facilities — *modern* means *up-to-date.*
13. Exact same thing — *Exact* means *same.*
14. Each and everyone will attend — *Each* means *everyone* in this context.
15. Complete and total results — *Complete* means *total.*
16. Estimated time of arrival is approximately — *Estimated* means *approximately.*

Although some degree of emphasis is achieved by using elements that are redundant, most of them are unnecessary and should not be used. Finally, do not confuse redundancy with repetition. Repetition refers to the use of the same word in a given sentence—redundancy refers to the repetition of the same *idea.*

Good writers also make certain that the data they include in their business communications are accurate. Business information is sometimes processed by several people and there are many opportunities to make mistakes. Words should be spelled correctly, of course, for we know that errors of this type reflect negatively on the image of the organization. Moreover, it is especially important that names, dates, and places be accurately recorded. Miscues on variable information such as these factors can be embarrassing and costly. Business depends upon accurate information, and misinformation requires the expenditure of more time, money, and effort. Doing the work correctly the first time pays big dividends in many ways.

Clarity

To be able to transfer meaning through written communication, the writer must be certain that the messages possess the quality of clarity. The reader must not be forced to struggle through cumbersome words, awkward phrases, extraneous information, or ambiguous references. Reading is an activity that requires effort, and anything the writer can do to reduce this work load will serve to improve communication skills.

Consider the following communication that was developed by a department manager and sent to all employees in his charge. Is it clear and easy to understand?

> Each person to whom this notice is addressed is entitled to submit to the District Director described above a comment on the question of whether the plan meets the requirements for qualification under Part I of Subchapter D or Chapter I of the Internal Revenue Code of 1954. Two or more such persons may join in a single comment or request. If such person or persons request the Department to submit a comment and that department declines to do so in respect of one or more matters raised in the request, the person or persons so requesting may submit a comment to the District Director in respect of the matters on which the Department declines to comment. A comment submitted to the District Director must be received by him on or before April 1. However, if it is being submitted on a matter on which the Department was first requested, but declined to comment, the comment must be received by the District Director on or before the date of April 1, or the 15th day after the day on which the Department notifies such person or persons that it declines to comment, but in no event later than May 7. A request of the Department to submit a comment must be received by that department on or before April 2, or, if the person or persons

making the request wish to preserve their right to submit a comment to the District Director in the event the Department declines to comment, on or before March 22.

Additional informational material regarding the plan and procedures to be followed in submitting, or requesting the Department to submit, a comment may be obtained at the principal office of the employer.

The quality of clarity is achieved through good planning and implementation. Good planning is important regardless of the type of activity we engage in. We have to know what it is we wish to accomplish, how we will accomplish our goal, and how we will evaluate our efforts. Earlier in this chapter we discussed the importance of the primary and secondary objectives—we need to know what it is we want to accomplish, and there must be no confusion or doubt in the mind of the writer. Certainly, if the writer is not clear as to the objectives, the reader will not be either. One of the greatest detriments to clear writing is the inclusion of information that does not pertain specifically to the intended purpose of the message. This extraneous information tends to distract, and it causes one to look for something that is not there. Knowing the objectives of the communication, then, is crucial to the quality of clarity.

The relationship between clarity and sound logic is significant and should be emphasized at this point. Logic is another word for reasoning, and all good communicators must incorporate this often elusive and ill-defined quality in their writing. Simply expressing ideas in correct grammatical form will not assure clarity.

One way to understand the importance of logic in communication is to identify those factors that result in impurities of logic. These impurities can result from several things, including:

- Poor word choice in relation to the situation
- Poor word placement within the sentence
- Poor use of techniques of emphasis and de-emphasis
- Loose arrangement of ideas within the message
- Inappropriate tone or attitude
- Insensitivity to the emotional dimension of the situation
- Defective reasoning or inappropriate assumptions

Naturally some overlap may exist between any one of these factors and any other in the list. However, we need not assign each violation of logic to any particular category. The important thing is that we be able to recognize illogical constructions when they do develop and that we correct them in our quest for clarity in writing. As we will note again further along, some of the rules of grammar have been determined rather arbitrarily, even though most have a logical basis. You will see in the examples presented below that many grammar errors are also logic errors. In other cases, the grammar is correct but the logic is incorrect.

Because of my schooling, the hours that I am at home are often erratic.

(Could imply that this person learned to be erratic by going to school.)

As a general rule, however, I am always home after 1:00 p.m.

(The word *general*, in this context, means *not* always.)

As you know, I have been impatiently waiting to use my new stove.

(Writer probably means "patiently waiting.")

As faculty advisor to my son, I am sure you are doing a good job.

(As stated, the faculty advisor is the parent.)

Under no circumstances do we publish any lies or rumors that will cause undue harm to those people.

(Could this statement imply that *only* harmless lies and rumors are published?)

We have been notified of the theft which took place from your vehicle stealing a CB radio and breaking a window to gain entry.

(How·can a vehicle steal a radio and break a window?)

To avoid any confusion, school will be dismissed on Tuesday for a teachers' meeting.

(Does this mean that we get confused by going to school or that "school" will avoid the confusion?)

(From a job application letter—)

I am preparing myself for a junior accountant.

(... and they lived happily ever after.)

I've narrowed my choice down to one company.

(Use of the word *narrowed* implies that more than one company is still being considered.)

I'm rather interested in some exciting new techniques in marketing.

(Is it possible to be *rather* interested about something that is exciting?)

Carefully check your writing to see that you observe the rules for logical development of ideas. An awareness of the importance of logic will help you make your writing more effective.

The readability of written material is certainly a measure of its clarity. If our written communications are to be effective, they must be understood by the reader. This understanding can be achieved only by having the messages presented at a level of difficulty that is within the range of reader ability. This measure of difficulty is called *readibility level.* A number of formulas have been developed which measure, with varying degrees of accuracy, the readability levels of written material. A formula often used is the Gunning Fog Index.[1] Consider the following formula and examples:

Simplified Formula for Fog Index: Fog Index = Average Sentence Length + Number of Difficult Words per 100 Words × 0.4

The index considers "difficult words" to be those that are three syllables or more in length. Do not count as difficult words a) those that become three syllables or more by combining two short words: ("what-

1. Robert Gunning, *The Technique of Clear Writing* (New York: McGraw-Hill Book Company, 1952), pp. 36-37.

ever," "bookkeeper"), b) those that are capitalized (unless capitalized only because it begins a sentence), or c) forms of verbs which become three syllables by adding -ed or -es ("sedated," "prorated").

Read the passage presented below and note how the simplified formula is used to determine the grade level of readability.

"Since the reader will be pleased to receive this kind of message, we should feel **confident** in **approaching** the message of our letter in a direct way (the **deductive** approach). We are **justified** in starting a letter with the key point if that is what the reader wants to hear. The cliche "time is money" may be **appropriate** in this instance. Letters written using the **deductive** approach will save everyone time and money because they move quickly to the essence of the message itself. The **psychology** of this direct approach does not mean that these letters should, of **necessity**, be short."

Number of words in passage _____100
Number of sentences in passage _____ 5
Average sentence length _____ 20
Number of difficult words in passage _____ 8
Total of average sentence length and difficult words _____ 28
$$\frac{\times\ .4}{11.2}$$
Grade level of readability =

Note: Generally we are more comfortable reading material that is somewhat below our level of ability; therefore, good writers will strive to keep the average sentence length and number of difficult or long words relatively small. When material has a readability level in excess of 11 or 12, the information will be beyond many readers.

Do not accept the results of any readability formula as final proof that written communications are either too high, too low, or just right. Other factors such as word choice and word order will naturally affect the understandability of a message. On the other hand, a proven formula such as the Gunning Fog will generally give one a good idea of the appropriateness of the level—particularly if the sample is representative of the entire written message.

Using this same formula, determine the readability level of other material that you have available. Determine what your own level of writing tends to be. Are you writing at a level that you feel will be appropriate for most of your readership? Are you using too many "big" words? Are the words in their proper sequence? Again, if you will empathize with your reader, your messages will probably be more likely to fall within the correct reading range.

While the approaches vary among the particular formulas, the overall objective remains essentially the same. Most readability measures include sentence length and number of difficult words or syllables. Sentence length is generally the most broadly applied determinant of level of difficulty. The longer the sentence is, the more difficult the material will be to read and comprehend. And, since big words are generally harder to understand than small words, this variable influences the material. A word of caution is in order at this point, however. The order in which words appear in a sentence may have more impact on readability than either sentence length or word length.

Most writing follows the "subject-verb-object" order, and we become accustomed to seeing words in this particular sequence. Whenever this sequence is interrupted, there is a possibility that readability will decrease. Questions typically interrupt this sequence, as do sentences which begin with *there*. Consider these examples:

The <u>Purchasing Department</u> <u>ordered</u> seven new <u>desks.</u>
(subject)   (verb)   (object)

Which room did the club use?

(The subject is *club,* the verb is *did use,* and the object is *room.*)

As our sentences become longer, the risk of illogical word order increases. The purpose here is not to encourage you to write only in short, simple sentences. In fact, more complex sentence structures can often show relationships between and among various ideas better than can several simple sentences. Rather, the objective is to emphasize that when sentences are too long and complex, the reader has a tendency to get lost in the process of reading. Furthermore, long sentences usually provide more opportunities for errors in grammar than do shorter ones.

Generally, the effective communicator will have little problem with sentence length if the material is written in a conversational manner, and if the thoughts are divided into logical units for presentation to the receiver. In this manner, communicators will avoid one of the most common errors in writing—saying too much in one sentence.

Readers generally have better comprehension rates if they are exposed to material somewhat below their level of ability. This lower level provides for ease of reading and permits one to "reflect on" or "process" the ideas that are being presented for consideration. Material that is too simplistic, however, can also be detrimental to effective communication. We should, therefore, know as much as possible about the abilities and background of our readership.

Conciseness, Completeness, and Concreteness

These terms refer to certain qualities of refinement that can help our letters achieve their primary objective. Business letters should be concise but not abrupt. Avoid using two pages to say something that can be said in one page. Be sure, however, that your message is complete. Too much information tends to confuse the reader who searches for meaning in the superfluous material. Too little information may elicit an incorrect response or require that the reader seek additional instructions. One way to assure both conciseness and completeness in your writing is to develop the element of concreteness.

Concreteness is the quality of precision our writing contains as a result of choosing words and expressions that are generally assigned similar meanings by most users. The following examples show the contrast between concreteness and vagueness.

Not: The new machine is really fast.
But: The new machine produces 80 copies per minute.

Not: The corporation settled for a large sum of money.
But: The corporation settled for $250,000.

Not: This new tire will give you tremendous mileage.
But: This new tire will last for at least 40,000 miles.

Not: The powerful motor drives the blade at a high rate of speed and will operated continuously.
But: The 1 H.P. Cont. Duty motor produces 4,800 strokes per minute.

The Secondary Objective—Promoting Goodwill

This secondary objective of our business communications would appear to be easy to achieve. All one would need, it seems, is the proper attitude toward the receiver of the message. To a large extent, this is true; but we can and often do fail to meet this objective for some very important reasons. Consideration and courtesy are key factors in a positive attitude. These factors include the elements of "reader" viewpoint, empathy, sincerity, tact, and other evidences of thoughtfulness and care in our writing. Writers can demonstrate them by careful proofreading, accuracy in spelling and grammar, and the proper use or avoidance of business jargon.

Reader Viewpoint and Empathy

Because viewpoint and empathy are so closely related, we should examine them concurrently. In fact, the "reader" viewpoint is a direct result of empathic behavior. Some writers refer to the "you" viewpoint, and the term is certainly appropriate. For our purpose, however, "reader" viewpoint seems to fit more closely with the reader-writer relationship being considered in our approach to effective business writing.

Empathy is defined as an awareness of another's state of mind. We can empathize with others by psychologically projecting ourselves into the role of the person with whom we are communicating. By so doing, we are better able to understand why one perceives a given situation in a particular way. Empathic behavior does not necessarily mean agreeing with someone. It means "seeing" another's perspective in order to understand that person's frame of reference. The ability to empathize is the mark of a mature person, and good interpersonal and organizational orderliness cannot exist without it. By having the ability to empathize, one will be able to develop communications from the point of view of the receiver (reader or listener). This orientation is, of course, called the "you" viewpoint or the "reader" viewpoint, and it is a vital quality of good communication.

Because each person perceives situations as they pertain to his or her own needs and desires, we should write to accommodate the reader. We must write with the needs, wants, and interests of our reader foremost in our mind. By so presenting our ideas, we will help the readers to understand the ideas we are transferring; and they will probably be more inclined to accept our message. The examples presented below emphasize these two different viewpoints.

Writer's Viewpoint	Reader's Viewpoint
I am happy to report that . . .	You will be happy to learn . . .
Our store will be open . . .	You can shop during . . .
We sell only the best . . .	You can choose from the best . . .
Our store needs this . . .	Your response to this . . .
We are now selling subscriptions for only 15¢ a week.	You can now order your subscription for only . . .
We invite you to come to our store and look over the wide selection of merchandise we have available.	You are invited to make your selections from a wide range of merchandise.
We have processed your application for credit. We are in a position to allow you to purchase merchandise on our convenient "Revolve" charge account.	Your application for credit has been approved. You may begin using your "Revolving" charge account at your convenience.

As we can see from the examples given, the elements of consideration and courtesy will generate messages that reflect "reader" viewpoint. Empathy is, of course, a key factor in this positive attitude toward those with whom we communicate.

Sincerity

To a certain extent, all communications are intended to persuade someone about something. We may desire to have someone accept our point of view on a controversial issue, we may want someone to buy something from us, or we may simply want a confirmation of information we believe to be true. The important element of persuasion will vary with the situation, but it does seem to exist to some degree. Because of this inherent need to persuade, one of the critical ingredients of a business message is *sincerity*.

If there is any reason to doubt the sincerity of the writer, the reader will not believe the message. Communications should, therefore, reflect this important quality. Stated another way, we should avoid including anything in our messages which will adversely affect sincerity. What are the qualities that will cause our messages to be believed?

Maintaining Basic Regard for Truth. If writers will maintain a basic regard for correctness and a willingness to provide accurate information, they will have the most essential qualities that will cause the readers to believe what is being said. Outright distortion of information, for example, will probably be detected by even the most casual reader. Any information that follows, accurate or not, will be questioned. Of course, this basic orientation to truth will not overcome the possibility of insincerity caused by other factors.

Avoiding Circumlocution. For a number of reasons, people sometimes seem to be talking in circles without ever really saying what they want to say. This habit may be caused by an inability to choose the appropriate words, a lack of understanding of the primary objective, or a reluctance to deal specifically with the situation. Whatever the reason, the reader will surely become confused and wonder why the writer has not been more specific. This bewilderment can jeopardize the intended sincerity of the message. Do not force the reader to guess what it is you are trying to say. Left to one's own estimate of the situation, a person may add meaning to your message that you do not want included. One way to minimize confusion is to use words which are not likely to be misinterpreted.

Not: Failure can never be measured in terms of one's overt performance because of varying levels of aspiration.

But: What is considered failure by one person may be success for another because their goals may be different.

Avoiding Misuse of Euphemisms. A euphemism is a word or phrase that is used in place of another for the purpose of making an idea seem less objectionable.

Mr. Jones died after he wrecked his car.

or

Mr. Jones passed away as a result of an automobile accident.

He applied for the job of dog catcher.

or

He applied for the position of Animal Control Director.

Use this deodorant for your armpits.

or

This deodorant is for underarm use.

Last week you said just the opposite of what you are saying now.

or

Earlier you supported a different point of view.

You may fly either First Class or Second Class.

or

You may choose from either First Class or Coach.

I worked as a flagman on a highway crew.

or

I have had work experience as a Traffic Control Director.

As you can see from these examples, euphemisms can be used to serve a useful and positive purpose or they can be used to deceive the reader. We should emphasize, then, that the mere use of a euphemism is inherently neither good nor bad; it all depends upon the intent of the writer.

An interesting characteristic of euphemistic expressions is that sooner or later they seem to take on connotations the same as those of the words and phrases they replaced. *Janitor*, for example, was replaced with *custodian*, and *custodian* was replaced with *maintenance engineer*. Many of these substitute words are so used in an effort to disguise the harsh realities of a given situation. Again, it is the intent of the writer that determines whether it is acceptable to use the less objectionable word or phrase in a particular context.

Tact

Tact is the skill we need to avoid doing or saying that which would offend or disturb someone. Good writers would not wish to be without this skill. Being tactless would seriously detract from the achievement of the secondary objective of the message—promotion of goodwill.

Proofreading

Once your communication has been thought through sufficiently, you need to commit the ideas to writing. In business communications,

Dear Mr. Whipple:

We have your letter in which you accuse us of not sending you the merchandise you ordered two weeks ago. We have proof that it was you who made the mistake and we have included copies of the purchase order for your information.

In checking your order and comparing it with what you said in your letter, we have discovered that you copied the wrong information from our catalog. If you want the situation corrected, send the goods back to our store and we will process a new order as soon as we can.

Cordially yours,

Accuse is a strong word with negative connotations.

Proof shows that the objective of the letter is to place blame, not to correct the situation. Including copies of the order reinforces the negative attitude.

You copied the wrong information places the blame once again. Indicates lack of cooperation in correcting the problem.

Now compare the preceding letter with the one that follows.[3]

Dear Mr. Whipple:

Your new order for merchandise is on its way to you by parcel post and should reach you within two days.

We appreciate your calling this situation to our attention and giving us an opportunity to correct the shipment to you.

Your new catalog for fall and winter has been sent to you. Check the items listed and let us know how we can serve you.

Cordially yours,

Opening paragraph refers to the subject of the letter without placing blame.

The emphasis is on service to the customer. Does not try to win any arguments regarding fault.

Closes on positive and forward-looking note.

3. Note: The letters included in the text are not presented in standard format. Dates, inside addresses, etc., have been omitted to facilitate your reading of the examples. The correct format for business letters is presented in chapter 6.

this usually involves the use of a typewriter. Regardless of who prepares the final typewritten copy, great care should be taken to determine that the document is free of errors. This "proofing" effort is often neglected, and serious or embarrassing errors are allowed to slip through to the readers.

Many reasons exist for this lack of proofreading, but few, if any, can be justified. Often we cite lack to time as the reason for not proofing the final copy. Some writers believe that the time required to identify and correct all errors (typographical, structural, or otherwise) is prohibitive when compared with the importance of other duties and responsibilities of the job. You will have to be the judge of these priorities.

The assumption that the material is correct before proofreading is another reason why errors often go undetected by the sender. We know from our own experience that this assumption is rarely warranted. Too many opportunities for mistakes occur between the development of an idea and the expression of it in printed form. This problem is magnified considerably when, as is usually the case, one person develops the message in idea form and another prepares the final copy in typewritten form. We know from our study of the communication process (as explained in the first chapter) that this involves another cycle of encoding and decoding. This additional cycle requires that interpretations be made by yet another person, creating at least one more opportunity for error.

There is a third important reason why errors are allowed to go undetected, even when a proofreading effort is made to assure accuracy. This reason is *the wrong attitude of the proofreader*. Let's examine the matter of attitude closely, because it is probably the most serious of the barriers to accuracy in written communications. Furthermore, developing the proper attitude about proofreading efforts will result in better communications and better use of time.

Most people who take the time to proofread their final copy probably do so *to make certain that the material is correct*. We feel that this is the wrong attitude to have while performing this very important task. Rather, one should proofread material *to detect and correct any errors that may exist*. Two significantly different attitudes are present in these statements about proofreading. The first one, *to make certain that the material is correct*, suggests that the material is probably correct and, therefore, no errors will be found. If this is the prevailing attitude, the reader proofing the material probably will not take the job as seriously as it should be taken. After all, if the material is probably correct, what need is there to be really concerned?

The second attitude, *to detect and correct any errors that may exist,* suggests that errors may be present and we should be serious about looking for them. (Perhaps this helps to explain why we miss seeing errors in our own work when others, such as classmates or teachers, seem to be able to find them.)

Consider these examples to see how easy it is to overlook mistakes in typewritten material.

> To feel the vibration, put you hand on the motor.
> A Thanksgiving dinner should include roast turnkey.
> Doesn't he have most the answers to solve the problem?
> The stage shows included several short skirts.
> Do you remember the saying, "A bird in the hand is
>   is worth two in the bush"?

In addition to correcting these kinds of errors, accurate proofreading will help us to correct errors in logic, grammar, and structure. Failure to proofread will communicate carelessness and will seriously hamper our objective of promoting goodwill.

Accuracy in Spelling

Over the past several years, we have witnessed a slackening of the hard, fast rules of grammar and writing. For example, we no longer seem to object to split infinitives, sentences that end with prepositions, or sentences that begin with conjunctions. Even the once "sacred" rules of punctuation have, in part, fallen to new methods of expression. One area that seems to have successfully withstood the pressures of change, however, is that of spelling. No matter how willing we seem to be to modify many of the old standards, we hold the line on spelling skills. We have never been willing to accept misspelled words, and hopefully we never will.

Writers have had much to say about the lack of spelling skills among students today. The educational system has been blamed for this deficiency; so have the influence of television, the lack of reading in the home, and the general attitude of carelessness of the younger generation. Whatever the cause or causes of the problem, an awareness of the situation is a prerequisite to solving the difficulty. Only by recognizing the problem can we begin to correct it.

By developing a positive attitude about the importance of correctness in spelling, one will be able to develop skills that will allow a rise in the level of competency considered acceptable in our society. An awareness of the problems caused by misspelled words in otherwise professional communications will give the effective writer adequate motivation to improve skills in this area.

Spelling rules or guidelines can help you to become a better speller. However, critics of these aids believe that your time would be better spent memorizing the specific words that are troublesome. These critics may have a point, but a little time spent studying rules and guidelines which are presented in the Appendix of this text will allow you to improve your spelling proficiency to an even greater extent than will memorization.

We have many troublesome words in our language. The word list in the Appendix presents words representative of those most often misspelled. A mastery of those words will help to overcome many of the spelling difficulties.

Business Jargon

Jargon is defined as specialized language of a particular job, position, or profession. This language has also been defined as gibberish, confused speech, and meaningless dialect. However it is defined, we know that some serious communication problems can be created if it is used in the wrong places or at the wrong time. Granted that there may be a time and place for using it, the effective writer will be wary of using it in any way that detracts from the process of communicating information.

Each specialized field of work seems to have developed a jargon unique to its own needs. Jargon can appear in the form of single words, phrases, clauses, or complete sentences. Accountants, for example, talk about "closing the books," "aging the accounts," and "footing and ticking." Retail clothiers talk about "mumsers," "pups," "double-headers," and "turnovers." The auto sales lingo includes such terms as "stroker," "double dip," "sled," and "homing pigeon."

Not everyone with whom you correspond will understand such highly specialized language, so you must adapt your technique of expression to the abilities of your receiver. Jargon, in and of itself, is neither good nor bad. If you are corresponding with someone in your own area of specialization, you may appropriately use jargon. If you

Hey Harry: Poach 2 on a side of little pigs, stack three high and a side of o.j.

Figure 3.1
Know your jargon

are reasonably certain the person will understand your "language," and if the circumstances of the situation seem to allow this level of expression, you will probably be safe to use it.

Buzz Words and Slang Expressions

Akin to jargon are buzz words and slang expressions that can and do communicate to those who understand the usage. Again, not all receivers will understand the meanings of these items and business writers need to exercise great caution if they use them.

Run it up a flagpole and see if anyone salutes it.

(Refers to the testing of an idea)

Let's put this on the back burner for a while.

(Refers to the need to hold an idea or a proposed action for a time)

We need to find out where it's at, reach deep, and get it all together.

(Refers to who knows what)

I mean like you know what I mean.

(Obviously this statement is used for filler)

This is meaningful at the gut level.

(Probably refers to the emotional dimension of another statement or situation)

Use of such terms in legitimate business communications is highly unlikely. A few thoughts about how your receiver will react to such language will undoubtedly suggest that you write at a more appropriate level.

Summary

All good business communications have at least two objectives—primary and secondary. The primary objective is to convey a particular message to the receiver, and the secondary objective is to create goodwill. Obviously, writers must know what these objectives are and keep them foremost in mind before and during the writing process.

Specific elements of writing that will allow us to achieve our objectives are *correctness, clarity, conciseness, completeness,* and *concreteness.* Also, writing that expresses the reader viewpoint and an empathic attitude will contribute toward the achievement of objectives.

Writing must be perceived as being sincere if readers are to believe the message. Sincerity is achieved by *maintaining a basic regard for truth, avoiding circumlocution,* and *avoiding the misuse of euphemisms.* Likewise, our messages must be written in a tactful manner.

Good writing habits also include good proofreading habits. Error-free writing communicates a positive attitude toward the reader in that it shows that the writer cares enough to make the writing correct. In a similar way, accuracy in spelling affects the writing.

Finally, good writing avoids the use of inappropriate jargon and buzz words.

Chapter Exercises

Select the correct word from the choices available in each of the following sentences.

1. How will the change in company policy (affect, effect) you?
2. Will the (affect, effect) of the new policy be significant?
3. The best way to (affect, effect) change involving personnel is to communicate with all workers in the organization.
4. I am (anxious, eager) for the meeting to begin. (Expecting a good result from the meeting)
5. We will (adapt, adopt) the new procedures at the beginning of the next quarter.
6. One should (adapt, adopt) his approach to meet the needs of each situation.
7. Everything will be (all right, alright, all-right) as soon as the new equipment is installed.
8. Do you think they will (accept, except) the new proposal?
9. They took (acception, exception) to three of the new rules.
10. (Accept, Except) for the honor, I would rather walk.
11. Seeking (advice, advise) can be painful and time-consuming, but it is often a good procedure to follow.
12. Please (advice, advise) me which car is the best buy.
13. A great (amount, number) of telephone calls came in during the late hours.
14. The (balance, remainder) of the wood can be stacked later.
15. He (can, may) go only when he has finished his practice.
16. He (can, may) enlist in the military service only when he reaches his majority.
17. His being unwilling to get involved suggests that he is (disinterested, uninterested) in the project.
18. Because he appears to be objective about the situation, he is probably (disinterested, uninterested) in the outcome.
19. She can throw the ball (farther, further) than any other person on the team.
20. Did you think the senator was (implying, inferring) that he knows more about the matter than he told the committee?
21. Can I (imply, infer) from your comments that you don't want to go?
22. He slipped from his horse and fell (in, into) the water.
23. She thinks that (its, it's) going to be a good contest.
24. Do you think she will (lend, loan) me five dollars until next week?
25. I (shall, will) see you in the morning.

Rewrite the following paragraphs to reflect the "reader" viewpoint.

To Our New Subscribers:

We welcome you to our growing family of subscribers. We believe we have put together one of the finest staffs in the newspaper business and we know you will enjoy our modern approach to keeping you informed. Our paper contains the standard format of current events plus some innovative features about which we are very proud. Our paper reaches more readers in the state than any other and we are confident that this position of leadership will be maintained.

Dear Mr. Harrison:

We would like to take this opportunity to inform you that we have approved your application for credit purchases at our store. We have many quality products for you to choose from and we will continue to provide you with a wide choice of items. Our store has been a leader in its field for years and you can be proud of any purchase you make.

Proofreading Exercise

The letter on the following page contains mistakes that should be detected by the careful proofreader. Identify all of the errors (spelling, punctuation, capitalization, etc.). Note: All business letters should be single-spaced unless they are so short that double-spacing is necessary for proper balance on the paper. This letter is double-spaced, however, for your convenience in identifying and marking the errors.

January 17, 19xx

Mr. Joe A. Brown

Personnel Director

Thorstein, Incorporated

Trenton, NJ   00000

Dear Mr. Brown:

On November 4, George Jodey was transfered to us here in El Paso. However, we have had to terminate his employment with our organization. It seems that he just makes too many misteaks.

We observed his work patters for two weeks and compared him with several other men in this position to see if his output was similiar. His work is far below the avarage, so we feal that this action was nesessary. Will you please put his termination in affect at once.

We are still intrested in finding a good clerk to handle the tiping, filing, and other office chores. The rite person will be payer a salery of $600 per month. We realize that it's very close to inventorytime, but there is enough time to train a new clerk if we atc soon.

Sincerely yours,

The sentences below contain redundancies. Evaluate each item and rewrite it so as to avoid this type of error. Do not change the meaning of the statement as you change the wording.

1. The tennis team members all know the basic fundamentals well.
2. A variety of different models are available for purchase.
3. Please repeat again the information I just shared with you.
4. I first began to feel the pain in my right elbow.
5. The consensus of opinion seems to be that we should move now.
6. We were able to escape because we were only partially surrounded.
7. She said the exact same thing when she heard the good news.
8. Submit your list of new innovations before March 22.
9. The modern, up-to-date methods should improve the work flow.
10. The two cars involved in the wreck were completely destroyed.
11. The new employees considered their orientation to be total and complete.
12. Each and every one of you will receive a substantial bonus.
13. His approach to solving that problem is most unique.
14. Seven problems still remain to be solved.
15. It has been raining outside for nearly four hours straight.
16. The snow has been coming down since before noon.
17. The annual meeting held each year attracts thousands of members.
18. Do not get involved with false deception as you work with them.
19. It seems to be damp and wet down here in the basement.
20. The organization is still flourishing today.
21. The animal ran until it was tired and exhausted.
22. First and foremost in our minds is the safety of the child.
23. Frequently, the drainage seeps through often.
24. She got back the tax rebate yesterday.
25. Please take immediate action on this matter at once.

The Foundation of Writing Skills

PART 3

The Fundamentals of Writing

4

In this chapter you will find the basics of writing. Specifically, you will learn:

1. that words do not have meaning by themselves—rather, we assign meaning to them.

2. the differences between concrete and abstract words and when to use each type.

3. to use the abstraction ladder to determine word choice.

4. the terminology of the parts of speech.

5. the definitions of phrases, clauses, and sentences.

6. the role modifiers play in effective, mature writing.

7. how to avoid common problems in sentence development.

8. how to build paragraphs that possess the many qualities of good writing.

Words represent the most fundamental of the symbols we use for our planned communication. Many of our other symbols such as gestures, facial expressions, and pictures help to convey the meaning of the word symbols we use. Because of the importance of words, they deserve special consideration.

Of the tens of thousands of words at our command, most people can effectively use only a few thousand in their communication. Does this mean, then, that we have too many words? We shall see that this is not the case. The problem lies in our failing to gain sufficient understanding of words and their functions to enable us to use them wisely in expressing our ideas to others.

A Word About Words

One of the frequent assumptions we make about words is that they have meaning. This assumption is faulty, and it will be worth our time to examine this idea further. Hopefully, we will see that words do not have meaning in and of themselves, but that we assign meaning to them. This distinction is very important because one of the greatest contributors to communication problems is the fact that senders and receivers of messages make incorrect assumptions about the agreement of meanings. In other words, we assume that the other person in the communication process is assigning the same meanings to words that we give to them. However, because of differences in culture, environment, prejudices, or countless other factors, no two words in any language can possibly have exactly the same meaning for two or more persons (fig. 4.1). Granted, the differences may be slight, but they are differences. At times these differences may be insignificant; at other times they may be critical to effective communication.

Figure 4.1
Big man in the community

Consider for a moment the word *right*. Depending upon how it is used, this word can pertain to moral law, propriety, fitness, suitability, how something is situated, straightness, political views, a claim or title, orderliness, or soundness of mind or body—to list only a few possibilities.

Most words have both *connotative* and *denotative* meaning. Connotative meaning refers to the emotional dimension of the word, whereas denotative meaning refers simply to the idea or thing itself. Denotative meaning is rather standard and common to nearly all persons in a given culture, but connotative meaning will vary considerably even within the same culture. It follows that different emotional qualities will be assigned to most of the words that we use. Because of variations in sender/receiver perceptions, then, appropriate word choice is vital to accurate transmission of information.

Concrete and Abstract Words

We know that some words are easier to "see" as we hear them than are others. Those that are easy to visualize are called *concrete* words; those that are not are called *abstract* words. Because we want our ideas to be understood, we should use words that others can "see." Study the following words and determine which are concrete and which are abstract.

books	ideas	table
pencils	beauty	anger
appreciation	work	understanding
love	car	transportation

We can almost see the objects some of these words are intended to represent, but others are difficult even to conceptualize. This is not to say that we should never use abstract words; it means merely that we should use them sparingly if we want to have any degree of precision in our communications.

An abstraction ladder may help to illustrate this comparison between concrete and abstract words. Consider the logical progression from concreteness (the lower rungs) to abstractness (the higher rungs) in the following sets:

concrete → abstract

environment	imagination	standard of living	human behavior
resources	creativity	products	extra-curricular activities
wood	music	office equipment	athletics
pencil	note	desk	football

Notice that in each of the examples we move from something that is easily visualized up to something that is vague and abstract. Probably senders and receivers will be closer to the intended meanings of words if concrete terms are used than if abstract terms are used. An advantage will be gained if we use vivid words in our writing, otherwise we are very limited in getting a confirmation that our communications are understood.

If you have a tendency to think that we have "just too many words" from which to choose, consider this problem. Start with two words—one at each extreme of a continuum. Then find a word to describe a point or condition that lies between them. The words *hot* and *cold* are good examples. What word describes something that is exactly between hot and cold? Lukewarm? Tepid? Warm? To start with, what do you mean by *hot?* How hot or how cold do you mean? Will these and other words mean the same thing to the receiver as they do to the sender of the message?

Many of our words really take on meaning only when we study them in context or when we see them in relationship to other words or other things. We can assure better communication, then, if we remember these relationships.

Word Classification

Words can be classified as parts of speech. These parts are nouns, pronouns, verbs, adjectives, adverbs, prepositions, conjunctions, and interjections. When we understand these terms, we can evaluate the contribution they make to a complete thought. As a good mechanic must know the parts of an engine, so a good writer must know the parts of speech.

A **noun** is a word that names a person, place, thing, or quality.

> **Billy** hit the **ball** out of the **park.**
> **Democracy** is a **way** of **life.**
> The **paper** arrived late in the **morning.**
> The **dog** was tied to a **fence** in the **yard.**

Pronouns are words used to take the place of nouns.

> **He** hit the ball after **it** was thrown to **him.**
> **She** knows all about **that.**
> When the bicycle arrived, **we** assembled **it.**

Verbs are words used to express action or a condition of being.

She **read** the book in one hour.
The typewriter **was broken** last week.
The shipment **arrived** late in the afternoon.

Adjectives are words that modify or describe nouns or pronouns. They are not used to modify any other words. Adjectives answer the questions *which, what kind of,* or *how many.*

The **old** automobile was repaired.
The **green** sedan had a **dented** bumper.
Seven days have passed since **that** secretary was hired.

Note: *A, an,* and *the,* referred to as **articles,** are also adjectives.

Adverbs are words that modify or describe verbs, adjectives or other adverbs. Adverbs answer the questions *when, why, where, how,* and *how much.*

The accident was reported **quickly.**
The **happily** married couple returned **yesterday.**
You will hear from us **very soon.**

Prepositions are words used to connect or show relationship between nouns or pronouns and some other word or words in a sentence.

He was **in** the house **for** a long time.
Put the book **on** the table.
The lady moved **toward** the last picture **on** the wall.

Note: The noun or pronoun usually following the preposition is its **object.**

Conjunctions are words that connect other words, phrases, or clauses in a sentence.

Several cows **and** horses were killed in the fire.
I would like to go with you, **but** I am too tired.
She has spoken only twice **since** she arrived.
The foreman lectured **and** the workers listened.

Interjections are words used to make exclamations.

Ouch, that hurts!
Oh, did you see that!
Wow!

What has been presented here is only a brief description of the parts of speech and a few examples of each. We will enlarge upon these descriptions and give additional examples as we consider how these parts of speech function within sentences.

The Sentence

A **sentence** is a word, or group of words usually containing a subject and a verb, that expresses a complete thought. This thought may be of any length, but it must be complete to be classified as a sentence.

I ran.

(This is a complete thought.)

While I ran.

(This is not a complete thought. It is dependent upon additional words for completion of the meaning.)

Each sentence contains various words that serve different functions. An understanding of these words and the functions they serve will allow us to develop a better understanding of sentence structure. As with the study of any topic, there are certain terms that will assist us in understanding the concepts relating to English usage. Learn these terms as we move through the chapter and your task will be much easier.

Of all the words that are contained in sentences, the subjects and verbs are probably the most important. They form the foundation of the sentence itself and communicate the writer's basic meaning. Therefore, we should learn to identify the subject and verb of each sentence.

Subjects   The subject of a sentence can be a word or group of words about which something is stated or asked.

> The **typewriter** is broken.
> The **walls** will be painted tomorrow.

A compound subject is one that contains two or more related words or groups of words. As you look for the subject of a sentence, be certain that you find the complete form and not just a portion of it.

> The **desk, chair,** and **books** are to be shipped today.
> The **form** and **content** are both correct.
> The **shipping** and **billing** are completed by two separate departments.

Clauses and Phrases

The words that are used to form sentences are often grouped together within the sentence to show relationship and to complete the meaning of certain words. Learn to distinguish between these word groups.

A clause is a group of related words that has its own subject and verb. A sentence may be composed of two or more clauses, which means that the sentence may have two or more sets of subjects and verbs. Notice that the definition for a clause is similar to that for a sentence. One difference is that a clause does not necessarily represent a complete thought. A clause that does express a complete thought and could, therefore, stand alone is said to be *independent*. A clause which could not stand alone but depends on the rest of the sentence to complete its thought is said to be *dependent*. The following examples show the use of clauses in sentences. All the subjects and verbs are underscored to help you identify them. A solid underscore shows each clause.

> The **accountants were interested,** so **management agreed** to the meeting.

> (This sentence contains two independent clauses joined by the conjunction *so*.)

> Because **we were** two hours late, the **bus left** without us.

(This sentence contains two clauses, but the first is dependent on the rest of the sentence for the completion of its meaning.)

Harland gave the picture to Janice.

(This sentence contains only one clause, so it is independent and can stand alone as a complete sentence.)

Whoever enters the room next **will receive** the door prize.

(Notice that in this sentence the clause *whoever enters the room next* is also the subject of the complete sentence. Its verb is *will receive.*)

A **phrase** is a group of related words that does not have its own subject and verb. Phrases, like clauses, can function as subjects of sentences or in other ways to connect or to modify. Two or more phrases can also function as compound subjects.

Running to the store keeps John busy.

(The phrase is also the subject of the sentence.)

The books are stored **in the shipping room.**
Hitting the ball and **running the bases** require much coordination.

(The two phrases function as the compound subject of the sentence.)

Remember that a clause contains a subject and a verb, but a phrase does not. In chapter 5 we will consider other functions of clauses and phrases, but the information given here will help you to recognize these kinds of word groups.

Verbs   Verbs are words used to express action or conditions of being. The action expressed may be performed *by* the subject or it may be done *to* the subject. Verbs fill the important role of giving "life" to every sentence.

The car **slid** from the road.
He **made** the telephone call during his lunch break.

The dog was taken for a walk in the park.
He will have finished the work by then.

She reads and writes manual shorthand.

(Compound verb)

Bill and Mary sing well together.

(Compound subject and simple verb)

Subjects and verbs can be either simple or compound, and they may be either singular or plural. In order for our sentences to be logical, it is imperative that there be *agreement* between these components. In other words, if the subject is singular, the verb must also be singular. If the subject is plural, the verb must be plural. This important requirement will be discussed thoroughly in chapter 5. In that chapter you will also learn about the properties (characteristics) of verbs.

Modifiers

In a grammatical sense, to modify means to qualify the meaning of a word or group of words. Through the use of modifiers we achieve many of the subtleties or refinements of our language. Modifiers can describe, restrict, or make more exact the meaning of another word. Proper use of modifiers will enable one to communicate ideas more effectively than would be possible without this skill. Correct usage of modifiers may be the mark of a mature, established writer.

Modifiers are generally classified as adjectives or adverbs. These modifiers include single words as well as phrases and clauses which function as adjectives or adverbs. The following sentences show some of the uses of modifiers.

Nine dollars is a large sum for the book.
Try to give an accurate description.
My assignment is to read this book by next week.
The French embassy was picketed by students.

In the above examples, single words are used as modifiers. Often two or more words may be combined to serve as a single modifier.

When this compound modifier comes before a noun or pronoun, it must be hyphenated. If the modifier comes after the noun or pronoun it should not be hyphenated.

part-time work	but	the work is part time
up-to-date plan	but	the plan is up to date
short-circuited wiring	but	the wiring is short circuited
well-planned effort	but	the effort was well planned

Further discussion of compound adjectives is found in the unit on punctuation in chapter 5.

When two or more words do not work jointly to modify a word, they are not hyphenated regardless of their placement.

The long, hard journey came to an end ten days later.
The old, worn roof was finally repaired last summer.
The dark green car was parked near the school.
The complacent, careless crew members were terminated.

To determine whether to place the comma between the two modifiers, see if the word *and* can be placed between the two words without changing the meaning of the sentence. If this can be done, use the comma in place of the *and*. In the first example, the journey was long *and* hard. However, the car in the third sentence was not dark *and* green. *Dark* is modifying *green;* therefore, the comma is not used.

Verbals as Modifiers   In addition to single words and compound adjectives, phrases and clauses may serve as modifiers. An important kind of phrase is the group called **verbals.** A verbal is a *verb form* (it has some properties of a verb) but it does not function as a verb. The three kinds of verbals are infinitives, gerunds, and participles. Verbals are so important to effective communication that we must learn to recognize them and to use them to increase our ability to express ourselves.

Infinitives are simple, uninflected (unchanged) forms of verbs that express action or a state of being. They do not refer to person, number, or tense and are usually preceded by *to:* to go, to run, to hit.

We want to go.

(The infinitive, to go, indicates action; however, the verb in the sentence is *want*.)

The teacher makes us think.

(*Think* is an infinitive even though it is not preceded by *to*.)

Infinitives and infinitive phrases may function either as adjectives or as adverbs. Remember that this functioning is determined by the kind of words they modify.

To enjoy good performance, you should service your car regularly.

(The infinitive phrase modifies *you*; therefore, it is an adjective because adjectives modify nouns and pronouns.)

He telephoned to explain the delay.

(The infinitive modifies the verb, telephoned; therefore, it is an adverb.)

Gerunds are verb forms ending in *ing* which function as nouns. Because gerunds are nouns, they seldom function as modifiers; however, a gerund phrase may be the object of a preposition and, as such, may serve as an adjective or adverb.

After meeting with each of the candidates, she announced her decision.

(The prepositional-gerund phrase serves as an adjective modifying *she*.)

He ended his report by summarizing his conclusions.

(The phrase serves as an adverb modifying *ended*.)

Participles are verb forms which function as adjectives. A participle is referred to as having *tense*, which will be explained in chapter 5. For now, consider the function of participles as they modify.

Smiling, the candidates awaited the judges' decision.

(The participle modifies *candidates.*)

The large room, **painted** and **decorated,** will be her new office.

(The participles modify *room.*)

Having been arrested three times, he feared the court's decision.

(The participle modifies *he.*)

Other Modifiers   Other phrases or clauses may serve as modifiers. For example, a prepositional phrase may serve as either an adjective or an adverb. Dependent clauses may also serve as adjectives or adverbs.

She gave the report to the man **in the last office.**

(The prepositional phrase is used as an adjective to modify *man.*)

They left **for the mainland** on the morning plane.

(The prepositional phrase is used as an adverb to modify *left.*)

This is the farm **where I spent my childhood.**

(The clause modifies *farm;* therefore, it is used as an adjective.)

We enjoyed the scenery **while we traveled.**

(The clause modifies *enjoyed;* therefore, it is an adverb.)

Distinguishing Between Adjectives and Adverbs   These examples show that many words and phrases may be either adjectives or adverbs, depending upon how they are used. Remember that adverbs modify adjectives, verbs, or other adverbs; adjectives modify nouns or pronouns. Read the following sentences that show the use of single words serving as adverbs.

Roscoe can run **faster** than his coach.

(Modifies the verb *run.*)

Each student should write **plainly.**

(Modifies the verb *write.*)

This is a **very** informative report.

(Modifies the adjective *informative.*)

The new secretary is doing **very** well.

(Modifies the adverb *well.*)

Notice that only one of the adverbs used in these sentences ends in *ly.* Yet, many writers have a tendency to assume that all adverbs end in *ly* and that all words ending in *ly* are adverbs. Each assumption is incorrect. Some adjectives end in *ly* (friendly, orderly, timely, etc.) and some adverbs do not end in *ly* (soon, often, very, etc.). Some words may function either as adjectives or as adverbs.

That is a **hard** decision.

(Adjective modifies the noun *decision.*)

He works **hard** for what he gets paid.

(Adverb modifies *works,* a verb.)

If you remember that adjectives modify nouns or pronouns and that adverbs modify adjectives, verbs, or other adverbs, you will have no trouble distinguishing between these two kinds of modifiers.

Special Problems With Modifiers   With an understanding of the kinds of modifiers and their functions, we are almost ready to start using them effectively in our writing. Some problems are still present, however, and we must solve them to be sure that the modifiers we use are doing the best job in our writing and speaking. Two of these problems relate to the proper placement of the modifier within the sentence, and the logical connection of the modifier with the other parts of the sentence. Grammatically speaking, the modifier may be *misplaced* or it may *dangle.* A sentence with either of these faults may be ambiguous, confusing, misleading, or unintentionally funny.

The burden rests with the writer to save the reader from the task of interpreting this kind of unclear writing. Special care should be taken to avoid misplaced or dangling modifiers. Because the writers know what they mean to say, they may not recognize the variety of interpretations that their writing may suggest to the reader. The following sentences may have been clear to the writer. Will the reader get the same meaning from them?

> The scouts came upon an unknown lake hiking in the woods.
> The secretary was startled by a noise in the outer office.
> Snarling and foaming at the mouth, the officer had to destroy the rabid dog.
> After being used by everyone in the office, the clerk found that the typewriter did not work properly.

Misplaced Modifiers. Modifiers should be placed as near as possible to the words that they modify. If other words intervene, the reader must search for the meaning and may assign the wrong word to the modifier.

Subjects and verbs of sentences should be close together. Wherever possible, avoid inserting modifiers between the subject and the verb.

> Not: The **committee,** having been briefed by the department managers and sales personnel, **convened** to discuss the alternatives.
> But: Having been briefed by the department managers and the sales personnel, the **committee convened** to discuss the alternatives.

Whether the modifier is a single word, a phrase, or a clause, it should be placed as close as possible to the word or phrase it modifies. The following sentences show some problems with misplaced modifiers and some revisions that correct the problem.

> Not: Please bring me a **cold** glass of water.
> But: Please bring me a glass of **cold** water.

> Not: We **almost** have enough money for our rent.
> But: We have **almost** enough money for our rent.

> Not: We **only** have two more weeks of school.
> But: We have **only** two more weeks of school.

Not: All of the cases were handled by the deputies **that were over two years old.**

But: All of the cases **that were over two years old** were handled by the deputies.

Most single-word modifiers should be placed immediately before the word they modify. Relative clauses, such as the modifier *that were over two years old*, should usually be placed immediately after the word they modify. An adverbial clause may be placed either before or after the main clause. Placing the adverbial clause first will put greater emphasis on the main clause. We may decide to place the adverbial clause at the end of the sentence to de-emphasize an unpleasant idea in the main clause.

Dangling Modifiers. Modifiers are said to dangle when they do not logically modify the subject of the main clause. If the writer fails to provide the modifier with anything to modify, it is forced to hang on to the nearest or most convenient word whether or not it can do so logically.

To get the most from this course, the exercises should be completed regularly.

The infinitive phrase, *to get the most from this course*, dangles because it does not logically modify *exercises*. To correct this sentence, we must change the subject of the main clause to one that is properly modified.

To get the most from this course, you should complete the exercises regularly.

In this sentence, the infinitive phrase correctly modifies *you* since it is *you*, not exercises, who seeks "to get the most from this course." Now, look carefully at the following sentence:

Under great pressure, many errors were made in the final report.

The prepositional phrase, *under great pressure*, is serving as a modifier. Can you pick out the word it modifies? Grammatically, it seems to be modifying *errors* since that is the subject of the main clause. But, is it logical to assume that *errors* were "under great pressure"? Since the phrase does not logically modify the subject of the main clause, it dangles. The sentence can be corrected by changing the subject of the main clause to one which is correctly modified by the prepositional phrase.

> **Under great pressure, the typist (or they, Mr. Jones, etc.) made many errors in the final report.**

Special attention to the placement and relationship of modifiers will give you more assurance that they are doing the job of adding meaning and clarity to the writing. If we use too few modifiers, our writing is drab and colorless; if we use too many, our writing may sound "gushy" or insincere.

Paragraphs

We have looked closely at words as communication symbols, at the classification of words, and at their function in forming sentences. A sentence represents a convenient package of words. Each of the words blends with each of the others to form a single, meaningful unit. Sometimes a single sentence is not sufficient to convey our idea, so we group the sentences about a single idea into a larger unit called the paragraph. Any number of paragraphs can be combined to form letters and reports.

The grouping of words, sentences, and paragraphs is of special help to the reader. This grouping helps to separate the ideas that are expressed into groups or patterns similar to those that existed in the mind of the writer. If this transfer of meaning is successful, we have accomplished the objectives of our communication effort.

For most business writing, paragraphs will be rather short—perhaps no more than six to eight lines in length. This length will give the writer and the reader closer control over the main thought and will promote better understanding.

Sometimes the writer may need to develop additional ideas about the main thought—more than can be conveniently included in one paragraph. The writer can help the reader to connect the ideas in these paragraphs by using words or expressions of transition. Examples of such transitional expressions include the following:

Furthermore,	Equally important . . .
In addition . . .	Again . . .
Besides . . .	Further . . .
Moreover,	Likewise . . .

At other times, it may be necessary to show a contrast between the idea in one paragraph and that of another. The writer can help the reader to make this change or to show cause-and-effect relationships between paragraphs by using carefully chosen transitional expressions. Consider the message that each of the following expressions would give to the reader who moves from one paragraph to another.

Consequently,	However,
At the same time,	On the other hand,
For this purpose,	Accordingly,
Hence,	After all,
Nevertheless,	On the contrary,
Therefore,	Still,

We have learned that our communications should have a primary and secondary objective. Careful construction of paragraphs along with the proper attention to the other writing fundamentals will help to achieve the primary objective and will lead to what we call *message unity*.

If we are writing a business letter about the refund of an overpayment for goods purchased from a supplier, the letter should not include information about an entirely unrelated subject. The letter should be unified in thought to the extent that the sentences and paragraphs all pertain to the same subject. This does not mean that we cannot make incidental reference to other topics; it does mean, however, that all ideas in the letter should in some way fit together. If incidental or extraneous information is included, it should probably appear in the closing paragraph where it can be used as a transitional device for future communication.

As you read the following letter, notice the lack of message unity. The paragraphs shift from one unrelated idea to another without any transitional helps. Furthermore, some of the ideas are so unrelated as to have no place in the letter.

Dear Mr. Johnston:

Your order for one gross of "Warm-Lite" lamps should reach you within one week. These particular lamps have been hard to keep in stock, but fortunately, you placed your order well ahead of others we received.

This opening paragraph is acceptable. Uses the direct approach.

The life of this lamp has been increased considerably by the redesign of the starter receptacle. We are confident, therefore, that you will be pleased with the service it gives you. Be sure to call us collect if you encounter any difficulties with this new dimension in home lighting.

This paragraph is also acceptable. Makes good use of transitional words.

Be careful not to give reader the impression that you do in fact expect difficulties to be "encountered."

Progress on our new plant has been halted due to the extended strike of Local 389. Delays of this nature can be very upsetting, especially during our busy season.

This paragraph does not belong in the letter. It violates concept of unity.

Thank you for your continued patronage, Mr. Johnston, and please let us know if we can serve you in any other way.

This paragraph is almost worthless. It is nothing more than a trite expression.

Very sincerely yours,

Now see if the rewrite of this letter corrects the problems identified above.

Dear Mr. Johnston:

Your order for one gross of "Warm-Lite" lamps should reach you within one week. These particular lamps have been hard to keep in stock, but fortunately, you placed your order well ahead of others we received.

The life of this lamp has been in-

No change needed in this paragraph.

creased considerably by the redesign of the starter receptacle. We are confident, therefore, that you will be pleased with the service it gives you. Be sure to call us collect if you need any assistance with this new dimension in home lighting.

A slight change in the wording here takes emphasis off of "difficulties."

Thank you for yet another order, Mr. Johnston, and please let us know when we might help again.

Goodwill objective appears to be met in this paragraph.

Very sincerely yours,

Summary

Words are powerful communication symbols. The more we understand about words, the better we are able to use them to transfer our thoughts and ideas to others. We have learned that words can be grouped into sentences, sentences into paragraphs, and paragraphs into a unit of communication. We have also learned that words can be classified according to certain functions they perform within the sentence.

The primary objective of communication is to convey a message. This objective is more easily achieved through the proper selection, modification, and organization of words, sentences, and paragraphs. The next step is to learn to apply the rules that will allow the refinement of our writing through a careful structuring of the parts of our language.

A good paragraph will contain a topic sentence, a single purpose, and a unity of thought. Each of these criteria is important to effective expression. The topic sentence generally appears at the beginning of the paragraph if the direct approach is used. If the message is written in indirect format, this sentence will appear at or near the end of the paragraph. The second criterion, a single purpose, refers to the objective of the writer. Each paragraph should possess only that wording which supports this single purpose. No other information should be included. Finally, the third criterion pertains to the quality of cohesiveness—the way the ideas are tied together. This unity of thought is best achieved through the use of appropriate transitional words.

Evaluate the preceding paragraph on the basis of the criteria mentioned in it. Identify the topic sentence, describe the single purpose, and list the transitional words which give the paragraph a unity of thought.

Paragraph Exercises

Evaluate the logic of the information presented in the following statements. Write a separate paragraph for each of the statements either by supporting or challenging the validity of the contents. Remember the criteria for good paragraph construction as you develop your responses.

Statement No. 1

Sarah Filer and Mary Peterson lived next door to each other in a ten-year-old housing development. Each bought new carpeting for her house in the month of February three years ago. Each household has four family members. Mrs. Filer's orlon carpeting is beginning to show signs of wear throughout her house while Mrs. Peterson's nylon floor covering appears to be in perfect condition. Mrs. Peterson concludes, therefore, that nylon carpeting provides better and longer service than does orlon carpeting.

Statement No. 2

A recent campus study revealed that college students who watch television programs between fifteen and twenty hours per week have higher grade point averages than those students who watch less than fifteen hours per week. They conclude that watching television is a good way to improve performance in the classroom.

Statement No. 3

Mr. Maurie Burns, Office Manager for Apel Corporation, sent a memorandum to all office personnel in his department telling them of a new procedure he has developed that changes the priorities for summer vacations. Since the notification was communicated to everyone over two months ago and nobody has complained to him, Mr. Burns believes that everyone considers the new policy to be acceptable.

Statement No. 4

Don Clayton and Clyde Chase each manage similar production divisions in the Corbone Company. They are both thirty-eight years old and have been with the organization the same number of years. Clayton, who is a "production" oriented manager, consistently gets greater productivity from his workers than does Chase who is a "people" oriented manager. The management group believe, therefore, that a "production" oriented type of supervision will yield better results than a "people" oriented type.

Statement No. 5

A recent analysis of hospital census figures shows that hospitals nearly always have fewer patients during the month of December than during any other month in the year. One observer stated that this phenomenon is probably due to the fact that the holiday season is more conducive to psychological health than is any other time period.

Statement No. 6

A researcher determined that the management of a particular company would have made the correct marketing decision 60 percent of the time without the benefit of supporting research. She concluded that the company would be money ahead if it depended solely upon the judgment of management and did not conduct research studies.

The following sentences illustrate problems with the use of modifiers. Indicate the nature of the problem and rewrite the sentence to correct the original statement. If the sentence does not have a modifier problem, indicate that the word order is correct as presented.

Sentence Rewrite Exercises

Example

   After spending $12 for lodging, George only had $6 left for food.

   (Misplaced modifier)

   After spending $12 for lodging, George had only $6 left for food.

1. She was almost married for seven years.
2. Snarling and frothing at the mouth, the officer had to destroy the rabid dog.
3. The person who learns to to this job well deserves a promotion.
4. He drank four cold glasses of water.
5. As soon as we receive an up-to-date report, we will make a decision on your application.
6. I was only gone for a few minutes when the fire broke out.
7. After completing the final sections, the report should be mailed to each stockholder.
8. To make the best use of your time, a schedule should be followed closely.
9. While hiking in the woods, an unnamed lake was found.
10. His remarks were well-received.

The Structure of Writing

5

In this chapter you will study the structure of written communications. Specifically, this study will include:

1. the proper sequence of the parts of speech.

2. the classification of sentences according to type.

3. the agreement of sentence parts.

4. the use of verbs.

5. a consideration of expression cast in active and passive voice.

6. an examination of the importance of parallel structure.

Chapter 4 described the parts of a sentence and the functions of those parts. Now we can consider the assembling of the parts into proper sequence to form effective sentences—sentences that convey the message (primary objective) and promote goodwill (secondary objective).

A good chef knows how to blend and serve certain food items to create a meal that is pleasing to the senses of sight, smell, and taste. A haphazard or careless blending of these same ingredients may destroy, rather than stimulate, our appetite.

Similarly, the good writer knows how to blend the elements of a sentence so that the message is clearly stated and is pleasing to the reader. The good writer knows that each part of the sentence complements the rest of the sentence and helps to bind it tightly into a unit. A careless or faulty blending of these parts results in a sentence that may be not only unclear but also misleading in its meaning to the reader. Just as the chef turns a piece of meat into a pleasing and tasty meal with a proper blend of spices, seasoning, and garnish, so the good writer blends words, modifiers, and sentences with a proper amount of grammar and psychology to turn a drab, routine message into a pleasant and profitable business experience.

A Practical Approach to Writing

Business writing should serve some practical purpose. The primary objective of business writing is to convey a message, so let's consider a practical approach to that objective. A student once remarked, "It don't matter HOW I say something, just as long as people can figure out WHAT I mean." Although this statement is grammatically incorrect, its philosophy may be correct if we make certain assumptions. For instance, we may assume that the receiver of the message does not recognize deficiencies in grammar or logic. We may also assume that the receiver does not object to being required to search for meaning, decipher incorrect sentence structure, and interpret the message he receives.

However, the letter writer seldom has information sufficient to permit these assumptions. The careful writer assumes that it DOES make a difference how the message is formed.

From a practical point of view, the business writer is not likely to be faced with the necessity of orating at length about split infinitives, pronoun-antecendent references, or dangling modifiers. But a knowledge of the part these elements play in effective communication will help in the construction of sentences, letters, and reports that are practical, clear, and effective.

Kinds of Sentences

In chapter 4 a sentence was described as a group of related words containing a subject and a verb and expressing a complete thought. A clause was described as a group of related words containing a subject and a verb. A clause is said to be *independent* when it makes a complete statement and is not introduced by any subordinating word. A clause of this kind, when it stands alone, is a simple sentence.

A *simple sentence* contains only one independent clause, but it may contain many phrases, a compound subject or verb, and many modifiers. Therefore, the simple sentence may be very short:

Linda watched.

or it may be quite long:

The accountants and computer analysts should request their vacation time in writing and should include two or more alternatives for consideration by the Personnel Department.

The first sentence consists of a subject (Linda) and a verb (watched). In the second sentence, the compound subject (accountants and analysts) and the verb (should request) are supported by a number of connectives, modifiers and phrases to clarify and complete the meaning of the sentence.

A *compound sentence* is one that contains two or more independent clauses. The independent clauses in a compound sentence may be joined by a conjunction:

> I studied for only two hours before the examination, so my score was no surprise.

The conjunction *so* joins the two independent clauses. Notice that without the conjunction either of the independent clauses could stand alone.

Not all independent clauses are joined in this way to form compound sentences. Consider the following examples. Each is a compound sentence, but the clauses are joined differently.

1. George wanted to leave on the next bus, but Harry wanted to wait until morning.
2. I would rather work alone; I do not need your help.
3. Rain threatened to delay the game; however, we finished by noon.
4. We worked and they watched.

Sentence 1 follows our first example with the two clauses joined by the conjunction *but*. Notice also that in these examples a comma precedes the conjunction to separate the two independent clauses.

Sentence 2 is also a compound sentence. However, these two clauses are joined by a semicolon. These clauses could stand separately as simple sentences, but the use of the semicolon to form the compound sentence shows a closer relationship between the thoughts expressed in the two clauses.

Sentence 3 is a compound sentence, but the clauses are joined by a conjunctive adverb. Conjunctive adverbs are used to join independent clauses and to show a relationship between them. Some examples of conjunctive adverbs are: *therefore, however, consequently, accordingly, furthermore, moreover, nevertheless*. When independent clauses are joined by a conjunctive adverb, it should be preceded by a semicolon and followed by a comma.

Although sentence 4 is very short, it is a compound sentence. These two clauses are joined by the conjunction *and*, but no comma is necessary because the clauses are so short. If the clauses are short enough and the relationship is clear enough, no punctuation is necessary.

Some sentences may contain *dependent* clauses as well as independent clauses. Sentences having one or more dependent clauses and one independent clause are *complex sentences*.

> **When we arrived at the conference room, we found the meeting in progress.**

In this sentence the introductory clause is dependent on the rest of the sentence to complete its meaning. The introductory word *when* attaches a condition which makes this clause dependent.

The fourth kind of sentence is the *compound-complex*. This type of sentence contains at least two independent clauses and one or more dependent clauses.

> **Since you are obviously not interested in our case, we will secure another attorney; you may bill us for your previous services.**

This sentence contains one dependent clause and two independent clauses. Can you identify them?

The writer who has a good understanding of the kinds of sentences is in a better position to add variety, interest, and fluency to writing. Read the following paragraph. Is it easy to read and understand? Is it interesting?

> **The entire student body turned out to welcome the team. They were returning from the national tournament. They had won the championship. The final game was won in overtime. The score was 94-93. A real team effort had made the difference.**

In this example the information is given in a series of short, simple sentences. Each sentence, if taken separately, is easy to understand. However, a reader may feel out of breath because of hopping from one short, choppy sentence to another. Another problem is that it is more difficult to show the relationship that one sentence has to another. Remember that one important function of connectives is to show this relationship. When writing includes the variety that results from using a blend of simple, compound, and complex sentences, this relationship can be shown by proper choice of connectives and clauses. Now, read the same information in a paragraph wherein these principles are applied.

> The entire student body turned out to welcome the team as they returned from the national tournament. They were the national champions, having won the final game 94-93 in overtime. A real team effort had made the difference.

These sentences show a relationship of ideas and help the reader to understand more about the message. Notice that the use of the simple sentence at the end causes the single idea in that clause to stand out more vividly. Later on we will talk about the use of sentence structure as one of the techniques for emphasizing or de-emphasizing an idea.

Agreement of the Parts of the Sentence

Our objective in writing is to transfer meaning from the mind of the writer to the mind of the reader. Writing is more likely to accomplish that objective when all the parts of writing—words, phrases, punctuation, etc.—are in *agreement* with each other. We may say that the parts of the sentence must be in harmony. The agreement of these sentence parts deserves special attention.

Agreement of Subject and Verb

The real "meat" of the sentence is shown in the agreement between the subject (the thing the sentence is about) and the verb (what the subject does or has done to it). This agreement of the subject and verb applies to the properties of *number* and *person*. If the subject is singular in number, the verb must be singular. If the subject is in the second person, the verb must be in the second person. Two problems for the writer are recognizing the real subject of the sentence and determining whether it is singular or plural. In most sentences these problems are easily solved, but consider the following example.

> Each of the men (**is or are**) expected to apply for (**his or their**) vacation before Tuesday.

Before we can determine which verb to use, we must identify the real subject. In this sentence, the real subject is *each*, which is singular. Therefore, our choice for the verb should be *is*. The correct pronoun is *his*, rather than *their*, because of the singular subject to which it refers. Each is one of a group of words sometimes referred to as *indefinite pronouns*. This group includes *each, either, every, neither, everyone, everybody, somebody, someone, anybody, anyone, no one, nobody*, and *a person*. These words are singular in meaning. Whenever one of them is used as the subject of a sentence, the verb must be singular.

Anyone who applies himself **is** sure to do well on the test.
Everybody was having a good time at the party.
No one is more interested in protecting your rights than I am.
Neither of us **was** willing to admit that he was wrong.

Any one of the clerks **is** eligible for promotion.

(*Any one* is written as two words when it is followed by a phrase.)

Even when two of these indefinite pronouns are joined by *and*, they remain singular. This situation differs from the normal rule for compound subjects.

Anyone and **everyone was** present for the hearing.
But: **He** and **I are** going to the convention.

A few words deserve special consideration. For example, *many a* is singular when it is the subject of a sentence, but *many* is plural. *More than one* is singular even though its meaning is plural. *A number* is plural, but *the number* is singular when these words are the subject of sentences. The words *both, few, several*, and *others* are plural.

Some other words which vary from the routine as subjects of sentences are included in the group called *collective nouns*. A collective names a group of people or things. A collective may be either singular or plural depending upon what is meant by the sentence. When the members of the group act as a unit, the collective is singular. When the members act individually, the collective is plural. Some examples of common collectives are: *jury, committee, class, family, group, couple*, and *pair*.

> The committee is visiting Hawthorne School this week.
> The jury are arguing about the evidence.
> Better: The members of the jury are arguing about the evidence.

Company names are collectives and may be either singular or plural, usually determined by the ending sound.

> Johnson Brothers have given their employees a Christmas bonus.
> Hollifield, Inc., ships its materials to seven foreign countries.

A few short words—though they are not collectives—are governed by the rules for collectives. That is, they are singular or plural depending upon the meaning of the sentence in which they are used. Some of these words are: *all, any, more, most, none, some, who,* and *which.* Usually the writer shows the intended meaning by the choice of verb. However, if a prepositional phrase follows one of these words, the noun in that phrase controls the number of the verb. Fractions also follow this rule.

> **Some** of the pencils **have** been lost.
> **Most** of the schedule **is** planned.
> **Which is** to be discarded? (Which one?)
> **Which are** to be discarded? (Which ones?)
> The **rest** of the meeting **was** a fiasco.
> The **rest** of the interviews were scheduled for Friday.
> **Three-fourths** of the load **was** lost.
> **Three-fourths** of his pigeons **were** destroyed.

When a number and a word are used as the subject to express a *unit* of measure, the subject is singular. However, when the term is used to express individual parts, the subject is plural and takes a plural verb.

> **Forty dollars is** a lot of money for her.

(Single unit)

> **Twenty dollars are** stacked on the counter.

(Individual parts)

Fifty push-ups **is** his goal for next week.

(Single unit)

Be sure to find the *real* subject of the sentence. This task may be a little more difficult when the verb precedes the subject or when the sentence starts with *where, here,* or *there.* Can you find the subject of the following sentence?

Here in the orientation session is our best opportunity to train the new clerk.

If you picked out *opportunity,* you are correct. The tendency to think that *here* is the subject would result in confusion in the selection of the proper verb.

Some of the words we use in our language have foreign or unusual plural forms. For example: *Analyses* is the plural of *analysis. Bases* is the plural of *basis. Phenomena* is the plural of *phenomenon. Criteria* is the plural of *criterion.*

Data is the plural of *datum;* however, it may be thought of as a collective noun. When we refer to *data* as a mass of facts (a unit), it may be treated as a singular form.

Memoranda is the Latin plural of *memorandum.* Through usage, the English plural, *memorandums,* has become more popular and is considered acceptable. In a like manner, *curriculum* (singular) has become *curriculums* (plural) in addition to *curricula* (plural also).

Agreement of Pronouns and Antecedents   Just as subjects and verbs must agree, pronouns and antecedents must agree and must show consistency within the sentence. One part of the problem in assuring this agreement is in the matching of the pronoun with its proper antecedent (the word to which it refers). In the sentence *Janet said that she was leaving, she* refers to *Janet;* therefore, *Janet* is the antecedent.

Which words would properly complete this sentence?
Many a person (feel, feels) strongly that (his, their) interests are not being represented.

Remember that *many a* is singular, so your choice for the verb should be *feels.* We must also choose the singular pronoun, *his,* which refers to the singular subject.

Once you have established a word as being singular or plural, you must be consistent in all references to that word throughout the sentence. All verbs and all pronouns that refer to the word must agree with it. Note the word choices in the following sentence:

Because this company bases its success on its ability to represent their clients, your suggestion is . . . .

In this sentence the first two pronouns refer to *company* as a singular form. However, the third pronoun, *their*, shifts to the plural form. This inconsistent use of the pronoun detracts from the effectiveness of the sentence. In the following sentences, can you identify the correct words?

Did either of the applicants bring (his/her, their) credentials?
Each of our supervisors expressed (his, their) opinion to the committee.
Notify the Personnel Manager if anyone changes (his, their) mind.

In each of these sentences, *his/her* is the correct choice because it agrees with the singular antecedents, *either, each,* and *anyone.*

Sometimes, because of placement or usage, pronouns may be vague or ambiguous.

The office manager told Mr. Johnson that he thought he would be promoted next week.

Who will be promoted? Mr. Johnson or the office manager? By repeating the antecedent or properly placing the pronoun, the meaning becomes clear.

The office manager said that he thought Mr. Johnson would be promoted next week.

Vague or implied antecedents may result in sentences that are not clear to the reader. The writer knows what is meant, but the reader must either guess as to the meaning or read unnecessarily long sentences. In the following pairs of examples, compare the clarity and conciseness when the sentence is properly worded.

Not: Your complaint has been referred to the Personnel Department, a copy of which is attached.

But: We have attached a copy of your complaint which was referred to the Personnel Department.

Not: In the newspaper, it says that we can expect the inflation rate to accelerate.

But: The newspaper reports that we can expect the inflation rate to accelerate.

These problems can be overcome by avoiding the use of pronouns that do not have antecedents, by placing the pronoun as close as possible to its antecedent, or by wording the sentence so that the pronoun reference is obvious.

Agreement by Case   Case is that property of nouns and pronouns which shows their relationship to other parts of the sentence. This relationship may be shown either by positioning within the sentence or by inflection, a change in form.

English grammar has three cases: nominative, objective, and possessive. All nouns and a few pronouns keep the same form in the nominative and the objective cases. The position of these words in the sentence indicates their function. Our only problem with these words is in their formation as possessives.

Most pronouns, however, change form in all three cases. This fact causes added trouble for the writer and results in frequent misuse of these words. The following chart shows the personal pronouns and the changes or inflections that are made to correctly show their relationship to number, person, and gender, as well as to case.

The *nominative case* is used primarily to name subjects of verbs or as a predicate complement after a linking verb (seem, appear, or any form of *be*).

He and **I** will be arriving late.

(Subject of sentence)

Please give this report to **whoever** calls for it.

(Subject of a relative clause. Notice that the verb of the relative clause is *calls* and that the entire relative clause, *whoever calls for it*, is the object of the preposition *to*.)

Case	Nominative		Possessive		Objective	
Number	Singular	Plural	Singular	Plural	Singular	Plural
First Person	I	we	my mine	our ours	me	us
Second Person	you	you	your yours	your yours	you	you
Third Person Masculine	he	they	his	their theirs	him	them
Feminine	she	they	her hers	their theirs	her	them
Neuter	it	they	its	their theirs	it	them

Martha is a better accountant than I.

(Subject of an implied clause, . . . than I *am*.)

Whoever is chosen will ride on the queen's float.

(Subject of a relative clause. Notice that the entire clause is the subject of the sentence.)

The auditors, Alan and he, will be here tomorrow.

(*Alan* and *he* is an appositive, which is a group of words standing next to another word and denoting the same person or thing. The appositive must always be in the same case as the word it is in apposition to—its antecedent. *Auditors*, the subject, is in the nominative case; therefore, the appositive must also be in the nominative case.)

Helen is the student who we suppose will score the highest on the test.

(*Who* is the subject of the relative clause and is not affected by the intervening words *we suppose*.)

The queen candidates are **Doris and she.**

(Predicate complement following the linking verb *are*. This structure is called a predicate nominative and is in the nominative case.)

The objective case is used to name words that function as objects. These words may be the objects of verbs, verbals, or prepositions.

The players lifted **him** to their shoulders.

(*Him* is in the objective case because it is the direct object of the verb *lifted*.)

The commissioners invited **her** and **me** to attend the hearing.

(The compound object *her* and *me* is the object of the verb *invited*.)

They expected **us** secretaries to work overtime without additional pay.

(*Us*, as well as its appositive *secretaries*, is the object of the verb *expected*.)

We had not planned to invite **them** to the conference.

(*Them* is the object of the infinitive *to invite*.)

We mailed a letter to the club thanking **them** for their help.

(*Them* is the object of the participle *thanking*.)

The controller gave **me** the financial report.

(*Me* is the indirect object of the verb *gave*.)

The telegram giving **him** the news was received yesterday.

(*Him* is the indirect object of the participle *giving*.)

To help **us** understand the company procedures, the office manager held an orientation session.

(*Us* is the indirect object of the infinitive *to help*.)

In each of the examples which follow, the pronoun is used as the object of a preposition. The preposition and its object are in bold type.

Will you please give the message **to him.**
Whom did you give the message **to?**
The person **for whom** your remarks are intended is no longer with our company.
The bulletin stated that the pay raise was **for us** engineers.

Everyone **but me** planned to attend the Miami convention.

(*But* is used here as a preposition, so its object *me* is in the objective case.)

Take your complaint to **whoever will listen.**

(Notice that the entire clause *whoever will listen* is the object of the preposition *to.* However, the relative pronoun *whoever* is in the nominative case because it is the subject of the clause.)

Remember that the subject of a verb is always in the nominative case. However, there are two situations in which the objective case is used as a subject. Subjects of infinitives and subjects of participles are in the objective case.

We expect her to be chosen.

(*Her* is the subject of the infinitive *to be.*)

Whom did they invite to speak at the dinner?

(*Whom* is the subject of the infinitive *to speak.*)

In each of these sentences the pronoun is the subject of the infinitive and not the object of the verb. In the first sentence the object of the verb *expect* is the entire phrase *her to be chosen.*

When the infinitive *to be* has a subject, the word following the infinitive must also be in the objective case.

They did not expect their competitors to be him and me.
Or: They did not expect him and me to be their competitors.

The subject of a participle is in the objective case. The writer may have a problem, however, in determining whether a verbal is a participle or a gerund since both may have the same form—the *ing* form of the verb. To solve this problem, determine whether the *doer* of the action or the *action* itself is being emphasized. If the emphasis is on the doer of the action, the verbal is a participle functioning as an adjective to modify a noun or pronoun. However, if the action itself is the important thing, the verbal is a gerund. Remember that gerunds are nouns and that nouns name *things*. The subject of a gerund is in the possessive case. The possessive case will be explained later, but the following sentences will help you to choose the correct case for gerunds and participles.

Imagine him asking for a raise.

(The emphasis here is on the pronoun *him*. Therefore, *asking* is a participle modifying *him* which is in the objective case.)

There is very little merit in his studying only ten minutes each day.

(Here the emphasis is on the practice of *studying only ten minutes each day*. The verbal *studying* is a gerund, and its subject, *his*, is in the possessive case.)

The possessive case is used to indicate possession. Most nouns and some pronouns retain the same form in the possessive case. For these words the possessive is formed by adding the apostrophe and an *s*.

the dog's collar; the secretary's chair

This principle of forming the possessive by adding an apostrophe and an *s* applies to singular nouns that do not end in *s*. To a great extent we can rely on the *sound* of words to determine the correct possessive form. For singular nouns that end in *s* the possessive is formed by adding the apostrophe alone if the possessive is not sounded with an additional *s-sound* or by adding the apostrophe and *s* if the pronunciation of the possessive includes an additional *s-sound*.

stewardess (stewardess'); boss (boss's)

This table shows some examples of the use of possessive case.

Singular	Possessive	Plural	Possessive
child	child's	children	children's
manager	manager's	managers	managers'
man	man's	men	men's
Jones	Jones's	Joneses	Joneses'
Turner	Turner's	Turners	Turners'
lady	lady's	ladies	ladies'

The personal pronouns do not require the apostrophe to form the possessive. Reference to the chart under "Agreement by Case" will help you choose the proper form for these possessives. For example, *it's* is a contraction for *it is* and should never be used in place of the possessive form *its*.

The company developed its own insurance program.

It's a good idea to prepare for emergencies.

(It is a good . . . .)

Standard usage considers it incorrect to use the apostrophe or the apostrophe and *s* to form the possessive of inanimate objects. Use an *of* phrase as shown in this example.

Not: The house's roof was made of red tile.
But: The roof of the house was made of red tile.

However, the apostrophe and *s* is used to form the possessive of inanimate objects denoting time, measurement, or space. For these words, the regular rules for possessives apply.

a day's pay	a dollar's worth
two weeks' notice	a stone's throw
a month's vacation	a six months' layoff

An *of* phrase should be used to avoid otherwise awkward constructions involving the use of possessives.

Not:	The supervisor's son's car was damaged.
But:	The car of the supervisor's son was damaged.
Not:	The Future Business Leaders of America's meeting was held in May.
But:	The meeting of the Future Business Leaders . . .

Form the possessive of compound words by adding the necessary sign of the possessive to the last word in the compound.

mother-in-law	mothers-in-law
(singular)	(plural)
mother-in-law's	mothers-in-law's
(singular possessive)	(plural possessive)

When two or more people possess the same thing jointly, show the possessive on the last word only. However, if the ownership is individual the possessive must be shown on each of the words in the series.

This is Robert and John's office.

(Robert and John share the same office.)

Robert's and John's offices are similar.

(Robert and John have separate offices.)

When a noun or pronoun immediately precedes a gerund, the noun or pronoun must be in the possessive case.

His telling the story convinced the jury.
You can depend on their giving good service.

Be careful to avoid confusing gerunds and participles. Remember that a gerund is a verbal noun, and a participle is a verbal adjective.

The improper use of case may be offensive to a reader or listener who is familiar with the rules of grammar. A good understanding of these rules will help the business writer to eliminate guesswork in the communication. Flexibility in writing and greater freedom of expression are additional rewards to the writer with an understanding of these principles.

Sexism in Written Communication

Writers have in recent years become particularly concerned with the sexist language that is used today. The term *sexist language* as used here refers to that wording which excludes women or which treats women or men unequally or unfairly. By merely being aware of the problem, a writer should be able to avoid the kind of sentence construction that creates the difficulty.

Perhaps the best way to deal with the matter of avoiding sexist language is to examine examples of it. Consider the following sentences that contain unequal or unfair wording either by statement or by implication. Note how the use of the masculine form creates the problem.

> The writer should do **his** best to express **his** ideas clearly.
> When one applies for a job, **he** should know the names and addresses of **his** former employers.
> Primitive **man** was concerned primarily with physiological needs.
> One's writing should be understood by the **man** in the street.
> Department Chair**men** should submit their budget requests by next week.

Careful writers can avoid the sexism in these statements rather easily. Note in the examples below how the problem is solved.

> Writers should do **their** best to express **their** ideas clearly.
> When applying for a job, **one** should know the names and addresses of former employers.
> Primitive **people** were concerned primarily with physiological needs.
> One's writing should be understood by the average **person.**
> Department **Chairpersons** should submit their budget requests by next week.

Many local, state, and federal agencies have provided leadership in changing the sexist language that had been used for many years. Job titles, for example, have been modified to reflect this concern for equal and fair treatment. Such terms as mailman, salesman, policeman, and foreman are being deleted from written communications. (Many man-hours are spent correcting this problem.) Gender-free titles are not particularly difficult to identify and use, and we are beginning to see more and more of them. As an effective business communicator, you need to develop an awareness of the problem presented by sexist language, and you need to use language that overcomes it.

As with almost any departure from common practice, we have a tendency to overcompensate in some instances. Do not overuse such terms as "person" or "persons" to the extent that your motivation to avoid sexist language predominates over your intent to communicate an idea to the reader. In other words, don't sound like the rancher who ended up advertising a job opening for a "cowperson."

Some writers strive for a balance between the masculine and feminine forms by intentionally using examples of each. This use, of course, is acceptable if for no other reason than the fact that it is realistic.

The Effective Use of Verbs

As we learned in chapter 4, verbs are vital to the meaning of our sentences. In fact, without verbs we would have only groups of meaningless words to represent our ideas. It is important, therefore, that we learn about the characteristics (properties) of these words to use them to our best advantage. These properties are *person, number, mood, voice,* and *tense*. Tense is probably the most troublesome of these properties.

Verb Tense

The three basic tenses are present, past, and future. These tenses refer to the basic *time* of an event or condition referred to in our sentences. In the following examples the *time* of the action or the condition is the present. The verb, therefore, is said to be in the present tense.

I am walking to school.
He is running through the park.
She is nineteen years old.
He feels better now.

Now see how the time of the action or condition shifts to some previous time period (past tense).

I walked to school.
He ran through the park.
She was nineteen years old.
He felt better yesterday.

All of these examples refer to some time before the present. Through the use of different verbs or through a change in the form of the same verb we are able to communicate these changes in our reference to time. Note how this same technique can be used to indicate a time in the future (future tense).

I shall walk to school.
He will run through the park.
She will be nineteen years old.
He will feel better soon.

Normally these three tenses are sufficient to enable us to communicate our ideas about when a particular action or condition occurred or existed. Three additional tenses allow us to achieve a greater degree of precision than do the simple tenses. These are called *perfect* (completed) *tenses*. They are identified by simply adding the term *perfect* to each of the simple tenses.

The *present perfect tense* refers to some action just completed or to some action which started in the past and continues into the present.

I have driven the car for four hours.
She has arrived from the meeting in Denver.
She has worked here for seven years.

The *past perfect tense* refers to an action in the past that occurred prior to another past action.

I had started the car before he arrived.

He had finished eating before the telephone rang.

She had worked for our company for two years.

The *future perfect tense* refers to an action or condition that will be completed by some specific time in the future.

I will have started the car before he arrives.

He will have finished eating by noon.

She will have worked here for eight years next month.

Each of the perfect tenses includes a form of an auxiliary verb. The auxiliary verbs are sometimes referred to as "helpers" because they help to complete the verb to express the tense, mood, or voice of the main verb. The ones used to form the perfect tenses are *has*, *have*, and *had*. Remembering this will help one to recognize the perfect tenses more quickly. For example, the past perfect tense always has the auxiliary verb *had* (had started, had been going, had left). The future perfect tense has the auxiliary verb *have* along with the verb *will* (or *shall*), and the present perfect tense uses the auxiliary verbs *has* or *have* as determined by the subject (I have driven . . . , but: He has driven . . .).

In addition to the verb tenses, there are two companion forms called the *progressive* and the *emphatic*. The progressive form tells the reader that the action referred to is, has been, or will be moving forward, or progressing, through the time indicated. The *ing* ending on the verb is used for the progressive form. Some examples are:

Present:	I am singing, she is singing
Present perfect:	I have been singing, she has been singing
Past:	I was singing, she was singing
Past perfect:	I had been singing, she had been singing
Future:	I will be singing, she will be singing
Future perfect:	I will have been singing, she will have been singing

The emphatic form is developed by adding the appropriate form of the verb *do* to form the complete verb. This adds emphasis to the action or condition as shown in the following examples.

He sings. He **does** sing.
They sit. They **do** sit.

Active and Passive Voice

The *voice* of a verb indicates whether the subject of the sentence is performing the action of the verb or whether it is being acted upon. If the subject is the *doer* of the action, the sentence is said to be in the *active voice.*

The boy caught the ball.

(The subject, *boy,* did the catching.)

The dog ran after the passing automobile.

(The subject, *dog,* did the running.)

He put the book on the table yesterday afternoon.
The **statue toppled** during the recent windstorm.
The **lightbulb burned out** after one year's use.
The **school employs** 150 part-time students each year.

If the subject is acted upon (receives the action of the verb), the verb is said to be in the *passive voice.*

The **ball was caught** by the boy.

(The subject, *ball,* was being caught, not doing the catching.)

The **book was put** on the table yesterday afternoon.

(The subject, *book,* was not doing the putting.)

The passive verbs consist of a form of the verb *be* plus a past participle. The forms of the verb *be* are: am, is, are, was, were, and been. This, then, makes possible a double test to determine whether a verb is in the active or passive voice. The following examples will help to illustrate this.

I am waiting for a ride.

(Active voice: Form of the verb *be* but no past participle.)

The report was mailed to the committee members.

(Passive voice: Form of the verb *be* and past participle *mailed.*)

The employees had been told about the change in vacation schedule.

(Passive voice: Form of the verb *be* and the past participle *told.*)

The students studied the problem carefully.

(Active voice: Past participle *studied* but no form of the verb *be.*)

Our original test is still valid for each of these sentences. We see that in the active voice the subject is performing the action indicated by the verb and in the passive voice the subject is receiving the action.

Remember that the passive voice is a legitimate form of English usage; however, we should avoid overusing it, particularly when the active voice will make our writing more effective. Use the passive voice when the doer of the action of the verb is to be de-emphasized. In the following sentences, note how the impact of the sentence changes as we move from the active to the passive voice.

The secretary made three errors in typing the document.
Three errors were made in typing the document.
She scored three goals in the game last week.
Three goals were scored in the game last week.
She turned out the lights before going home from work.
The lights were turned out before going home from work.

In each of these examples we shift the emphasis from one noun to another as we move from the active to the passive voice. Either voice is acceptable as long as it serves the writer's purpose best.

The careful business writer will avoid shifts between active and passive voice within the same sentence. Some sentences have two or more clauses and, therefore, have more than one set of subjects and verbs. We must take care to be consistent in using only one voice for all clauses within the same sentence. This consistency should be maintained not only for grammatical correctness but also for ease of reading. The reader expects ideas to be presented in a logical format (i.e., all active or all passive); so when the writer deviates from this pattern of expression, it is disruptive to the person who is reading the material. We cannot always easily detect shifts in voice, but the careful writer will see to it that this type of error does not occur. Let's consider some multiple-clause sentences that contain shifts in voice.

After he finished Step 1, Step 2 was started.

(Shift from active to passive voice.)

After he finished Step 1, he started Step 2.

(No shift in voice.)

An office memo will be typed, and then we will mail it.

(Shift from passive to active voice.)

An office memo will be typed, and then will be mailed.

(No shift)

We drove the car all morning, and then it was parked in the driveway.

(Shift from active to passive voice.)

We drove the car all morning and then parked it in the driveway.

(No shift)

Generally, writing in the active voice gives our ideas more vitality than if we express them in passive voice. Use of the passive voice often sounds too formal and pretentious for effective business correspondence. Remember, your reader will probably be a busy person and will want to keep his reading time to a minimum. If you write your ideas in the active voice, you will help your reader accomplish the task much faster.

Parallel Structure

Much of our communication requires that we write sentences and paragraphs which contain ideas of equal rank and importance. If we are to achieve the best results from such writing, it is imperative that these ideas be expressed in similar grammatical form. This similarity of form gives our writing a smoothness and cohesiveness that facilitates reading and understanding. Conversely, ideas that are expressed in grammatically inconsistent ways generally prove to disrupt the flow of key ideas and lower comprehension and retention. Having ideas of equal rank expressed in the same grammatical form is called *parallel structure*. Consider the following examples of this form.

> **Our instructions were to drive to the shopping center, pick up the packages, and return home.**

Note that the instructions called for us to do three things: drive, pick up, and return. As the reader moves through the words in the sentence, it is expected that these ideas will be presented in a consistent and similar format. Specifically, if the reader has read that we were to *drive* and *pick* up, then it is reasonable to expect that the next form will be *return*.

Now consider the same ideas expressed in unparallel form.

> **Our instructions were to drive to the shopping center, pick up the packages, and that we should return home.**

Notice how disjointed this last example is. In a sense, we have thrown the reader a "curve." We have used a form of expression that is not consistent with the other two and we have surprised the reader. Naturally, this break in the flow of our ideas results in awkward writing that distracts the reader.

The good writer will proofread the material to make certain that the parallel ideas included in the communications are expressed in parallel form. This precaution will help to assure the grammatical correctness of what has been written. Furthermore, there should be a review of the material to determine if parallel structure has been used where it would be advantageous to do so. Of course, parallel structure involves more than just the form itself. In some instances, the absence of this form will weaken our writing as much as will structural errors, even though the sentence may be correct grammatically. Use the parallel form of writing to strengthen your ideas. Your reader will be better able to remember those ideas that are cast by this method than those presented in a disjointed fashion.

Summary

The parts of a sentence must be placed in the proper sequence to form effective sentences. A good writer will know how to blend the elements of a sentence in such a way that the objective of the communication is achieved.

A knowledge of the kinds of sentences we use will help us blend these elements. The four kinds of sentences are *simple, compound, complex,* and *compound-complex.* Each type serves a special purpose in writing. For these sentences to be useful and correct, their parts must agree with each other; in other words, the parts of the sentence must be in harmony.

Verbs are vital to the meaning of sentences, and their properties of *person, number, mood, voice,* and *tense* help us to achieve particular meanings. Tense deserves special attention because it is often the most troublesome of all the properties.

Parallel structure allows us to develop forceful messages, and correct use of this technique is the mark of polished writers.[1] The essence of parallel structure is that all ideas of equal rank and importance must be expressed in similar format.

1. For additional information regarding parallel structure, refer to Dr. Calvin D. Linton's article in Appendix D.

Classify the sentences below as to whether they are simple, compound, complex, or compound-complex.

1. She went to the store and purchased two loaves of bread, four pounds of hamburger, and one head of lettuce.
2. The guitar had a pretty design on the front, but the sound seemed muted.
3. The high schools wanted the orientation periods scheduled later in the month, but the colleges would be closed by then.
4. He has been a steady customer, although he hasn't been in lately.
5. After the basic overview of the manual has been presented, the instructor will announce a short break.
6. Since that model fits your immediate needs, you should consider buying it; we believe you will be happy with its performance.
7. The car ran off the road and slid to a stop at the edge of a cliff.
8. He ran down the road away from the gathering crowd.
9. She will pick you up in the morning, or I will stop by later.
10. The chair was placed next to the fireplace, but it had to be moved.
11. Although you have just returned from that part of the state, I would appreciate it if you would make another trip up there; let me know if you can do it.
12. The wallpaper had an interesting pattern.
13. The packet of table napkins was purchased by the lady wearing the green suit.
14. The typewriter was equipped with correcting tape, and the desk had two pedestals.
15. Although the books were sent to the correct address, they arrived too late to be used in the workshop.
16. When she arrived to speak to the association members, she met with a standing ovation.
17. Whenever you decide to make the adjustment, please call my office.

In the sentences below, select the correct verb to match the subject of the sentence.

1. The table and the lamp that sits on it (is, are) to be sold at the auction.
2. The wheels on the front of the truck (squeak, squeaks) when the brakes are applied.
3. One of the three ladies who (was, were) at the meeting (is, are) available for discussion.

Chapter Exercises

Subject/Verb Agreement Exercises

4. Everyone in attendance (is, are) to receive a summary of the day's activities.
5. Either of the two three-way speakers (is, are) for sale now.
6. Neither of the typewriters (work, works) well.
7. Either Mary or her sons (has, have) the car today.
8. Every representative and every delegate (is, are) asked to be present during the orientation session.
9. The nature of her questions (seem, seems) unusual.
10. *Marketing Principles* (is, are) the best of all the books available.
11. Some of the barrels (has, have) leaks in their spouts.
12. Some of the sugar (has, have) been spilled.
13. A vocabulary of easy-to-understand words (is, are) important to good business writers.
14. Each of the men on the team (refuse, refuses) to accept the idea of losing the game.
15. If either (refuse, refuses) to go, please call me.
16. Twenty dollars (is, are) a lot of money for that particular set.
17. The rest of the children (was, were) still in camp.
18. The rest of the children's camping gear (was, were) left behind.
19. Two-thirds of the paper (was, were) devoted to advertisements.
20. Which (is, are) to be remodeled? (Which one?)
21. The criterion (is, are) to be determined by Mr. Spofford.
22. What criteria (is, are) considered appropriate for performance appraisal?
23. The curricula (is, are) set by school board policy.
24. Accurate data (is, are) a primary consideration in determining the quality of a report.
25. The consensus (is, are) that two employees will be chosen to be on the committee.

Case Exercises

Select the correct word or words in each sentence to demonstrate your understanding of the case.

1. Either (she, her) or (I, me) will conduct the meeting next week.
2. The ambassadors from our school, Lisa and (I, me), will submit a report at the end of the semester.
3. Neither (he, him) nor (she, her) will disagree with whatever decision you make.
4. Clarissa is the person (who, whom) we feel is next in line for a promotion.
5. (Whoever, Whomever) is answering the phone on that day will get credit for the order.
6. Choose (whomever, whoever) you think will do the best job for us.

7. He is only seven months older than (her, she).
8. Floyd is a better boxer than either Tom or (I, me).
9. The teacher likes the work better than (I, me). (In relation to how much I like the work)
10. The teacher likes the work better than (I, me). (In comparison to how the teacher feels toward me)
11. The winner was thought to be (her, she).
12. Was that (her, she) who called?
13. This is (he, him) speaking.
14. He thought it was (I, me) who called.
15. Give the message to (whoever, whomever) you believe will not misinterpret it.
16. It was (I, me) who wanted the information.
17. The new chairpersons were Mildred and (he, him).
18. He hopes the work will be assigned to you and (I, me).
19. The new vacation policy was a welcome change to (we, us) who work in the filing and records management division.
20. The manager called (he, him) and (I, me) as soon as the new order had been verified.
21. Was it (they, them) who called while no one was in the office?
22. (We, Us), rather than (they, them), should be given first choice of the new work assignments.
23. The office crew picked Harold and (she, her) as candidates for "Boss of the Year."
24. (He, him) and (I, me) launched the boat without any help from the rest of the crew.
25. The individual to (who, whom) this letter is addressed will be surprised and happy to receive it.
26. Just between you and (I, me), case is an important part of grammar.
27. They thought her to be (she, me).
28. (Whom, Who) do they expect will be elected at the meeting?
29. Alex and Ceedy are two people (who, whom) we enjoy being with.
30. With (who, whom) will I be speaking tomorrow evening?
31. (Its, It's) going to be a long time before we see another winter like this one.
32. (Its, It's) cover is slightly torn from the rough treatment it has received.
33. The plural possessive of *men* is (men's, mens').
34. The (mother-in-law's, mother's-in-law) other son was still living at home.
35. Employees should give (two week's, two weeks') notice before they stop working for the company.

36. The (manager's secretary's typewriter, typewriter of the manager's secretary) was stolen right out of the front office.
37. The (house's insulation, insulation of the house) was inadequate for those extreme temperatures.
38. The (father's-in-laws, fathers-in-law's) attitudes toward the marriage were quite similar.
39. Helen and Bill share the same office; therefore, it is rightfully (Helen and Bill's, Helen's and Bill's) office.
40. The (secretarys', secretaries') collective efforts were appreciated by everyone in the association.

Verb/Tense Exercises

Classify the sentences below according to the three basic tenses (present, past, future) and the three perfected tenses (present perfect, past perfect, and future perfect). Also indicate *progressive* and *emphatic.*

1. I *have finished* painting half of the room.
2. He *ran* the entire operation as though he *had done* it before.
3. I *have been walking* to work for almost seven years now.
4. She *smiled* at me when I *looked* up from my work.
5. By then, I *will have read* nearly 400 pages.
6. Over half of the wall *had collapsed* before we *could stop* the slide.
7. I *do take* exception to what the speaker presented.
8. She *is taking* all the necessary precautions to avoid the flu.
9. Francis Bacon *challenged* the method of deductive reasoning.
10. The accountant *was preparing* the final draft of the report.
11. The supervisor of the night shift *will talk* with the new employees within the week.
12. I *shall have bought* all the needed supplies before Friday.
13. The television set *had stopped* working properly before then.
14. Ralph *is completing* his assignment now.
15. All of the uniforms *will have been* turned in by April 1.
16. Most state governments *have* legislative auditors.
17. I *had figured* on being with her during March and April.
18. The dictation *will have been* transcribed by then.
19. She *is* not *going* to town today.
20. Mr. Peterson *transferred* his bank account to First Federal.

Parallel Structure Exercises

The following sentences illustrate problems caused by unparallel structure. Rewrite the sentences in correct form. If a sentence does not have unparallel structure, indicate that it is OK.

1. A good paragraph will contain a topic sentence, a single purpose, and unity of thought will be emphasized.
2. Her main strengths are that she is honest and her attitude is good.
3. Bill is a person of great capability, but he is not highly motivated.
4. He said that he had followed all of the instructions, but the pieces still couldn't be put together properly.
5. The product is designed not only to function properly but also it costs considerably less than other models.
6. His response was not only accurate but also complete.
7. The inside address of a letter should contain the addressee's name and title, his street address, his city and state, and the ZIP number placed at the end.
8. Finding the problem with her sales approach was not difficult, but to get her to correct the problem was almost impossible.
9. An effective communicator will organize the message, plan for an efficient method of delivery, and not forget the importance of a good summary.
10. The scientific method of inquiry requires that we identify the problem, collect the facts, form and test hypotheses, and reach a conclusion.

The following sentences illustrate problems caused by a shift in voice. Indicate the nature of the problem and rewrite the sentence in correct form. If a sentence does not have a shift, indicate that it is OK.

Voice Exercises

Example

As soon as we receive the authorization from the auditor's office, the checks will be issued to the contractors.

(Shift: First verb is active; second verb is passive.)

As soon as we receive the authorization from the auditor's office, we will issue the checks to the contractors.

1. The first series of lights burned brightly for 72 hours; all other lights were dimmed after the first day.
2. You should record your analysis of the problem on a separate sheet of paper, and the report should be mailed to us no later than Tuesday.
3. Most books of this size can be read in less than three sittings, but I required six for this one.

4. The financial audit was conducted by senior accountants, and the junior accountants conducted all procedural audits.
5. Your choice of colors should be shown in the right-hand column, and the quantity is listed in the left-hand column.
6. If you pass this business communications course, you should take the report writing course next semester.
7. Your expenses should be recorded as they are incurred; otherwise, you may overlook them.
8. Our report was considered by the committee, but they made no definite recommendations.
9. As soon as we receive your budget request, we can prepare our final report.
10. Sign the enclosed form and return it with your check.

The Techniques
of Business Writing

The Mechanics of Writing

6

As you study the material in this chapter, you will:

1. learn of the effect that nonverbal communication has on business correspondence.

2. concentrate on the physical properties of stationery.

3. review writing style and business letter format.

4. develop more precision in the use of various punctuation marks.

5. understand that punctuation is not an "add-on" feature of writing, but is, on the contrary, an integral part of the entire process of expressing ideas.

If we understand the objectives of communication, we are ready to consider the physical plan by which these objectives may be met. The theory of communication helps us to understand the many ways in which communication is taking place around us. We see that only a part of our message is in the form of words or other symbols and that even the words themselves may communicate a variety of ideas to an audience. Consider now how these principles of communication apply to the writing of business letters.

In chapter 2 we learned that much communication takes place "between the lines." The things that are *not* said often speak more firmly than those that are said. Even though looks may be deceiving, we often pride ourselves in being able to tell a great deal about people by their appearance. Consider then the impression that may be made by the letter which represents us to a reader or group of readers. Perhaps it may help to consider yourself as the recipient of messages from persons you do not know. As you read your morning mail, what impressions do you get from the letters you read? Your first impression of any letter will likely be reached before you actually read the message. What mental picture do you have of the person who wrote the letter that has the smudged mark of a finger on one side? The typing may be a bit faint, and several erasure smudges attract your attention. Perhaps the color of the stationery is unusual or dull. You may also see that the message is crowded toward the top of the page and is not centered on the sheet. In a split second your mind takes in all these "messages" about the person who wrote the letter. What kind of person is this writer? Careful? Considerate? Sloppy? Careless? Will you trust this person with your next important order for goods or services?

Whether we like it or not, our letters convey a message by their appearance as well as by their words. These "other messages" may be even more important than the one intended because of the important first impression the reader gets from the appearance of the letter. Good writers will make certain that this first impression is a positive one.

Appearance

If we were to make a personal visit to business associates, suppliers, potential customers, or others who are important to us in our business and social life, we would naturally want to make a good impression. We would want to present ourselves at our best because others can and do make judgments about us on the basis of how we look. When we send written communications to represent us, we should take steps to project the "good appearance" image. Factors that affect the appearance of our written communications include the quality of paper, the design of the stationery, the characteristics of the typing, and the physical format of the document itself.

Properties of Paper

Paper can be made from wood pulp, cotton rags, and various combinations of chemicals. Most of the ordinary paper we see today is made from pulp, least expensive of the papermaking processes, and the product is generally of adequate quality for the purposes it serves. Newspapers, for example, do not require superior raw materials. On the other hand, high-quality paper such as that used for many business communications is often made from rags because of their durability. Firms need to maintain certain records for many years in order to meet the operational requirements of business and the regulations of the government. Information of this nature should be recorded on a substance that can be preserved over long periods of time.

A good bond paper will receive the imprint from a carbon or fiber ribbon better than will a substance of lesser quality. Since the way that paper receives the print can affect the appearance of the written message, we should take care in selecting the stationery for our communications.

Design of Stationery

Most business organizations have stationery which bears information about the firm. This information will appear on the paper, on the envelope, or on both. The letterhead will contain the name and address of the firm, telephone numbers, and perhaps a brief phrase describing the products or services offered. Also, some letterhead designs show the logo (or trademark) of the business. This letterhead not only provides information but also serves to enhance the appearance of the document. Note the variations in letterhead design that appear in the examples presented by figures 6.1 and 6.2.

Letter Format

The format of a letter refers to the actual placement of the typewritten word. While there are numerous variations of basic letter format, we will limit our analysis to only the most common ones. Note that some business organizations have their own format, which is used for all written communications initiating from their offices. In most cases, these individual styles derive from one of the basic forms we will discuss in this unit.

Before we illustrate the forms that communications may take, however, we need to identify the parts of the letter itself. Nearly all business letters that are sent to others outside the firm (to suppliers, customers, etc.) will contain a date, inside address, salutation, body, complimentary close, and dictator's name and title. Optional parts include the attention line, subject line, dictator/stenographer initials, enclosure notations, carbon copy listings, and postscript.

Dateline. The date the letter is written should be placed on this line. As we will see, there is some flexibility in the placement of this item. Use the conventional order of month, date, and year (January 28, 19xx).

Inside address. Information in this part can include the name and title of the person to whom you are writing, the name of the company, street address, city, state, and ZIP Code number. Not all addressees will have titles, of course (beyond Mr., Mrs., Miss, Ms.), nor will all letters be written to business firms. Because information in the inside address will vary in space requirements, typists should exercise care in balancing the layout.

Not: Mr. James P. Johnston, Vice President
ABC Company
2507 North Street
Meridian, VT 00000

Allstate®

Home Office
Allstate Plaza
Northbrook, Illinois 60062

Dear Policyholder:

Thank you for choosing Allstate to provide your Homeowners insurance. Your policy has been carefully designed to provide the protection you need--at a reasonable cost.

One valuable feature I'd like to remind you about is the "Property Insurance Adjustment Endorsement." Here's how it works.

> Each year, the amount of insurance on your home will be adjusted on the anniversary date of your policy, if necessary, to reflect changes in construction costs. Any changes will be based on the Composite Construction Cost Index published by the U.S. Department of Commerce.

This means the amount of your insurance stands a better chance of keeping pace with the cost of repairing any insured damage. It helps make sure you don't have to pay thousands of dollars out of your own pocket because you didn't have enough insurance.

Your endorsement shows which coverages will be changed and how the premium will be adjusted. Any change we make, however, is optional. If you don't agree with it, just let us know. We'll adjust your insurance to the amount you need.

Even with this endorsement, we encourage you to review your insurance periodically. There are a number of reasons why the value of your home may be increasing at a faster pace. Major re-modeling such as a room addition is a good example. If so, you may want to consider additional adjustments in your insurance.

If you have any questions about the "Property Insurance Adjustment Endorsement" or any questions about your insurance, please let us know. Just contact your Allstate agent or your Regional Office. We want you to be completely satisfied with your Allstate protection.

Sincerely,

R.B. Sheppard
President

WKA

Figure 6.1
Example of well-spaced
letter with letter head

Figure 6.2
A collage of letterheads

But: Mr. James P. Johnston
      Vice President
      ABC Company
      2507 North Street
      Meridian, VT 00000

The data included in the inside address should be accurate and complete because it will appear on the file copy, which often serves as the basis of information for future correspondence.

Attention line. As the name suggests, the attention line will serve to direct the correspondence to a particular individual or unit within the organization. Many organizations process a considerable amount of mail each day and they can save much time, both in handling and response, if writers will provide a specific destination (within the organization) for the letter. Place the attention line on the second line below the inside address.

ABC Company		ABC Company
2507 North Street		2507 North Street
Meridian, VT 00000	or	Meridian, VT 00000
Attention: Mr. James P. Johnston		Attention: Purchasing Agent
Gentlemen:		Gentlemen:

Salutation. The salutation serves to direct the letter to a particular reader or group of readers. This letter part also serves to introduce an appropriate amount of courtesy and begins the communication on a positive note. This courtesy can be expressed in a variety of ways.

Dear Mr. Jones:	Dear Mrs. Jones:
My dear Mr. Jones:	Dear Miss Smith:
Sir:	Dear Ms. Jones:
Dear Sir:	My dear Ms. Jones:
Gentlemen:	Madam:
Dear Richard:	My dear Madam:
My dear Richard:	My dear Frances:

The courtesy titles of Messrs. (plural of the title, Mr.), Mesdames (plural of Mrs.), and Misses (plural of Miss) are also appropriate titles. Some business communicators consider these titles to be too formal under most circumstances and, therefore, do not wish to use them. Similarly, the saluations of Dear Sir, Sir, and Madam may possess a degree of formality not desired in some situations.

Some salutations involve titles and require a somewhat different wording.

The Reverend John Mitchell	(Dear Reverend Mitchell)
Professor Harriet L. Payne	(Dear Professor Payne)
The Honorable Jay B. Dunn	(Dear Mr. Dunn)
Doctor Susan Brender	(Dear Doctor Brender)
	or
	(Dear Dr. Brender)

Sometimes we use abbreviations for these titles, although the complete spelling is preferred.

Subject Line. Often a notation indicating the subject of the letter will be included. This information should be placed on the second line *below* the salutation and can be blocked to the left margin or centered between the left and right margin. The word SUBJECT is followed by a colon.

Dear Mrs. Casillas:
SUBJECT: Purchase Order No. 48971

Individual Paragraphs. The body of a letter is made up of paragraphs. Techniques of paragraph development are considered in another unit of this text, but a few comments about them are in order at this point. The first paragraph of a letter should be relatively short. This paragraph should serve only to identify the subject of the letter and should not include too much information.

The paragraphs should be varied in length to avoid a "prepackaged" look. Paragraphs will automatically vary in length if the writer will concentrate on the primary objectives of the letter. Because of the uniqueness of each paragraph and its contents, writers generally need not worry about length.

As with the opening paragraph, the closing paragraph should be short. Information about the primary objective will have been stated previously; this will allow the writer to make an expression of good will and close the message on a positive note.

Complimentary Close. After the primary message has been expressed in the body of the letter, the writer needs to close with a courteous word or phrase. Numerous thoughts may be expressed in this closing including:

Cordially yours,	Yours truly,
Sincerely,	Sincerely yours,
Respectfully,	Respectfully yours,
Warmest regards,	Yours respectfully,
Very sincerely yours,	Respectfully submitted,

Complimentary closings that include the word *respectfully* are most often used when the writer wishes to be especially formal. This degree of formality may be appropriate for communications that accompany reports or other documents of an official nature. Finally, the complimentary closing is placed on the second line below the last line of the last paragraph.

Company Name. Another option available to writers is the use of the company name presented on the second line below the complimentary closing. The company name should be placed even with the starting of the complimentary closing and should be typed in all capital letters. Do not allow the company name to extend so far that it extends into the right margin.

Dictator's Signature, Typed Name, and Title. After allowing three blank lines below the company name, type the name of the dictator or writer of the letter. Type the writer's title (Vice President, Sales Manager, etc.) immediately below the typed name. (See examples of following pages.)

Special Notations. Dictator's and stenographer's initials usually appear on the second line below the dictator's title (or below the dictator's typed name if titles are not used). These initials can be typed either in upper or lower case and placed even with the starting point of the typed material immediately above it.

Mr. Patrick S. Adams
Sales Manager
PSA:RC

Other forms acceptable for business usage include:

PSA:rc   psa:rc   P.S. Adams:rc

A special notation indicating the existence of carbon copies is represented by the letters *cc.* Generally the name of the person or persons to whom the carbon copies are sent appears after the *cc* letters. *X Copy* can be used to denote copy machine reproductions.

When enclosures accompany a letter, an enclosure notation is typed below the carbon copy designation. Use *Attached* or *Enclosure(s)* or *Encl:* to show both the person preparing the material for mailing and the recipient of the information that enclosures are a part of the communication.

Special mailing instructions such as "certified mail," "air mail," or "registered mail" may be placed below the carbon copy notation or below the dateline toward the top of the page.

Postscript or P.S. information may be added as the last item on the letter. While this information may be typed or handwritten, most formal business communications present it in typed form. (Note: Use of the postscript is an effective method of emphasizing a point you especially want your reader to remember—though the technique should not be overused.)

For examples of each of the notations presented above, refer to figures 6.3, 6.4, 6.5, 6.6. Keep in mind that individual organizations may prefer some variation in one or more of the suggested forms shown. Learn the specific format preferred by your organization and prepare your communications accordingly.

Letter Placement

The physical distribution of information on a letter form is important to the overall appearance of the communication. Generally, we should strive to "frame" the message on the stationery by allowing for relatively even margins on all sides. Margin widths of from 1 to 1½ inches on the sides and bottom provide a well-balanced look. The size of the top margin will be determined by the particular layout of the letterhead. Generally, if the date is typed on the 13th line from the top of the paper, the boundaries will be fairly well established.

The standard typewriter provides for six *vertical* spaces to the inch. Therefore, the total number of lines on the long edge of a sheet 8½ x 11 inches is 66. The middle point of the sheet is on approximately the 33rd line.

The number of *horizontal* spaces on a typewriter will vary according to the kind of type in the machine. With Pica Type there are ten horizontal spaces to the inch and with Elite Type there are twelve spaces to the inch.[1] Compare the spacing requirements for Pica Type and Elite Type in the following samples:

```
Pica Type uses 10 spaces to the horizontal inch.

Elite Type uses 12 spaces to the horizontal inch.
```

Now study the illustrations that follow. Note the placement of the information (fig. 6.7) and the various parts of standard business correspondence.

1. Many of the newer typewriters provide a "dual pitch" that allows the user to change the spacing from ten spaces to the inch to twelve spaces to the inch.

```
Mr. Dale R. Chappell
Northwestern Insurance Associates
1359 South Pike Street
Portland, OR  97229

Dear Mr. Chappell

Subject:  The Full-Blocked Letter Style

The full-blocked letter with open punctuation is perhaps
the most efficient letter style from the typist's point of
view.  This letter displays that style.

In the full-blocked format, every typed line starts at the
left margin; therefore, there are no tabulations to set or
manipulate.  The open punctuation style includes no punc-
tuation after the salutation or the complimentary close.
This example also shows one arrangement for subject line
which is always typed a double space below the salutation.
The subject line may be underscored or typed in all capi-
tals.

The efficiency of this letter style makes it a popular ap-
proach to the traditional format for letters.

Sincerely yours


Richard R. Kayser
Assistant Director

RRK:dm
```

Figure 6.3
Example of block style—
the basis format

October 12, 1977

Northwestern Insurance Associates
1359 South Pike Street
Portland, OR 97229

Attention: Mr. Dale R. Chappell

Gentlemen:

   This letter shows one of the variations of the basic
letter style. The dateline may be typed to end even with
the right margin, as shown, or centered.

   With this leeter style, the first line of each paragraph is indented (usually about five spaces). Notice the
position of the attention line with a double space sepa-
rating it on each side from the inside address and the salutation. This line may be centered, may be typed in all
capitals, or may be underscored. Many letter writers choose
to center it in keeping with the modification of the blocked
style. The salutation agrees with the first line of the inside address by using the traditional "Gentlemen." In this
example, the salutation is followed by a colon, and the
complimentary close is followed by a comma. Variations in
these marks are not considered appropriate.

   The closing lines start at the center to give the letter a well-balanced appearance on the page.

                        Very truly yours,

                        Richard R. Kayser
                        Assistant Director

RRK:dm

Figure 6.4
Modified block style with
indented paragraphs

```
                         October 12, 1977



Miss Irene L. Patterson
4890 West Parkside
Montgomery, AL  36109

Dear Miss Patterson:

This letter style is similar in many ways to the block
style.  Only the date line and the closing lines are dif-
ferent.

The date line may be centered, as shown, or typed to end
even with the right margin.  The closing lines are started
at the center.  This example also shows the mixed punc-
tuation principle with a colon following the salutation and
a comma following the complimentary close.  Open punctua-
tion may be used if preferred.  The enclosure notation is
typed a double space below the reference initials at the
left margin.

A postscript may be typed a double space below the last
typed line and may be indented or blocked to agree with
the rest of the letter. The letters P.S. may or may not
precede the notation.

                         Sincerely yours,



                         Mary A. Dahlquist

dm

Enclosure

P.S.  Variations for the enclosure notation include: Enc.,
Encs. 3, Enclosures 2, and Enclosure: Invoice.
```

Figure 6.5
Modified block style with
blocked paragraphs

October 12, 1977

Mr. R.J. Roberts, Director
Arco Distribution Company
3792 Highlands Avenue
Tulsa, OK 74114

AMS SIMPLIFIED LETTER STYLE

As the name implies, this is a time-saving letter style
recommended by the Administrative Management Society. The
following characteristics typify this style:

1. All typed lines, including enumerated items, are blocked
   at the left margin.

2. The salutation and complimentary close are omitted; a
   subject heading in all capital letters is typed between
   the inside address and the body of the letter with a
   triple space before and after.

3. The writer's name and title are typed in all capital
   letters three to six lines below the body of the letter.

4. Placement of reference initials and other notations are
   the same as for other letter styles.

This letter style, while being simplified, has good eye
appeal and should help to reduce letter-writing costs.

MARK H. ABRAMS--GENERAL MANAGER

rts

xc Stewart H. Worley

Figure **6.6**
The AMS simplified letter
style

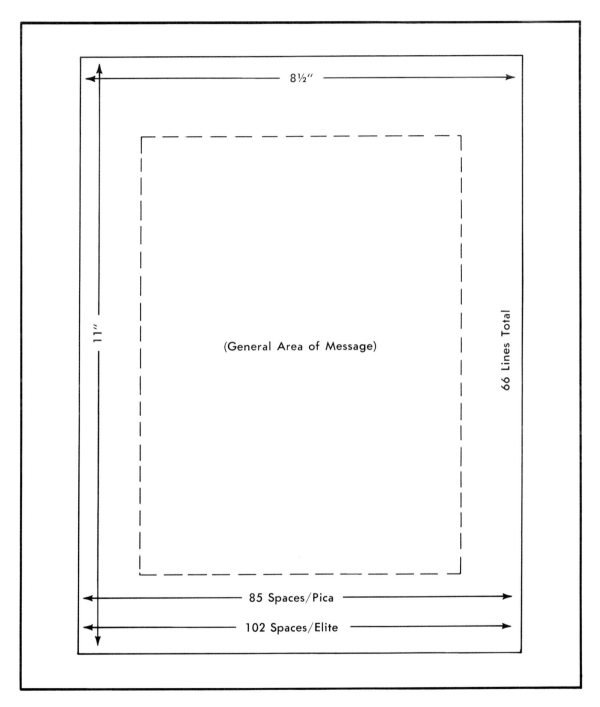

8½"

11"

66 Lines Total

(General Area of Message)

85 Spaces/Pica

102 Spaces/Elite

Figure 6.7
Letter placement on
standard size paper

Letters will vary in length and we need to estimate the amount of material that will appear on the page. The actual placement of the typewritten words on the page can be influenced by two factors—margin width and number of spaces allowed between the dateline and the inside address. Wider margins, of course, will give shorter line length and this will "stretch" the letter from top to bottom. We can achieve this effect, for example, by setting our margins at 1½ inches rather than at 1 inch. (See figures 6.8, 6.9.)

Punctuation

Any information on the mechanics of writing would not be complete without some attention to the subject of punctuation. An understanding of a few punctuation principles will help us to develop

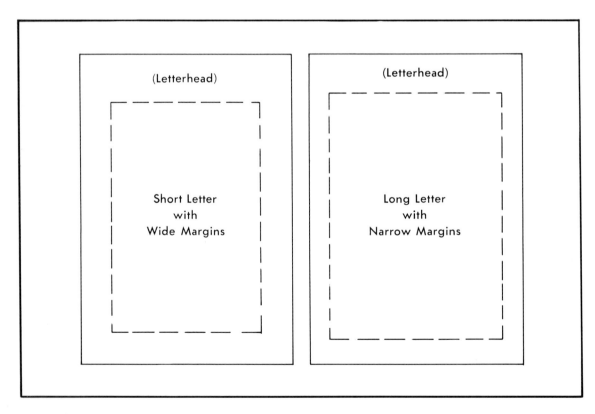

(Letterhead)

Short Letter
with
Wide Margins

(Letterhead)

Long Letter
with
Narrow Margins

Figure 6.8
Relative margins for short
and long letters

(3 Blank Lines)

Long Letter

Figure 6.9
Relative appearance of
short and long letters

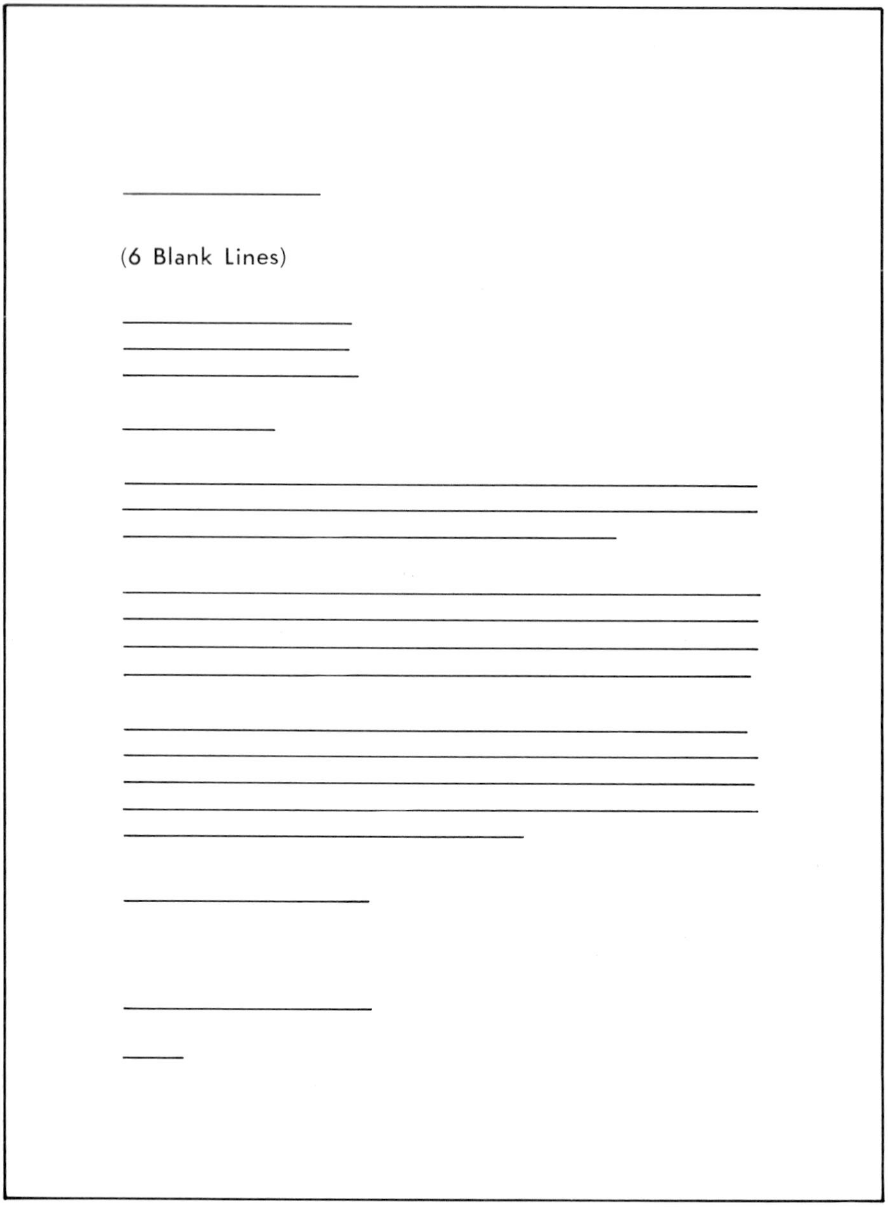

(6 Blank Lines)

Short Letter

Figure 6.9
Continued

business letters that show the proper use of this important element of writing.

The most-used punctuation marks are periods and commas. The period is used as terminal punctuation for most sentences that represent statements, requests, or commands.

Please leave the package on the table.
Here are the pages which were missing.
Don't be late for work.

The period is also used in writing abbreviations. However, an increasing number of abbreviations have become so common to everyday usage that no period is necessary to express them accurately. Some examples are ICC, AFL-CIO, FBI, CIA, and NATO. If you are in doubt, however, use a period even for these abbreviations.

Some sentences ask a direct question. These should be punctuated with a *question mark*. The writer should be careful to use the question mark only if the sentence is a direct question.

Will you please close the car door.

(A period is used because this is a courteous request—not a direct question.)

What time is it?

(The sentence asks a direct question.)

If you are in doubt, consider the nature of the response that the sentence elicits. If a direct answer is called for, use a question mark. If the response is expected to be some physical reaction, use a period (Will you close the door.). For some sentences, the question mark may be used to show the writer's intent.

You didn't hear me call you?

When we make a statement that expresses strong feeling or great excitement, we can show this intense feeling by the use of the *exclamation point* (!). Too frequent use of this mark, however, is likely to destroy its effectiveness as an emphasis technique.

Watch out!
Help!
Now is your chance!
Look at that!

The period, question mark, and exclamation point are the marks of terminal punctuation for sentences. Within the sentence several additional punctuation marks are available to give our sentences clarity and emphasis, and to help show proper relationship of the sentence parts. These marks include commas, parentheses, dashes, colons, semicolons, and quotation marks.

The *comma* is one of the most useful of the punctuation marks for giving clarity to sentences.

The plumbers agreeing with the decision returned to work.
The plumbers, agreeing with the decision, returned to work.

In the first sentence, we are talking about a limited number of plumbers. Only those agreeing with the decision returned to work; the others did not. The second sentence states that all of the plumbers agreed with the decision and returned to work. Just by the proper use of the comma, the intended meaning can be precisely shown.

The comma has two primary functions. It separates certain elements within the sentence that show relationships, and it sets off elements that interrupt the flow of the thought of the sentence. The comma is used to separate items in a series.

All men, women, and children are to be evacuated.
The recipe included fish, beef, and ham.
Salespeople on the road, workers in the office, and workers in the plant are all required to take this training.

We also use the comma to separate two or more words for which the conjunction has been omitted. In this use we may say that the comma is taking the place of the missing word.

He is a conscientious, faithful employee.

(*and* is omitted)

She is a fast, efficient key punch operator.

(*and* is omitted)

The comma should be used to separate the two independent clauses in a compound sentence when the clauses are joined by a coordinate conjunction. However, if the clauses are not joined by a conjunction, separate the two clauses with a semicolon. We will learn more about the semicolon later, but it will help to consider this particular use now.

> The meeting was adjourned at 3 P.M., and we reported our findings before leaving the office.
> The weather was warm and pleasant, but we knew that it would soon change.
> The parents waited nervously; the news would soon arrive.
> Please send your remittance at once, or we shall place your account in the hands of our attorneys.
> We stood on the corner for three hours and waited for the bus.

(No comma is necessary in this example because *waited for the bus* is not a clause.)

If the independent clauses are very short, and if the meaning is otherwise clear, no comma is needed.

> Their prices are low and their service is good.
> Her work is accurate and her attitude is good.

Use the comma to separate introductory words, phrases, or clauses from the rest of the sentence.

> Furthermore, we will expect your report to be on time.
> In the meantime, we used whatever help we could find.
> Before we can make a decision, we must have all the facts.
> Hoping the tip was accurate, he placed his money on Big Boy in the fifth race.
> Upon leaving, secure all windows and lock the door.
> To make a long story short, he forgot to mail the letter.
> To satisfy the coach is not going to be easy.

(In this last sentence, the infinitive phrase is the subject. Since it does not serve as an introductory phrase, it is not separated by a comma.)

Use the comma to separate the items in dates, names, and addresses. The military practice of writing the day of the month first eliminates the need for a comma; however, in traditional format, we use the comma.

Our next reunion will be July 12, 1981.
July 4, 1776, is a date we shall always remember.
Richard C. Parker, Jr., is likely to be the next Division Manager.
The new plant will be built on Frontenac Road, Tulsa, Oklahoma.

In addition to functioning as separate elements in a sentence, commas also set off. For this function, two commas are usually required. Use commas to set off appositives and parenthetical words, phrases, or clauses. An appositive is a word or phrase that is placed beside another word or phrase to rename or explain the first.

Doris, my administrative assistant, arrived early.
Harry, our Credit Manager, left town on Monday.

In the first example, *my administrative assistant* is in apposition to *Doris*. In the second example, *our Credit Manager* is in apposition to *Harry*. Neither the meaning of the sentence nor the clarity would be changed by omission of the appositive. However, the appositive does rename the subject, which may be helpful to the listener or reader.

A parenthetical expression is one that gives additional or qualifying information about some other element in the sentence. These expressions may sometimes be set off by parentheses, as the name indicates; however, a closer relationship to the rest of the sentence can be shown by the use of commas. A word or group of words placed in parentheses is further removed from the meaning of the sentence than is a word or words set off by commas. Both of these devices (commas and parentheses) are even further removed than are words that are restrictive and that do not call for *any* punctuation.

The secretary who is sitting near the window wrote that letter.

(*Who is sitting near the window* is a restrictive adjective clause. Because it is necessary to identify which secretary we mean, it is not set off by commas.)

Miss Robbins, who is sitting near the window, wrote that letter.

(In this sentence, the clause is nonrestrictive because it merely renames *Miss Robbins*. Therefore, the commas are necessary.)

A restrictive modifier or appositive is essential to the meaning of the sentence because it "restricts" or limits the word preceding it. We show this vital nature by omitting the commas.

Nonrestrictive modifiers do not restrict the meaning of the sentence. They merely add interesting or helpful information about the preceding word, or they rename it. This idea of secondary importance is shown by setting off these elements with commas.

Commas are useful tools in that they allow us to show the meaning of what we write. Their proper use will make possible a more precise communication of meaning from the writer to the reader. The careful writer will learn these rules, as well as a few others, governing the use of the comma. Commas may sometimes be used merely to prevent the misreading of sentences, to identify quoted expressions, or to give emphasis to certain elements in our writing. If they are used improperly, the result will be ambiguity or confusion.

In determining the punctuation for appositives and parenthetical expressions, the writer must first decide whether they are restrictive (essential) or nonrestrictive (nonessential). If the element is necessary to specifically identify the word it modifies, it is restrictive. If it merely furnishes additional information about the word, the element is said to be nonrestrictive. Because nonrestrictive elements are not vital to the meaning of the sentence, we can show this loose relationship by setting them off with commas. The following examples show these uses of the comma in sentences involving appositives and parenthetical expressions.

John Gray, our director, will be here on Tuesday.

(The appositive, *our director*, renames the subject.)

Scientists in New York, like those in California, must confine their control of the weather to worry.

(The parenthetical expression, *like those in California*, is only loosely connected to the sentence.)

Exercises in tabulation, however, should receive greater consideration.

(The parenthetical expression, *however,* shows relationship of the parts of the sentence. It could be left out without affecting the meaning of the sentence.)

The word **technology** has many meanings.

(*Technology* is an appositive; however, it is vital to the real meaning of the sentence. It is not set off by commas.)

My cousin James will graduate on Saturday.

(The appositive, *James,* is correctly shown without commas if James is one of several cousins.)

The *semicolon* has several uses that should be understood in our quest for good writing habits. This punctuation mark is used to separate one element of a sentence from other elements.

Use the semicolon to separate the independent clauses of a compound sentence when the clauses are not joined by a conjunction.

We have finished our investigation; you may expect our decision by Tuesday morning.

They had done their best; they believed the victory was theirs.

Be certain to be at the meeting; you will be asked to say a few words.

Use the semicolon to separate two independent clauses that are joined by a conjunctive adverb. (Conjunctive adverbs are words that not only join but also modify the elements of the sentence.)

The merchandise was shipped f.o.b. Buffalo, New York; **consequently,** title to the inventory transferred to us at that time.

Our report is due on July 20; **therefore,** we will need your data before July 10.

Your vacation is scheduled for May 10; **however,** you may be asked to postpone it for two weeks.

When one or both of the main clauses contain commas, separate them with a semicolon even though they may be joined by a conjunction.

> You will, of course, have to study; and, with proper attention to details, you can expect to pass.
>
> Naturally, they will want us to attend; and, because of our vested interest in the project, we should go.

This same rule helps us to separate items in a series when the items contain internal commas.

> My schedule will take me to Harrisburg, Pennsylvania; Deseret, Utah; and Sun City, Arizona.

The *colon* is used following the salutation of most business letters. It is also used following an expression that introduces a quotation, a salutation, a list, or an explanation.

> Dear Ms. Brown:
>
> This new glue has three outstanding qualities: strength, durability, and elasticity.
>
> Please ship the following items: one three-ring binder, six reams of 20-pound bond paper, and one gross of No. 2 pencils.

The *dash* is used mainly for emphasis. We can use it to emphasize parenthetical elements or appositives that would normally be set off by commas. We also use it to set off these elements if the modifier contains internal commas. The dash may also be used between main clauses when the second clause explains or summarizes the first.

> Only one secretary—Mary Rawlins—was late for work.
>
> Tell him to ask Mr. Becket—who has the authority to decide—how to handle the termination.
>
> Tyndall University—established, it is reported, in 1874—has ceased its operation.
>
> His real feelings were obvious—he resented the suggestion and the person who gave it.

The dash should be used sparingly. Since it is used primarily for emphasis, this mark will lose its effectiveness through overuse. For most situations, the comma will serve better to punctuate.

The *hyphen* is used primarily to separate compound adjectives that immediately precede a noun.

The well-written report . . .		The report was well written.
The long-overdue account . . .	but	The account was long overdue.
A part-time job was . . .		The work is only part time.
An up-to-date account . . .		The account was up to date.

However, when one of the compound modifiers is an adverb that ends in *ly*, do not use the hyphen.

A highly reliable source . . . .
The especially careful investor . . . .
An intensely heated debate . . . .

The hyphen is also used when expressing numbers from twenty-one through ninety-nine. This rule applies no matter where the numbers appear in the writing.

Some flexibility in the use of the hyphen does exist, however. Some writers will always hyphenate prefixes that end with the same letter that begins the main word.

re-evaluate
re-examine

Others will choose to omit the hyphen.

reentering
reenforce

The hyphen should be used to separate the prefixes *ex* (meaning former) and *self;* use the hyphen to separate a word and the suffix *elect.*

ex-president
ex-officio
self-fulfilling
president-elect

Finally, the hyphen is used to divide words that cannot be fitted at the end of a written line. Words may be divided between syllables (fashion-able, state-ment), between double consonants that are part of two syllables (question-naire, syl-lable, bor-row, but not fussy or fulfill). Do not leave a single letter on one line, or carry it over to the next line (e-lated or culminat-e). Divide previously hyphenated words (self-appointed) only at the hyphen. If a vowel in a word is a syllable by itself, do not hyphenate immediately before it (not germ-inate, but germi-nate).

Parentheses are used to enclose elements that are very loosely connected with the idea expressed in the sentence. These elements could often be set off with commas or dashes. Parentheses serve to de-emphasize what they enclose and may serve the writer better than the other marks of punctuation.

> The financial statements (delivered just this morning) were mailed to all the stockholders.

Quotation marks are other important punctuation devices. One obvious use of the quotation marks, as the name indicates, is to enclose material which is directly quoted from some other source. The use of quotation marks indicates that the material is precisely quoted—even including errors, if there are any—from the original source.

The quoted material may be a single word, a sentence, a group of words, or several paragraphs. When several paragraphs are quoted, quotation marks should be placed before each of the paragraphs but after only the final paragraph. For other uses, beginning and ending quotation marks are used.

In addition to their use for identifying quoted material, quotation marks are used to enclose certain titles of articles, names of chapters, or poems from a collection where the items are a part of a larger work.

> You can find this reference in "What About Computers" in the March issue of **Modern Technology.**
> "This company will meet its competition squarely but fairly," said James Schwab.
> This is what I heard him say: "Just sign for me this one time. It won't happen again."

> (Two sentences quoted, but only one set of quotation marks is necessary.)

> "We are all in this together," he remarked, "and with all your help, we will see it through."

> The last paragraph stated: "Freud once said that he could not see universal love as man's highest form of behavior, and then he added dourly: 'A love that does not discriminate seems to me to forfeit a part of its own value, by doing an injustice to its object; and secondly, not all men are worthy of love.' "

Note: All periods and commas are inside the final quotation marks. Question marks and exclamation marks are placed inside the quotation marks also, provided that they are part of the quoted material, but outside them if they are part of the original sentence. The semicolon and colon are placed outside the quotation marks unless they are part of the quoted matter. Notice also that the quotation *within the quotation* in the last example (above) is indicated by the use of the single quotation marks.

> As soon as he arrived, he asked, "Where are the others?"
> Who said, "Give me liberty or give me death"?
> "I don't care who gave you permission," he shouted; "you can't do it!"

Obviously, punctuation is an important part of our writing. The marks of punctuation are not something that should be "plugged in" as afterthoughts; instead, they should be included as a part of the original effort to express our ideas in written form. Punctuation marks are mechanical tools that allow us to express our meaning much more precisely than we could without them.

Summary

Included as a part of the mechanics of writing are the elements of appearance, letter format, and punctuation. They are effective in putting the finishing touches on the writing effort.

Appearance refers initially to the eye appeal that our writing may have. Business letters should be well dressed to elicit from the reader a favorable first impression. Consider such important factors as color and design of stationery—even the properties of the paper on which we write.

Letter format should follow a consistent pattern within each letter. The variations in style may be determined by the company or the situation. The basic parts of the letter should be assigned a place within a letter that is balanced by proper placement upon the page.

Punctuation is not a supplement to our writing—it is basic to it. By using the marks properly, the writer can indicate to the reader what the writing really means. The successful writer will become familiar with these helpful tools and apply them to the writing.

Chapter Exercises

The lines presented below represent various parts of the standard business letter. Identify these numbered parts to demonstrate your understanding of basic letter format.

1._____

2._____
_____
_____
_____

3._____

4._____

5._____

6._____
_____.
_____
_____
_____.
_____
_____
_____.

7._____

8._____

9._____

10._____

11._____:

Punctuation Exercises

Provide the necessary punctuation for the sentences that appear on the following pages.

1. The pens pencils and paper will be delivered to your office by Friday January 14.

2. Mr Jackson who will be on leave for the next two months will provide you with the necessary documentation.
3. Her mother arrived yesterday and she will stay for at least three weeks.
4. The men who worked on the project during December January and part of February will be reimbursed for all out of pocket expenses.
5. To order simply return the enclosed coupon in the addressed postage paid envelope.
6. I went home but she stayed on.
7. The men who delivered your new sofa when asked when the reclining chair would arrive told us it would be here tomorrow.
8. Of all the cities listed in the brochure only three Trenton Bloomington and Grand Rapids qualify for the awards.
9. Making the right decision requires that you obtain all of the relevant information organize it into a logical format identify possible alternatives and test these alternatives in a sound and consistent manner.
10. In spite of a severe drop in market prices investors continued to buy on margin.
11. An up to date report will be prepared after the audit has been completed.
12. The new employee appeared to be confident competent and competitive.
13. My brother who lives just around the corner often visits us in the evenings. (Assume there is only one brother.)
14. My brother who lives just around the corner often visits us in the evenings. (Assume there are two brothers.)
15. A hard sell approach may appeal to some customers but most prefer an opportunity to make their own decisions.
16. The work is only part time but it will give you something to do until a permanent position becomes available.
17. Three young ladies Janet Susan and Helen will be competing for the scholarship.
18. Manual Supplement No. 7 which replaces all previous handouts is ready for distribution.
19. In fact you will probably want to return next year.
20. While the *Courier* published by Dawson Enterprises has higher advertising rates it has more circulation than any of its competitors.
21. Model No. 435 has three unique features automatic closure standard threading and conversion capability.
22. Please send the following items two fabric ribbons four reams of bond paper and one box of offset masters.

23. He said tell her to come to work at noon tomorrow.
24. He said to tell her to come to work at noon tomorrow.
25. She asked when will you be able to begin.

The Psychology
of Letter Writing

7

In studying this chapter material, we will:

1. examine the nature of the message and the reader's reaction to it.

2. learn the meaning and format of the deductive and inductive approaches to letter writing.

3. review the techniques of emphasis in written expression.

4. see how "worn-out" terminology diminishes good writing.

Thus far we have considered the ways we communicate in business, the objectives of communication, the fundamentals and mechanics of expressing our ideas, and the structure of our language. We are now ready to learn how to tie together all of these elements of good expression, and we will learn to do this within the framework of the psychology of letter writing.

The Message and the Reader's Reaction

We must be able to predict the way in which our message will affect the reader, because reader reaction will determine the specific approach that should be used in putting ideas together. Being able to predict this reaction requires that we know something about the reader, the nature of the message, and the possible alternatives available under the circumstances. The ability to empathize with our reader, then, becomes especially important as we try to determine a particular reaction to a given situation. We must be able to "see" things from the other person's frame of reference. In other words, what are the reader's interests in this situation, and what will be the impact of that which we are going to say?

Basically, the two extremes of reader reaction are: (1) the reader will react favorably to our message, and (2) the reader will react unfavorably to our message. Naturally, a reader's reaction can fall anywhere between these extremes, and it is the writer's responsibility to make such a determination. The diagram below shows only some of the reactions a reader could have to a particular message. Remember that we are, at this point, talking about the reaction to the *message* (primary objective) of the letter. Our concern for the reader's goodwill (secondary objective) will determine *how* we express this message in view of the reader's expected reaction.

A Continuum of Possible Reader Reactions

| Very Favorable | Somewhat Favorable | Somewhat Unfavorable | Very Unfavorable |

While it is not always possible to predict the reader's reaction, an effective writer can usually estimate it with a fairly high degree of accuracy. The ability to empathize with the reader will help considerably. Good letters, then, will reflect this concern for the psychology of reader reaction.

The Deductive (Direct) Approach

Most of the communications in business will receive some degree of favorable reaction from the reader. This reaction occurs because communications of this nature generally provide information that is needed by the reader to achieve personal objectives. We can expect, therefore, that the reader will be pleased to receive the message.

Since the reader will be pleased to receive this kind of message, we should feel confident in approaching the message of our letter in a direct way (the deductive approach). We are justified in starting a letter with the key point if that is what the reader wants to hear. The cliché "time is money" may be appropriate in this instance. Letters written using the deductive approach will save everyone time and money because they move quickly to the essence of the message itself. The psychology of this direct approach does not mean that these letters should of necessity be short, or that they should ever be abrupt. Many letters that follow this format are, in fact, quite long and involved. The following outline explains the format generally used for writing a letter that uses the deductive approach.

(Date)
(Inside Address)
(Salutation)

The opening statement should be used to communicate the essence of the entire letter. Write directly to the point or purpose of the message itself.

Subsequent paragraphs should be used to provide the reader with the explanatory information necessary to support the statements or ideas presented in the first paragraph. One or more paragraphs may be devoted to this purpose.

The closing paragraph should be used to conclude the message and to develop the goodwill factor.

(Complimentary Close)

Even though this direct approach is preferred for most of our business writing, writers traditionally have been inclined to express their ideas in an indirect way even when it would be to their advantage to do otherwise. If you are one of those people, make a concerted effort to break this habit. If you consider the effects of using the psychology of the direct approach when the situation calls for it, you will realize the benefits that derive from such action. Let's examine some examples of business letters that follow the direct approach.

Dear Mr. Grayson:

Your order for 12 Whirly lawn mowers was shipped to you today by Barrett Freight.

The Whirly represents the latest in lawnmowing ease, economy, and precision. The unique design with a minimum of moving parts assures your customers years of trouble-free performance. The enclosed brochures will help you to promote the Whirly for your Grand Opening sale.

Remember Garco Sales for all your yard and garden equipment. We wish you success in your new business.

Sincerely yours,

Letter starts with the "gist" of the message. No need to keep reader in suspense as to the status of his order.

Additional details and supporting information will help Grayson and reassure him of his wise choice of mowers.

Pleasant closing anticipates future business. Notice the "reader viewpoint" throughout the letter.

The example above shows how a letter using the direct format can be written. Of course, this is not the *only* way to write a letter of this nature. The letter could be written with different wording and writing style to reflect the personality of the writer. The letter should, however, follow the direct approach.

Now consider the following letter, which is written in response to the same business situation.

Dear Mr. Grayson:

We have received your order for 12 Whirly lawn mowers.

We would like to thank you for your order and assure you that the Whirly will measure up to your expectations. We have enclosed some brochures to explain the many features of our lawn mower.

Your order was shipped today by Barrett Freight. We look forward to your continued patronage.

Sincerely yours,

This is obvious. Otherwise, we would not be responding to his order.

Mr. Grayson may say, "Okay. Go ahead and thank me since you would like to." Also the details are vague.

We finally get around to telling him what he wanted to hear. Which viewpoint is stressed throughout the letter? The final sentence is a wornout expression to "limp" out of the letter.

Now can you furnish the analysis for the following letter? Check it for format, viewpoint, and other qualities, and include your comments on a separate sheet of paper.

Dear Mr. Adams:

We were thrilled to receive your order for our Red-red Raspberries. The plants are on their way to you.

Since you live in Minnesota, you will have to protect these plants for a week or two after they are planted, or they will die. If you have any trouble, get in touch with us.

Lots of luck with your berries, and thanks again for your order.

Sincerely yours,

The Inductive (Indirect) Approach

Not all business situations are pleasant. At times it is not logical to present the main idea in a direct opening statement if the nature of the message will cause an unfavorable reaction by the reader. Good psychology prepares the reader for the unfavorable or undesirable information so that the unpleasant news does not come as a complete surprise. We need to "lead" the reader to the main objective of the message. The letter format presented here is for those business situations that should usually be handled with letters written in the indirect (inductive) order.

(Date)

(Inside Address)

(Salutation)

This first paragraph should serve as a buffer zone in which you make a neutral, but relevant, reference to the subject of your letter. The paragraph should be short, and it should be constructed to lead logically to an explanation or to supporting details. Do not give the reader the impression in this first paragraph that the message is favorable.

Use the next paragraph(s) to provide your reader with the reasons or details that will support the refusal or unfavorable information which is about to come. State the reasons for your action or decision before presenting the negative message itself. Generally, if we give the reasons first, the reader will be in a better position to understand and accept our point of view. Proper use of the techniques for emphasis and de-emphasis will help us to state our message effectively.

In the closing, avoid any reference to the unfavorable message mentioned earlier. Use this space to develop a favorable or forward-looking comment that will, hopefully, leave the reader in a positive position.

(Complimentary Close)

Let's assume that Mr. Grayson's order for 12 lawn mowers cannot be shipped for two weeks. That is not news that he wants to hear. If we give him that information in the opening statement of our letter to him, his disappointment may prevent him from listening to our reasons or explanation of alternatives. We can prepare him to listen to our side with a neutral, on-subject comment or to some statement on which we mutually agree. Our explanation should follow. This explanation should lead the reader to see our side and prepare him to hear the unpleasant news.

Dear Mr. Grayson:

When we received your order for 12 Whirly lawn mowers, we immediately placed it in our schedule for shipment to you.

States receipt of the order and indicates our interest in handling it efficiently.

The lightweight durability and the ease of operation are some of the features

Reassures Mr. Grayson of his wise choice (resale) and introduces reason that have made the Whirly the most popular lawn mower for this spring. Consequently, the requests for this mower have exceeded our supply. We have increased our production and have now scheduled your order for shipment to you on March 20. We are, however, shipping one Whirly mower to you now for your use as a floor model during your Spring Sale. The balance of your order should arrive at your store for your customers within one week after your sale.

We appreciate this opportunity to participate with you in what we are sure will be a successful Spring Sale. Think of Whirly for all your yard and garden equipment needs.
Sincerely yours,

why his order cannot be shipped now. States the delayed shipping date in positive language and explains an alternate step we are taking to serve him. Offers suggestion on how to maximize results of receiving only a part of his shipment.

Closing assures him of our goodwill and anticipates future business relationships.

You will not gain from "dwelling" on the problem nor from making endless apologies that remind the customer of the difficulty. Now, consider the letter that the careless writer may have written.

Dear Mr. Grayson:

We regret that we cannot ship the 12 Whirly lawn mowers to you before March 20.

The popularity of the Whirly has pushed sales beyond our expectations. When we received your order, we had one Whirly mower in stock. We will ship it to you today and hope that it may help somewhat in your Spring Sale. The rest of your order cannot be shipped until later.

We are sorry for this delay and look forward to many opportunities to serve you in the future.
Sincerely yours,

Opens with a direct reference to the bad news. Mr. Grayson may not be receptive to the rest of the message after this negative beginning.

Notice the "writer" viewpoint. The letter fails to capitalize on the benefits of receiving at least one mower of his order Repeats the bad news.

Closes with an apology reminding him of the problem and sounds insincere in looking forward to more opportunities to serve.

Better organization of one's ideas and more consideration for the reader's feelings can turn an otherwise disappointing situation into a pleasant business experience. Often it is just a question of *how* we say something that makes the difference.

Analyze the following letter to see how it measures up to the guidelines we have discussed.

Dear Mr. Harden:

Thank you for giving Robbins, Inc., an opportunity to serve you.

Unfortunately, we cannot approve your credit application now. Your ratio of assets to liabilities is below the recommended level. Until this is corrected, may we sell to you on our liberal cash terms?

Just let us know how we may serve you until we can approve your credit.

Sincerely yours,

While the examples that have been given generally fit into the pattern of the deductive or the inductive approach, there may be many variations of these two styles. We must be concerned not only with the order in which we present our ideas but also with how we express those ideas within our selected outline. Our next step is to consider some of the techniques that will increase the effectiveness of all our writing.

Techniques of Emphasis

All communications, regardless of their form, are intended in some way to persuade the audience. This fact is true of spoken communication, and we see evidence of it nearly every day. We note, for example, that we can raise the pitch of our voice, increase the volume, vary the rate of delivery, speak softly at certain points in our presentation, use gestures, or ask our listener for immediate feedback. All of these devices are intended to stress certain information that we wish to have stand out above the rest. What techniques of emphasis do we have for stressing key points that are presented in writing? Can we, in other words, develop written communications that contain the power we need to emphasize certain ideas? Of course we can, and the effective writer will take advantage of all such devices.

Certain *mechanical devices* that are available to us can add power to our writing. Varying the length of our sentences will attract the reader's attention. If some sentences are particularly short, for example, they will seem to stand out and ask for attention. An especially short paragraph, one or two sentences in length, will achieve a similar effect. By increasing the margin width (shortening the line length) we can make an idea more noticeable than the general text of the letter or report. This is another way of telling the reader that the material is particularly important.

Other mechanical techniques include the use of underscoring, capital letters, parentheses, dashes, quotation marks, and different colors of ink. Of course, overuse of any of these mechanical devices will result in decreasing emphasis, so they should be used sparingly.

Another important way of achieving emphasis is through *sentence structure*. Sentences that contain both dependent and independent clauses can be used very effectively to make an important idea stand out. The idea you wish to have dominate the sentence should be placed in the independent clause. This automatically subordinates the other idea contained in the sentence. Consider the following examples to see the difference sentence structure makes. The independent clause with the emphatic idea in bold face.

> **He has missed many payments because of illness,** even though he is a good credit risk.
>
> **He is a good credit risk,** even though he has missed many payments because of illness.
>
> Although he is only sixteen years old, **the quality of his work is good.**
>
> Although the quality of his work is good, **he is only sixteen years old.**

Position also determines the amount of emphasis a particular point will receive. Generally we remember best those ideas that appear first and/or last in written communications. It follows, therefore, that we should reserve the beginning and ending of our letters for that information we want to emphasize. However, too many business letters waste these valuable positions by filling them with information the reader already possesses or does not particularly care to have. Consider the traditional opening paragraph of a business letter as presented here:

> Thank you for your letter dated March 15 in which you indicated that you would like to have us come to your home and repair the fan which we installed last month.

The person who would receive this letter would in all likelihood be aware that the letter was written to us on March 15 and that it had referred to the repair of the fan that was installed last month. Why, then, merely repeat this information and waste the position of emphasis? Use this position for information that deserves to be emphasized. For example, if we are going to repair the fan, we can use this position to tell the reader when we will do it.

Now consider the following closing paragraph. Remember that the closing is another position of emphasis.

> **If we can be of further assistance to you do not hesitate to call us at your earliest convenience.**

This closing paragraph is probably the last thing the reader will read, so it is likely to be remembered longer than any other part. Why waste this important position on a trite expression that says almost nothing? Rather, use this position to make a forward-looking statement or to provide the reader with additional information that may not be available to him.

Another technique we can use to emphasize certain points is to *repeat the information* in another part of the message. By referring to it more than once, we tell the reader that the idea is important. Also the idea is reinforced each time the reader refers to it. It is possible, of course, to emphasize an idea simply by saying that it is important.

We have already mentioned the importance of writing in the active voice for most of our communications. This technique is worth mentioning again because it does represent another method of emphasizing something. Usually, information expressed in the active voice will carry more power with it than will the same information couched in passive voice. The active voice is that form in which the subject does the acting rather than receives the action.

Finally, the specific words that we choose to do our bidding will influence the amount of emphasis we achieve in the message. *Concrete words*—as opposed to abstract words—are more vivid and more easily understood by our readers. We may at times have to use abstract words to communicate our ideas, but the concrete word will generally serve us best. Check your writing to determine whether you are using the most powerful and appropriate words available.

Techniques of De-emphasis

While all of our messages should be designed to persuade the reader, not all of them should use the most emphatic techniques to establish our key points. In providing our reader with unpleasant information, for example, we will not wish to dwell on the subject or reinforce it in any way. Our objective should be to communicate the ideas in the most efficient way and promptly move on to more favorable aspects of the situation. In those instances where bad news is being communicated, we should attempt to minimize the impact it will have on the reader.

In most instances we can minimize this impact by doing just the opposite of what we would do if we wanted to emphasize the material. Instead of making the information stand out by using certain mechanical devices such as underscoring or variations in margin widths, we can maintain consistent format throughout the letter. We can place ideas to be de-emphasized in the dependent clauses. Similarly, we can de-emphasize information by "burying" it in the middle of a paragraph rather than by assigning it a prominent first or last position. Also, we can use the passive voice in constructing the sentences. Generally this form will carry less power than the active voice. We should use words that are not powerful or forceful, and we can do this by choosing words that are relatively high on the abstraction ladder. Finally, when it is appropriate, we can leave the key idea to implication. If our case has been well developed, our reader will get the message without our stating it in so many words. We must be careful here, however, that we do not leave the reader in the dark, guessing at what we really mean.

The Reader Viewpoint

As we noted in the first chapter, one has a tendency to perceive situations as they pertain to his or her own frame of reference. This tendency often manifests itself in the communications we develop and transmit to others. All too often we express our ideas as they relate to ourselves rather than to the receiver of our message. While this is a natural tendency, the "writer" viewpoint adversely affects the quality of the communication, and effective writing will suffer from it.

If our writing is to be persuasive and interesting to our reader, it must be structured with that individual in mind. Perhaps the best way to establish this point is to study examples of different viewpoints and weigh their impact on the message.

Writer Viewpoint:
I am pleased to be able to tell you that we have examined your application for credit. We are now in a position to sell you our quality merchandise at substantial savings.

Reader Viewpoint:
You will be pleased to learn that your application for credit has been approved. You may now buy quality merchandise at substantial savings.

Writer Viewpoint:
Our organization is sponsoring a drive to obtain funds for needy children in the community. We can achieve our goal if you will help us. We need to have all pledges of support in our office by May 1 if we are to have time to process them by May 15.

Reader Viewpoint:
You can help meet the goal of serving the needy children in the community by sending your pledge to us by May 1.

If we write letters from our point of view, we may be telling our reader that we believe we are most important. If we are, in effect, wanting the reader to do something or asking that something be believed, we will have to show how it pertains to or benefits his or her own situation. The reader will have difficulty in seeing the benefit from something if the writer puts himself in the "limelight" of the letter. Go back now to the preceding viewpoint examples and notice how the focus shifts from one person to the other.

Letter Tone

As the reader interprets the information you have provided, the attitude you had when the letter was written will be detected. You may have intended for the reader to sense your feelings, but it could also be that you revealed them inadvertently. Whichever is the case, it is vital to the success of the letter that you consider the tone (attitude) of the communication.

Variations of letter tone include:

1. a positive attitude
2. a negative attitude
3. an indifferent attitude
4. a condescending attitude
5. a patronizing attitude
6. an attitude of superiority
7. an attitude of inferiority

Hopefully all of our communications will convey a positive attitude, regardless of the circumstances. Anything less than a positive orientation toward the problem at hand will result in diminishing the effectiveness of the transaction. It is surprisingly easy for a reader to determine the feelings of the writer. Through the use of positive language we will be better able to convey the proper attitude for any situation. Consider the attitude reflected in the following expressions and note how easy it is to shift from the negative to the positive by changing the wording only slightly.

We cannot repair your broken window for two days.
We can repair your broken window within two days.
A new window can be installed for you within two days.

Notice that the third example reflects reader viewpoint and also refers to the new window (positive) rather than to the broken window (negative).

We are unable to ship the supplies you ordered because we have not received them from our wholesaler.
The supplies you ordered will be shipped to you as soon as they are received from our wholesaler.
You will receive your supplies as soon as the wholesaler releases them to us.

(This last sentence is stated in the active voice.)

Our stores are closed until 9:00 a.m. and after 6:00 p.m.
Our stores are open from 9:00 a.m. to 6:00 p.m.

Most of our ideas can be stated positively rather than negatively. Often it is simply a matter of telling the reader what we *can* do rather than what we *cannot* do.

As discussed earlier, it is to our advantage to know as much as possible about the person with whom we are communicating. A knowledge of the receiver allows us to tailor the messages according to the reader's frame of reference and background of information on the subject. Naturally, we have to make some assumptions about the individual's knowledge of the subject. If we assume that the reader has more knowledge of the situation than is actually possessed, we may write above the level of understanding. Similarly, there will be difficulties if we assume one has less background and understanding than actually exists. In this instance we run the risk of being too simplistic or of forcing one to read more material than necessary.

While there is no clear-cut answer or formula that will allow us to write directly to the reader's level of ability, we will probably achieve our objective if we think in terms of the reader rather than in terms of the writer. Empathize!!

What would be your reaction if you received the following letter? How many attitudes can you identify?

Dear Mr. Dillon:

We have received your letter in which you ask us to sell you our Lansing brand appliances.

We are one of the largest manufacturers of quality home appliances and have achieved this enviable position by choosing our distributors very carefully. According to our information, you are not qualified to be a distributor even though you have done well as a retailer.

Because we must deal in volume, we cannot sell to you directly. We are happy, however, to give you the name of our distributor in your area. Just write to John Draper, Inc., 1223 Mesa Dr., Tulsa, OK 48293. He may be interested in selling to you as a retailer.

Let us know when we can help you again.

Sincerely yours,

If you were Mr. Dillon, how would you respond to this letter? How would you feel about Lansing products? Now consider the following analysis, which points out some of the attitudes that the receiver of this letter might observe.

Analysis: The writer opens with a statement of the obvious. Of course he received my letter. Otherwise he would not be answering it.

Note the writer viewpoint throughout the letter. An attitude of superiority is evident in the second paragraph. The writer boasts of his "enviable position" and his careful selection of distributors. The second sentence is insulting at first, then condescending as the writer acknowledges my accomplishments as a retailer. The sentence is also negative in telling me I am not qualified.

The third paragraph is insulting and negative. The second sentence shows a patronizing attitude. The last line of this paragraph is insulting and gives a rather hopeless outlook for my chances of doing business with Lansing products.

The last line of the letter is an example of wasting a position of emphasis with a statement that is destructive of goodwill. Since I have certainly not been helped as yet by this letter, why should I ask the writer for some more of the same insulting statements?

Now, see how this same situation might have been handled by a careful, thoughtful writer.

Dear Mr. Dillon:

We were pleased to receive your letter indicating an interest in a distributorship for Lansing brand appliances.

Our distributors are very special to us, Mr. Dillon. Their right to sell Lansing products in an assigned area is protected. As sales potential grows, as population patterns change, or as marketing procedures improve, franchise areas are divided and new distributors are chosen. Your area is one of those being considered for expansion, and your success as a retailer shows your great potential as a distributor for Lansing products. For now, we suggest that you write to our distributor, John Draper, Inc., 1223 Mesa Dr., Tulsa, OK 48293, for your purchases of Lansing appliances. You will be pleased with his service and you'll have a chance to test Lansing's marketability. Then we will call on you to discuss further the possibility of a distributorship for the future.

Our catalog is on its way to you as a start toward a pleasant and profitable relationship with your company.

Sincerely yours,

Remember that no letter is necessarily the *perfect* one. The one above, however, will convey a friendly, cooperative attitude to the reader. It sounds helpful and encouraging. Mr. Dillion knows that if he becomes one of our distributors, we will protect his rights as we now protect our present distributors.

Trite Expressions

The term *trite* means hackneyed or common, and it implies the absence of freshness and originality. Therefore, such expressions can do little to add to the quality of our writing. Before discussing further problems presented by using trite expressions, we should list some examples. How many of these have been in letters you received? Have you used any of them?

> Please be advised that . . . .
> We regret to inform you . . . .
> Enclosed please find . . . .
> Please do not hesitate to call if . . . .
> Trusting that you will . . . .
> Enclosed herewith . . . .
> . . . is being mailed to you under separate cover.
> . . . at your earliest convenience.

Many of the business letters written today still contain these trite expressions. Even though they may possess many of the qualities of good writing, such letters could be strengthened by replacing expressions like these with more imaginative and informative wording. Remember, our reader will expect to receive a letter that has been prepared especially to meet *his* needs. By including terms that have been worn out through excessive use, we are indicating in a very subtle way that everyone receives the same treatment.

Give consideration to your reader and write to specific needs. Make a special effort to avoid expressions that are overworked and that have lost the personal qualities our writing should have. Again, by thinking of the reader's needs, we will be in a good position to meet them.

Summary

In this chapter we have learned that there is a certain psychology of letter writing that communicators must recognize in order to be effective. Business writers need to anticipate a reader's reaction to the message and use appropriate logic in expressing ideas. The two possible extremes of reader reaction are a very favorable response and a very unfavorable response. There are, of course, several other possible reactions between these extremes.

Based on these response expectations, a writer will generally follow a deductive (direct) or inductive (indirect) approach to the letter format. The deductive approach will generally be used in situations that generate favorable responses, and the inductive approach will be used for those that generate unfavorable responses.

Several techniques are available that allow the writer to add power or emphasis to selected points in the communication. Good writers will learn to use such things as active voice, mechanical devices, subordination of ideas in a sentence, position, repetition of key ideas, sentence structure, and concrete words to increase the impact of their writing. In a reverse manner, writers can de-emphasize certain elements in their writing. The application of all of these techniques will be shown in later chapters.

To be effective, our communication should be written from the reader's point of view. The tendency for writers to construct ideas based upon their own perspectives can often detract from the overall effectiveness of their efforts to communicate and persuade others. Similarly, the tone of a letter is an important factor in writing, and readers can detect this tone rather quickly. The careful writers will consider the importance of tone as they express the ideas.

Finally, we have learned that trite expressions abound in business writing and that they generally detract from the overall effectiveness of the communication. Trite expressions lack the freshness and originality required of good writing and should be avoided.

With this general background, we are ready to examine the application of these principles in writing letters about specific business situations.

Chapter Exercises

1. Discuss how it may be possible for writers to determine what a reader's reaction to the message will be.
2. Do you think it is possible to ignore possible reader reaction and still have an effective communication?
3. In the context of this chapter material, what is another word for *deductive?* For *inductive?*
4. Will the reaction readers have to business messages be mostly favorable or unfavorable? Why?
5. Discuss the general flow of ideas in a letter that is written in the deductive or direct format. For the inductive or indirect format.
6. Why is the goodwill portion of a letter generally reserved for the closing paragraph?
7. Is there any way for the goodwill attitude to be included or reflected throughout the letter?
8. Describe the function of the first paragraph of a letter written in the inductive manner.
9. Why should the writer of a letter of refusal not refer to the actual refusal in the closing paragraph?
10. Why is it a good technique to present the details of a negative message prior to the negative message itself?
11. What does it mean to "leave the refusal or negative message to implication"?
12. Do you think the indirect approach is simply a way to "weasel" out of a bad situation?
13. Compare the techniques of emphasis that are available to us when we speak with those we have when we write.
14. Do you think it is possible that some messages, when written, could actually be more emphatic than the same messages would be when spoken?
15. How is it possible to *de-emphasize* an idea in writing?
16. How can sentence structure be used to emphasize or de-emphasize an idea?
17. Define "letter tone."
18. What specifically contributes to the tone of a written message?
19. What can the writer do to assure that the tone of the letter is appropriate to the situation and is, in fact, what is desired?
20. Do you think it is possible to cast every idea that has a negative connotation into a positive framework?
21. Search letters and reports that you have available (direct mail from business firms, letters that you receive from others, etc.) and try to identify any trite expressions or words that detract from message effectiveness.
22. Why do you think speakers and writers persist in using trite expressions?

The Principles of Effective Letter Writing Applied

As you study the material in this chapter you will:

1. learn to identify the various kinds of business letters.

2. be able to categorize business writing situations requiring the direct approach.

3. be able to categorize business writing situations requiring the indirect approach.

4. learn to apply good writing principles to letters requesting information and merchandise, letters of acknowledgment, letters about adjustments and claims, letters refusing credit, letters concerning backorders, memorandums, letters of congratulations, and others.

It is one thing to learn the facts that accompany a certain principle, and often quite another to apply those facts—to put into practice
the things we believe to be correct procedure. Here we will bring
together all the elements of good writing we have discussed so far
and use them to produce letters that will achieve the objectives of
written communication.

Before we can apply these writing principles to develop good
business letters, we need to consider the kinds of business situations
that may require the writing of letters. When we understand the nature of the business situation, we can then make a decision as to
which approach will best achieve our objectives.

Kinds of Business Letters

Most lists enumerating the various kinds of business letters would
be either infinitely long or so short as to eliminate some of the types
of messages we may be called upon to write during any given week
of our business experience. Perhaps, then, we can group our letters into
a few convenient categories. From this grouping, the business writer
can establish some guidelines for the writing of each unique letter.

As discussed earlier, the messages of most business letters are
likely to elicit a favorable reaction. These letters would include those
written to make routine requests for information or merchandise, or
letters acknowledging these requests.

Other kinds of business messages include those to grant or refuse
claim adjustments, to grant or refuse credit privileges, letters transmitting information regarding orders and back-ordered merchandise, and
other letters to decline requests or to handle a combination of matters.

Letters Using the Direct Approach

Merely assigning a name to a certain category of letters does not give any assurance that all those containing information about the subject are going to elicit the same reaction. The first group of letters to which we can apply these writing principles should be, however, that group which should generally be written in the direct order.

Requests for Information

Many businesses and individuals find it necessary to write for information. This information may pertain to prices or availability of merchandise, recommendations for product usage, production schedules, or it may be for information about a prospective employee. Whatever the reason, this kind of letter is likely to be received favorably or at least with interest. This kind of letter is usually best written in the direct order.

Gentlemen:

Will you please send me your latest price list on Flightwing shotguns.

Based on market projections, we plan to sell over 100 shotguns this fall. The pump action is the most popular in our area, followed by the automatic and single action. Can you also tell us when your new customized 12-ga. double-barrel will be available?

This information will help us to make plans for placing our initial order for fall needs.

Sincerely,

Opening remark states the primary objective of the letter.

Details and additional information provided to help the reader respond fully to our request.

Closing emphasizes our needs and looks forward to business transactions.

Gentlemen:

We have just been awarded the contract for construction of the new high school in our city. This high school, which

The opening remarks avoid the primary objective of the letter. This is superfluous information, or information that is sorely needed for a growing community, will include the largest auditorium in the state.

We are interested in getting bids for the acoustical tile in this auditorium. We will need 9,000 square feet, and it must meet the specifications on the attached sketch. We would like to ask you to send us your best price and delivery date for this tile.

Your early reply will be greatly appreciated.
Cordially,

could be included as part of the explanatory detail.

Vague reference to the main idea of the letter. When the writer finally gets to the point of the letter, he does so in a vague statement rather than a direct request.

Closing paragraph is a trite expression.

Gentlemen:

Will you please send me your price for 9,000 square feet of Audio-lux acoustical tile.

The attached sketch gives the specifications for this tile which is to be installed in a high school auditorium.

Your response by July 28 will be appreciated.
Cordially,

The main idea of the letter is contained in the first sentence.

Precise information given in the second paragraph will help the reader to respond fully to our request.

Closing gives additional information and anticipates receipt of the data.

Gentlemen:

We have been in the business of selling home furnishings to residents of the area for over 34 years. During this time we have strived to provide the best products and service possible.

Do you sell the Muldoon Pattern floor covering which is now being advertised on national television? We are beginning to receive requests for this new product in our three outlets. This new covering appears to have many new characteristics which appeal to homeowners everywhere. Naturally, we wish to stock quality products such as Muldoon,

Uses the indirect approach in a situation that calls for directness. Also, too writer centered.

Lacks transition from first paragraph. Again, the indirect approach is used.

No specific call for action. Writer should be specific and tell or ask the

and we will be interested in obtaining them as soon as possible.
Cordially,

reader to take action of some kind.

Gentlemen:

Can you supply us with the new Muldoon Pattern floor covering which is now being advertised on national television? We are beginning to receive requests for this product in our three retail outlets here in the valley, and we wish to place an order as soon as possible.

This new floor covering appears to have many characteristics which appeal to modern homemakers, and I expect there will be a large demand for the product soon. Please send me any information you have on Muldoon, including prices and delivery dates.
Cordially,

This letter uses the direct approach by referring to the objective in the first paragraph.

Transition between paragraph achieved by using the phrase "This new floor covering . . ."

Adequate explanatory information provided in second paragraph.

A specific call for action is made in the closing.

Orders For Merchandise

When an order for merchandise is sent to a business, we can be certain that it will be received favorably. References to the desired merchandise should be made early in the letter. Generally, there is little need for explanatory information unless it has a particular bearing on the order itself. In fact, too much additional data may serve only to confuse those who are to fill the request. Order letters should contain information regarding the specific merchandise desired, pricing, shipping dates and delivery arrangements.

Gentlemen:

I would like to order the following for delivery before the end of June.

6 — No. 4309 Hose Assembly

12 — No. 80 Hose Bibbs

8 — No. 426 Check Valves, ½"

Sincerely yours,

This letter is certainly short. Is it as direct as it could be? What can you say about the opening sentence? Is any other information needed?

You probably noticed that the opening statement of the letter would be improved if it were in the form of a polite request rather than a vague statement of what we would like. For instance, say "Please ship the following . . . ." The listing here with quantity, numbers, and size would help the reader to respond. Presumably, the number for each of the first two items indicates the size. If this is not so, that information should be given to avoid the delay of additional communication cycles to get the complete information.

Letters About People

Other requests may seek information about people. Since these messages may be of a personal or confidential nature, we should exercise care in explaining the reason for the request and the use to which we will put the information. The direct approach may still work well in most cases. Other situations, however, may require a more indirect approach to help the reader understand the request and be prepared for it. The following examples show these two possibilities.

Dear Mr. Gibbons:

Will you please send me what credit information you may have on the Ralph Dalton Enterprises.

Mr. Dalton has given your name as one of the companies with whom he has transacted credit business. The usual credit report indicating the extent of credit extended and the paying habits will help us. You may count on us for similar help at any time.

Sincerely yours,

Although the direct approach is used, the opening appears to be too blunt. Perhaps we should indicate why we need the information.

Tone of this inquiry seems too casual and routine for such an important situation.

Also, poor word choice—"extent" and "extended"—creates a lack of smoothness. Information requested is too general to be of any real value.

Dear Mr. Stephens:

Mr. Burl R. Johnson has applied for work with our company and has given us your name as one with whom he has worked during the past five years.

Even though Mr. Johnson's education

This letter is written in a more indirect order. We establish the initial base for the purpose of the letter.

Here we give Mr. Stevens informais in engineering, he has applied for the position of Purchasing Agent for our firm. We need someone with Mr. Johnson's background to direct the purchasing of hydraulic equipment for our defense contracts. What can you tell us about Mr. Johnson's work habits, his character, and his skills? Does he work well with other people? How does he handle pressure? Is there any reason to question his honesty or dependability? Will you please tell us what your observation has been and whether you believe that Mr. Johnson can handle the type of work we have described.

Whatever help you can give us will be treated confidentially and will help us in making this important decision. Whenever we can help you in a similar way, please call on us.

Sincerely yours,

tion that will help him understand what it is we are looking for.

He can relate this to his knowledge of Mr. Johnson. Some specific questions will help Mr. Stephens to respond more fully to our needs. After giving certain details we request the information—the specific objective of our letter.

Even though Mr. Stephens may assume we will be discreet in our handling of this information, it is probably helpful to say so.

Each of these two letters could have been written either in the direct or indirect order. However, most of these situations will be looked upon favorably or with interest by the reader and may likely be handled better in the direct order.

Remember that business firms are in the habit of giving information about products, services, or people. In fact, that may be their business. Therefore, you should expect that such requests will be best handled by the direct approach.

Many companies write enough letters requesting information for them to develop form letters for this purpose. A proper form letter is usually helpful to both the sender and the receiver because it may provide for more specific details or easier-to-answer questions. The following is an example of a form letter requesting credit information.

Gentlemen:

Will you please give us the confidential information requested below?

The applicant has given us your name as a credit reference. We shall appreciate your help. You may count on us whenever you need similar assistance.

Name: Gerald R. Browning_____

Highest Credit Amount_____Current Amount_____

Amount Past Due_____Normal Pay Habits_____

Length of time as a credit buyer_____

Remarks_____

_____

Signed_____

Title _____

This form may vary considerably depending upon the requirements of each company. In any event, the document should be brief, asking for only that information which will be of use.

Claims Letters

Whether as a consumer, retailer, or wholesaler, you are likely to be faced with the need for writing letters to seek adjustments, refunds, or replacements for products or services that are damaged or defective. Some logical thinking about the nature of such claims will help you to write more effectively when the need arises.

Generally, those who sell products are interested in seeing that those products perform satisfactorily. If anything happens to disrupt the flow of favorable feedback from users of the product, the seller is interested in doing whatever is necessary and is consistent with good business practice to correct the problem and to reestablish the flow of goodwill.

Now consider the seller's reaction to a letter that asks for an adjustment on defective merchandise. Although the response may not be one of pleasure, you can assume that the reader will be interested and is likely to react favorably to the request. The reader will not have to be persuaded to see your side of the problem unless some unusual circumstances prevail. In fact, too much persuasive effort is likely to arouse suspicion. You will do well, then, to be forthright and confident in your writing of such letters. You will also need to be realistic about the matter.

The handling of claims is a routine phase of the business of many companies. Some maintain special departments with trained personnel to process this kind of company business. The finesse with which these problems are handled will be likely to have a bearing on the reputation and subsequent sales of the company.

Despite the soundness of this logic, many people find it difficult to approach this chore in a positive, confident manner. The result may be letters which are threatening, apologetic, evasive, rude, or fraught with any number of other faults so as to render them punchless in getting the results sought. How would you respond if you received the following letter?

Gentlemen:

What kind of outfit are you anyway? The controls on the refrigerator-freezer I ordered from you are so fouled up you must have been asleep when you figured them out. I plugged the unit in, filled the freezer with ice cream and frozen vegetables, and put some milk and other items in the refrigerator section. The next morning when I opened the freezer door, a gush of white, brown, and pink froth poured out all over the kitchen floor. The ice cream had melted and made one big mess.

I'd like to know what you intend to do about this. I'm a man of some influence and I will expect you to make it right.

This opening will likely put the reader immediately on the defensive.

Even after all the explanation, the writer doesn't really ask for an adjustment, repairs, or any other kind of settlement.

The letter ends with what appears to be a threat.

The above letter is so crudely written as to appear to be a joke. However, letters like this are all too real. In most of these situations, the company will respond favorably in *spite* of the letter, but certainly not *because* of it. A rational, well-thought-out approach would request a repair or replacement of the defective control.

Now read the letter that might have been written for this problem.

Gentlemen:

Will you please repair or replace what appears to be a defective thermostat or control switch for the new TR-16 refrigerator-freezer.

This letter in the direct order gets right to the problem with a polite request for settlement.

I purchased this unit last Saturday. It seemed to be working when I plugged it in, but imagine my surprise when I opened the freezer door the next morning and was met by a gush of melted ice cream. Apparently the temperature in the freezer section does not go down below freezing. I assume that your warranty policy will also reimburse me for the loss of the three gallons of ice cream at $1.45 each.

These details may help the company to determine the nature of the problem to make the necessary adjustment.

Reference to the ice cream indicates our confidence that the seller will respond favorably to our loss.

Your help in correcting this problem before next Saturday will be appreciated. Sincerely yours,

The closing is friendly and gives additional information by referring to the time when we expect the repairs to be done.

If you know what is wrong, make a direct request for a reasonable adjustment. If you do not know what is wrong, do your best to explain what you have observed or what you think is the problem. You may have to ask the company to make an inspection in order to determine the cause of the problem.

Many other kinds of claim situations do exist, of course. For most of them, the direct approach will get the results you want, and you will feel better for having "kept your cool." Because your attitude is likely to show in the letters you write, refrain from writing the letter when you are angry or upset. Above all, try to empathize with the person who will read your message. The reader had nothing to do directly with causing your problem. This person is interested, however, in working out a solution to restore your confidence and goodwill in the company.

Now is an ideal time to consider the letter that should be written in reply to a request for an adjustment. Most companies take the stand that the customer is honest in the appeal for an adjustment and that it is in the best interest of the company to respond favorably. This may not always be the case, and we will discuss these other possibilities later. For now, let us consider how to handle these routine adjustments in a positive, friendly manner.

Since the customer has made a request and we are going to respond favorably, we are writing a message of good news. This kind of letter should certainly be written in the direct order. There is no reason to keep the customer in suspense as to what we intend to do. If we offer lengthy explanations first, our settlement will appear to have been reached grudgingly. And, we will have to be selective in our choice of words to refer to the customer's request. Certain words and phrases have a grudging tone and should be avoided. Study the following for so-called hidden meanings:

You claim	sorry
Your fault	inconvenience
We are amazed	trouble
regret	You accuse us of . . .

While some of these words are threatening and unfriendly, others are simply negative or stand as reminders to the customer of the inconvenience that caused the need for an adjustment. Rather than tell a customer to "return the defective merchandise," we will do better to tell how to "return the original shipment" or to use some other appropriate phrase that does not call attention to the problem.

The following letter was written in response to a letter requesting a replacement for a tent that had ripped as a result of a hard wind.

Dear Mr. Avery:

A new CWT1012 tent was shipped to you today by Fleetside Freight. It should reach you in plenty of time for your outing on August 12.

We have asked the carrier to pick up your present tent and return it to us. This pick-up will spare you from having to return it to us and will give us an oppor-

This direct approach gives Mr. Avery the good news in the beginning.

The writer shows interest in helping to get the "defective" tent returned. Notice that the letter does not refer to "defective" or any other negative idea.

tunity to inspect it to determine how we can improve upon the quality of all our tents.

The enclosed catalog shows some of our other camping items which will be featured during our Hunters' Special next month.

Sincerely yours,

The letter closes on a pleasant, forward-looking idea and assures Mr. Avery of our goodwill.

Letters of Acknowledgment

Often there is a need to respond to a letter simply for the purpose of letting the writer know that the message has been received and acted upon. When merchandise is ordered, when a favor has been requested, or when favorable information has been received, a company has an excellent opportunity to promote goodwill by sending an acknowledgment. The purpose of the acknowledgment may be to let the person know that you have received the communication and that you have taken appropriate action on it. Since the reader's reaction to this type of letter will undoubtedly be favorable, the message should go directly to the primary objective of the communication. The following letter does this and saves the reader the trouble of having to wade through unnecessary explanations or information.

Dear Ms. Cosgrove:

Your letter telling us how much you are enjoying your new electric range is the kind of feedback we enjoy receiving from our customers. We promise to be just as thoughtful if you ever need service or assistance with any of your appliances.

Stop by our store whenever you are in our area and we will keep you informed about any new products which may interest you. In the meantime, you will continue to receive our regular mailings announcing special sales and promotion items.

Sincerely yours,

This letter begins with the objective and develops the positive attitude. Does the opening sound sincere?

Additional information is given the reader which provides the basis for more business opportunities.

The Memorandum

Many employees make jokes about the interoffice memo. One worker is reputed to have said, for example, "Something must be wrong around here, I haven't received a memo from anybody for nearly two days." Comments like this are understandable when we think of the actual number of communications that are written in this form. The implications of these great numbers of memos are significant.

One of these implications is that we depend quite heavily on the memo as a form of intraorganizational communication. This form can be fast, efficient, and relatively inexpensive. Memos are generally short messages that communicate information that is needed between various work units in the firm. Transmission time required for their distribution is short, and no postage is necessary.

Another implication is that once the memo is written and sent, the message has been communicated. This assumption is not always warranted, however. In actuality, it may be that the person(s) for whom the message was intended never received it. It may be that those who should have been sent the information were not included in its distribution. Furthermore, it could be that those who received it and read it never really understood it. These problems must be recognized by anyone who writes these kinds of messages.

Let's consider the standard memo and examine its characteristics. Interoffice memorandums can be viewed from the standpoint of format, content, and attitude. We can use the following example for our evaluation.

KRBA ENTERPRISES, INCORPORATED
Interoffice Memorandum

TO: Al Ferguson, Director of In-service Training
FROM: Mark K. Smith, Personnel Services
DATE: May 19, 19xx
SUBJECT: Follow-up of Communications Workshop

We have received the evaluations of the Workshop you co-ordinated last week, and I want to share the information with you. Obviously, these opinions and comments are important to us in that we are planning to continue with additional programs in communication.

Overall, the employees were very satisfied with the total effort. Naturally, some parts of the session were stronger than others, and we can improve our efforts by looking closely at those things that need to be modified.

Please let me know when your schedule will allow us to get together for a discussion of these matters.

Note that the format provides for the "fill in" of routine information. Although the actual placement of this information may vary, it always appears toward the top of the sheet and is clearly identified. Standard paragraphing is appropriate for this type of message.

The content of an interoffice memorandum should meet the same requirements—accuracy, completeness, clarity, coherence, and correctness—that pertain to any communication. Perhaps the only difference regarding content would relate to the nature of the information. Generally, interoffice memos deal with rather routine information that is not particularly detailed to the extent that a report would be. However, the memorandum can be used to communicate almost any type of information that the sender deems appropriate. Typically the memorandum will include such things as follow-ups of various project activities, requests for information, responses to requests for information, notice of policy or procedure change, and certain modifications in organizational plans or activities. Communications requiring any degree of confidential treatment or detail may be transmitted more appropriately in other forms, such as personal mail or formal reports.

One very important consideration regarding the memo is its tone or attitude. As we have already learned, nearly all communications will reflect some degree of feeling (positive, neutral, or negative) to the reader. Memo writers must be equally aware of this fact and develop communications that reveal the appropriate feeling. If, for example, management has a condescending attitude toward employees, this attitude might easily be communicated through the memo. Or, if the feeling is one of harshness or dislike, this, too, will be apparent to the reader. Similar attitudes will also be transmitted from one department to another. Hopefully, all memorandums will reflect a positive, constructive attitude that will allow people to work together in a productive effort.

Congratulatory Messages

Letters of congratulations are certainly a part of business com-

May 24, 19xx

Miss Marjorie Callanan

Administrative Assistant

Futura Industries

95 Buxton Place

Memphis, Tennessee 00000

Dear Marjorie:

Congratulations on your promotion to Administrative Assistant. Having had the opportunity to work with you over the past four years, I know you are deserving of it.

We hope that you will still have time to see us on occasion, even though your new responsibilities will demand much of your time. We look forward to meeting and working with your replacement in the Purchasing Department, and, of course, we hope that person will be as pleasant to work with as you have been.

Sincerely,

Jim Coulter

Sales Manager

JC:bl

P.S. I have enclosed your picture which appeared in "Business Briefs" of the local newspaper--thought you might like to have it.

munications. These letters can be written to deserving individuals for any number of reasons. Justification for letters of this nature include promotions, special awards or recognition, authorship of professional publications, speeches, seminars, workshops, and personal matters such as weddings, birth announcements, and civic contributions.

Naturally, these letters should be written in good taste, should be appropriate to the situation, and should possess the quality of sincerity. Congratulatory messages should not be especially long. While the message should contain some reference to the nature of the event, the intent should be to provide the reader with the deserved recognition.

The example presented below serves as a message of congratulations to an individual who has just been promoted to an administrative position within an organization.

Letters Using the Indirect Approach

The realities of business sometimes require the communication of disappointing or unpleasant information. For these situations, the indirect approach will do a better job of serving our needs. Merchandise cannot be shipped as ordered, application for credit must be refused, or a claim for adjustment must be denied.

Letters About Merchandise Orders

When companies receive orders for merchandise, they make every effort to ship as soon as possible. Circumstances about the order or the availability of the merchandise, however, may delay or even negate the shipment as requested. When this happens, the company must explain the problem so that goodwill is retained. The following letter was written to a retail store owner who had ordered merchandise from a manufacturing firm. The retailer had ordered thirty suits—seven of them had to be back-ordered.

Dear Mr. Stimson:

Twenty-three Wearloom suits requested in your order of June 15 were shipped to you today. The colors, sizes, and styles are just as you ordered, and

This letter starts with a statement about the positive—part of the order is being shipped.

the suits should reach you by Thursday morning.

The other suits you ordered will be shipped to you on June 29. These suits have proved to be so popular that our production is running slightly behind the demand. We have stepped up our production schedule, however, and will give your next order the careful attention you expect.

In a positive way, we tell the reader about the part of the order that is to arrive later. The letter gives him assurance that we can handle his future orders.

The enclosed brochure describes the entire line of fall styles we have for you to choose from. Look them over and let us help you with your fall selections.
Sincerely yours,

The letter closes on a positive, friendly tone with no reminder of the back-ordered suits.

Notice that the letter does not stop by simply stating when the suits were shipped. The reader is more interested in knowing when the suits will reach the store, so this information should be given if it is available. In this letter, we have some good news as well as some disappointing news. The reader will be more receptive to our explanation and more understanding of our problem if we give the good news first. The use of the passive voice helps here to put the emphasis on the product rather than on our inability to make shipment.

Sometimes a retailer orders merchandise that cannot be shipped. The manufacturer may sell only to franchised distributors, or maybe none of the merchandise is available. In such situations, we will use the indirect approach to help explain the matter to the reader.

The following letter is written by a wholesaler in response to an order for merchandise that is sold to customers only through the regular retail distributorship. The letter must refuse the order, but it must also attempt to preserve the prospective sale by referring the reader to the dealer who can provide help.

Dear Mr. Emery:

Thanks for considering the Guardian dishwasher for your home. It should give you years of trouble-free service.

We have found that the best way to

The opening paragraph is on target but does not refer to the negative element in the message. Is this opening positive or negative? Too positive?

build and maintain the reputation of dependability and service is to provide retail sales outlets throughout the region. Your needs can best be met if you have someone nearby who can sell and service the products you choose for your home.

Mr. Nells Gourley is the Manager of Home Appliance Company at 102 Albright in Overland, Idaho (208-375-4456). He has been notified of your order and is looking forward to hearing from you. He will determine a delivery date that is convenient for you.

We hope that you continue to look to Guardian for your appliance needs. Sincerely yours,

This section begins to lead the reader through the logic of the refusal. Does the letter specifically state the refusal—or does it imply it? Is the technique of de-emphasis used in this letter?

At this point, the reader is given assistance regarding what to do next. Notice how the positive approach is used. The writer assumes Mr. Emery will still want the unit.

Closing is personalized and does not include any trite expressions.

The soundness of the logic involved in the inductive or indirect approach has been demonstrated many times and in many ways. It just makes sense to "prepare the reader's ego" before presenting the negative or bad-news information. If the reader is first given the reasons for the refusal, there will probably be more willingness to accept the decision than there would be if the psychology were reversed. After all, who can honestly argue with sound reasoning? Do not, on the other hand, confuse the logic of the indirect format with the questionable technique of "skirting the issue." The indirect format is simply a method of delivering bad news in a good way—it is not an attempt to avoid the issue itself or to make the reader believe something that is not true. Most readers will detect the insincerity of attempts to write around the problem.

Letters Refusing Claims and Requests

As indicated earlier, we have valuable guidelines that apply to nearly all indirect-type letters. However, because each business situation is unique, we must remember to address the specific needs of each one. Note the similarities between claim and request letters that appear below and the previous messages that also contain negative responses.

Dear Mr. Mott:

Your damaged Babe Tipton Autograph tennis racket has been examined by our Testing and Standards Department. I am enclosing a copy of their report with this letter.

This opening is relevant to the situation, but it is neutral as to purpose.

The essence of the report is that your racket was used to hit something much harder than a tennis ball. Pieces of gravel and glass were found in the outer part of the frame in the same general area where the break occurred. Our guarantee, of course, covers defects in workmanship and materials only.

This paragraph leads to the refusal by providing an interpretation of the report findings.

Refusal left to implication.

I have enclosed a copy of our newest brochure which shows the improved models of field hockey sticks. You may wish to consider the purchase of one of these items for your next outing.
Sincerely yours,

This is a risky closing. Be certain that your comments cannot be misinterpreted.

The following letter answers a request from a basketball coach who has asked that a particular film be reserved for his use. In a sense, this might be considered as if it were an order for merchandise. The treatment of this situation is similar to that of the merchandise order. You may wish to evaluate this letter individually, in small groups, or with the entire class. Apply the criteria you have learned thus far to determine whether this is a well-written letter.

Dear Coach:

Your request that we reserve for you the basketball film, "Run The Offense," shows that you really appreciate the classics in audio-visual aids. This film has been in great demand for years—in fact, it is the only one that some coaches seem to use.

Films like this one which have been shown so many times eventually lose their elasticity and have to be discarded. Such has been the case with "Run The Offense." Our evaluation team decided it was time to retire this old standby in favor of more current productions.

A new film catalog is being sent under separate cover. If you are interested in something a bit on the humorous side, may we recommend the film strip entitled "Wait 'til Next Year."

Good luck in your coming season.

Cordially yours,

Letters Refusing Credit

Certainly a most delicate letter to write is the one that refuses a person the opportunity to make purchases on credit. This refusal could be a reflection on the applicant's character, because the seller may be implying that there is too much risk involved. The seller must write an especially good communication because of a desire to promote business on a cash basis, and a need to create goodwill. In writing this type of letter, we will want to take advantage of techniques of subordination and de-emphasis. The reader will want to know the reasons why the application for credit has been refused. It is through our writing techniques that we can communicate these reasons without causing undue harm or ill feelings. The following letter attempts to relate the reasons for the refusal without offending the reader.

Dear Mr. Standle:

Thank you for completing the credit application and related forms we sent to you on March 18.

One of the criteria we have for extending credit to new customers is a record of continuous employment. Those who buy on credit without the availability of a steady income often have difficulty in making their monthly payments. Our experience suggests that sales on a cash basis are in order until your circumstances improve in this regard.

Opening broaches the subject of credit and is neutral in content.

Indirect approach takes the reader through the rationale for the refusal.

Please notify us of any change in your employment status so we can make arrangements to send your charge cards to you.

Sincerely yours,

Closing paragraph is positive and forward looking.

Summary

With certain exceptions, business letters can be grouped into convenient categories. For each of these categories we can identify sound guidelines that serve us well as we communicate our ideas to others. The two broad categories we have considered in the chapter are letters using the direct approach and letters using the indirect approach. Each of these classifications is further structured according to specific types of business situations.

Letters using the direct approach include requests for information, orders for merchandise, claim letters, acknowledgment letters, memorandums, and congratulatory letters. The psychology to be used in writing these letters is that of directness. The major objective should be stated rather early in the message and should be followed by adequate supporting information. Its orientation should be positive overall, and the letter should be written from the reader's point of view.

Letters using the indirect approach include those about merchandise orders that cannot be filled, those refusing claims and requests, and those refusing credit applications. These letters should generally follow the indirect format by beginning with a buffer paragraph followed by a presentation of the reasons for the refusal. The refusal or the negative information should be left to tactful implication whenever possible. The closing paragraph should not refer to the bad news but should contain statements pertaining to acceptable alternatives for the reader or to some forward-looking dimension of their business relationship.

Chapter Exercises

The letter problems presented below include a wide variety of situations that are representative of those you will find in many businesses today. Some of these situations call for a response that is direct and to the point, while others call for indirectness. Your assignment, in each case, will be to determine first of all which approach will be best for the reader.

After you have determined the appropriate psychology for your response to a specific problem, organize your thoughts in such a manner that you can incorporate the several writing skills that you have developed thus far. Take advantage of the techniques of emphasis (and techniques of de-emphasis where needed), for example, and develop a message that will "speak" to your reader.

Be certain to use good grammar and effective word order in expressing your ideas. Consider the need to empathize with the receiver of the message, and, of course, be certain that the communications are expressed with the "reader viewpoint." Remember the relationship between readability levels and the all-important factors of sentence length and difficult words. Note, too, that concrete words are generally more easily understood than are abstract words.

Once your written responses have been fully developed, check your work very carefully to determine that there are no spelling or proofreading errors.

1. Mr. George Blackham recently purchased a second home in the mountains about two hundred miles from his primary residence. The mortgage requirements specify that adequate fire insurance be carried on the property throughout the life of the indebtedness. It is standard operating procedure for the new homeowner to pay for the first year of insurance by sending his premium directly to the insurance company. Subsequent coverage will be paid for out of the monthly installments that will be sent to the lending agency and kept in an escrow account.

   In obtaining the necessary insurance coverage, Mr. Blackham made a telephone call to his agent, Mr. Bob Brenner, and gave him the specific address and legal description of the second home, along with instructions regarding the type and amount of insurance desired. Mr. Brenner issued an immediate binder and sent a copy of the transaction to Mr. Blackham's mortgagee, Second Federal Savings & Loan Association. Mr. Blackham was told that he would receive a bill for the first year's premium and that he would have thirty days in which to pay it.

   A copy of the binder was sent to the lending agency, but no mention was made of the billing procedure. Consequently, the finance officer of the Second Federal Savings & Loan Association did not know that Mr. Blackham was aware of who must pay this first premium.

a. As the finance officer, write a letter to Mr. Blackham at 346 North Blaine Street to let him know that he is to pay the first premium amounting to $104.

b. As Mr. Blackham, write a letter in response to the correspondence from the finance officer and let him know that you are aware of the procedure and that you will pay the premium when you receive the billing from the insurance company.

c. Nearly one month has passed and Mr. Blackham has not received a bill from the insurance company for coverage on his second home. He is beginning to wonder if there has been some clerical error or misunderstanding that has caused this delay. Fearing that his mountain property may not be insured, Mr. Blackham decides to write to the Mutual Insurance Company at Mutual Plaza in Cincinnati, Ohio and get some kind of verification regarding his coverage. Write the letter expressing your concern over the matter and ask the company to give you something "in writing" to show that you are in fact covered.

d. As the Customer Services Manager of Mutual Insurance Company, write a letter to Mr. Blackham in which you assure him that his property *is* covered. Tell him that there is normally a three- to four-week processing period required for new policies. Tell him further that all the necessary papers will be sent to him and to his lending agency.

2. Last Christmas you received a Unitronix pocket calculator as a present. It had a 90-day guarantee against faulty workmanship and mechanical or electronic defects. Approximately five months after the unit was purchased, it began to malfunction. Specifically, you could not get the machine to accept figures when the keys were depressed. According to the instructions contained in the shipping box, owners were required to send a check or money order along with the defective unit to the Service Center located at 2115 Broadben in New York City. The unit would then be repaired and returned to the owner.

You followed the instructions and, after almost four months of waiting, the company returned your calculator to you. When you tried to use the unit, you discovered that it would not work; in fact, it had the same problem that it had when you sent it in to be repaired.

a. Write a letter to the company and ask them what you should do next. You do not wish to send in another $9.50, but you do feel they should fix the machine. (Note: The purchase price of the calculator was $50.)

    b. Two months have passed since you wrote the company and you have not heard anything from them. Before taking other courses of action, write them one more letter and let them know how you feel about the matter and specifically what you want them to do for you. You may wish to indicate to them the alternatives available to consumers.

3. As adjustment manager for Whiffle, Inc., you recently received a letter from Armand Legg. It seems that Mr. Legg purchased your L-280 room air conditioner for which he paid $300. He installed the unit in his kitchen window and turned on the switch. It seemed to work well for about a minute. Suddenly, loud noises started coming from the motor and fan area. Before the air conditioner could be turned off, the fan became disengaged from the shaft and caused considerable damage to the interior of the air conditioner. Mr. Legg wants his money back or a new air conditioner.

    When you check with your shipping department, you are told that several air conditioners were shipped without final inspection which includes any necessary tightening of the fan on the shaft. According to the serial number, Mr. Legg received one of these units. Obviously, then, you may be hearing from some other customers who experience similar problems (although the fans are usually firmly installed and need no tightening during final inspection).

    The settlement of Mr. Legg's claim should include an explanation. Write the letter that will adequately handle this problem. If you decide to ship a new unit to him, who will pay the freight charges? What do you want him to do with the damaged unit? What can you tell him that will retain his goodwill and secure his future business?

4. Mrs. Harriet Montgomery of 2000 Warm Springs Avenue in Hagerstown, Maryland, recently paid the American Glass Company a total of $43.98 for the replacement of a window in the family room of her home. A window was broken recently when a ladder fell against it. A copy of the bill, along with a letter that explained the circumstances and asked for reimbursement, was sent to her insurance company, Mutual of Maryland at Capitol 1 Center in Baltimore, Maryland.

    a. Write the letter for Mrs. Montgomery and ask for the reimbursement.

    b. As Claims Officer of Mutual of Maryland, write to Mrs. Montgomery explaining that the "all-perils" coverage she chose has a $50-deductible clause, which means that the company pays only for those amounts over $50.

5. Write a letter "To The Editor" of your local newspaper and express your feelings regarding any issue or problem that interests or concerns you. (For example, violence on T.V., property taxes, sex education.)

6. Mr. Clyde Chase, who lives at 123 Mesa Drive in Pendleton, Oregon, made reservations for a party of six to attend a dinner-show in Lost Wages, Nevada. These reservations were made through Centrex Reservations, Inc., located in Lost Wages. Centrex sells tickets, the price of which includes the dinner, gratuities, taxes, and show.

When Mr. Chase and his friends appeared at the casino for the dinner-show, the maitre d' hotel admitted them and turned them over to one of the many waiters who escorted them to their seats. Apparently the extent and quality of service to patrons is determined by "who" you are and/or what type of reservation you have.

When it was determined that the amount of the gratuity was based on a percentage of ticket price and would, therefore, not vary according to the quality of seating arrangements or service, the attitude and demeanor of the casino employees changed drastically.

The table at which Mr. Chase and his party were seated was out of the "mainstream" and off to one side of the great hall that holds approximately 1000 people. No one in the party of six had a good position from which to view the show that was to follow the dinner. The place settings were jammed together, allowing barely enough room for everyone to eat the meal. Furthermore, no choice of salad dressing was allowed—everyone was required to have the same kind. Finally, when refills of coffee and water were poured, several of the party members were splattered because of the waiter's rush to serve the more lucrative tables.

Mr. Chase feels that Centrex should know about this second-class treatment even though he realizes that they may already be aware of it, and even though they may not be able to do anything about it. Write the letter to Mrs. Pat Lung, Manager of Centrex Reservations, Incorporated.

7. Ms. Jones recently returned to town after a summer away and called the telephone company to request that a phone be installed. She had followed this procedure, as outlined by the phone company, for the past three summers. Ms. Jones requested that a dial

phone be installed in the living room. She would not be home during the day so the installer would have to get the apartment manager to let him in. This information was given when the installation request was made.

Two days later, Ms. Jones came home to discover a touch-tone unit (more expensive) installed in the kitchen. A call to the company brought little satisfaction. Ms. Jones was told that phones were never installed when a person was not home (even though this *had* been the practice for the past three summers), that perhaps the apartment manager did not want phones in the living room, and that if the service was to be changed, a second installation charge would be necessary.

Write a letter to the manager of the telephone company saying that you do not believe the second installation charge should be levied since the company made the mistake that called for the extra service.

8. On September 3, you special ordered 14 yards of upholstery fabric through a large local department store. This type of order was normal procedure since the store stocked only a sample of each fabric. The clerk said it would take about fourteen days to get the merchandise.

After an appropriate waiting period, you call the store and find that the merchandise has not arrived. In another week you call again—and still no merchandise. During the next two weeks, six more phone calls were made and the answer was always the same, "The merchandise has not yet arrived."

Since five weeks have passed, you call the store and ask to speak to the department manager, only to be told it was his day off. The next day you are told the same thing, and on the third day you call, finally get the manager, and learn that he has been on a buying trip. He is very helpful and offers to check into the matter. Three days later he calls to say your merchandise has arrived.

During this six-week period, you have been charged interest on your charge account because you have not paid for this merchandise. (The charge for the merchandise was made when you first ordered it.)

After receiving the call, you rush to the store to pick up the fabric before it disappears. Stapled to the package is an invoice indicating that the merchandise was ordered by telephone only three days previously, and was air-freighted to the store.

Write a letter to the manager of the store suggesting that this sale might have been handled more efficiently and that you do not intend to pay the interest on your bill.

9. Write a letter to Literary Incorporated at 1974 Bookman Rd. in Great Neck, New York, informing them that the one-volume encyclopedia they sent you as a "bonus purchase" is missing nearly 60 pages. Because of other purchases you made, you were able to buy this volume at only a portion of its original selling price; however, the bonus is of limited value in its present form. Ask the company to send you a new encyclopedia and to let you know what to do with the faulty one you now have.

10. The order you sent to Old World Art Forms at 3333 North Goslin in Topeka, Kansas, arrived yesterday. The shipment contained five dozen statuettes of which nearly three dozen were broken or fractured. You need the merchandise for your spring sale which will begin in two weeks. Your store, Finch's Gift Shop, caters to an exclusive clientele, and you want to have a wide assortment of high-quality gifts to offer.

   The sale will be advertised in the local newspaper and you want to make certain that the products you offer will be in stock. Write to your supplier and explain the problem. Ask him to replace the damaged shipment with salable merchandise in time for the sale. Naturally, because of the time limitation, this order will need to be processed immediately. Ask that they send the shipment by parcel post directly to your main store at 102 North 10th Street in Lakeland, Florida.

11. Write a letter for Walker and Brown, Inc., to Richard R. Louis (make up an address). Mr. Louis has written to you asking for information and prices on your Model WP3200 water purifier. He asked you to send one of these units to him, C.O.D., if the price was less than $30. Your price is $26.95, and the shipping and C.O.D. charges are $2.80. The water purifier can be shipped tomorrow by parcel post.

12. Three months ago you purchased a complete set of Dorchester water-free cookware. The cookware is coated with nonstick Tefloff, which is as hard "as a sapphire" and is guaranteed against all defects and wear for a period of five years. One of the pans was slightly nicked when you received the shipment and now the Tefloff coating is disappearing from another of the pans.

   The lid does not seal properly on the pan that is nicked, and you feel that the other pan should be replaced because the coating is apparently defective. In all other ways, you are happy with the cookware. It performs as the salesman said, cooks vegetables with no water at very low temperature, and the taste of the food is better than you expected. So you want to keep the set and you'll continue with your regular payments, but you do want these two pans replaced. You can't remember whether the salesman said that the company or you should pay for any shipping expenses. Write to the Adjustment Manager of Dorchester, Inc., 1458 Norwood Avenue, Baltimore, Maryland, to ask for your replacements.

13. Assume that the following letter was written to you (just change the name mentally) in response to your request for information about your past-due account. When you bought your garden tractor for $695 three months ago, you understood that a handy little two-wheel trailer for your tractor was included at that price. You have made the first payment of $100 (after your down payment of $195) but have written to ask the company to send you the trailer, without charge, before you make the rest of your payments. Here is the letter you receive.

Dear Mr. Browning:

We are in receipt of your letter of February 15. In your letter you asked us to send you our TR-15 trailer free of charge. There must be some misunderstanding.

The TR-15 only sells for $68, which is plenty cheap considering what our competition is selling. The tractor which you bought did not include the trailer, and nearly all of our customers purchase the trailer when they get the tractor. This was clearly explained to you when you signed the contract, and we don't see why this question should have come up.

You will find us fair and reasonable in every way, but we cannot agree with you on this point. Will you please send your payment for $200 to bring your account up-to-date.

If there is anything else we can do to help, please let us know.

Sincerely yours,

U. R. Stuck

Answer the following questions about the letter:

1. What kinds of reactions and emotions could you identify as you read the letter?
2. Is it necessary for Mr. Stuck to tell you that he received your letter or to tell you what you said in your letter?
3. How well does the third sentence prepare you for the bad news to come?
4. How many problems in this letter relate to modifiers being misplaced or incorrectly used? Identify these problems.

5. What problems with logic can you identify from this letter?
6. Do the connectives show proper relationship of the clauses they connect?
7. Was Mr. Stuck successful in motivating you to purchase the trailer as an accessory? What should he have done?
8. How effective is the last sentence in promoting further favorable relations?

After you have answered these questions, rewrite the letter the way you think it should have been written. Try to determine what the objectives of this letter should be and see that your letter achieves those objectives. Type the letter on a separate sheet of paper and include another sheet with your answers to the questions about the original letter.

14. As an accountant for the Goldfarber Department Stores, Goldfarber Plaza, Lexington, KY, you have just completed a comprehensive study of the various amounts of energy required to operate the different electric appliances that are sold by your organization. After working in conjunction with the Public Utilities Commission, you have written a report that provides the detail necessary for a complete analysis for top management. Your presentation includes all of the consumption figures for lighting, food preparation, entertainment, grooming, laundry, comfort, and housewares.

The estimates of energy usage are based on local and national statistics but, of course, do not provide for the variable of individual operation. The kilowatt hour (KWH) is used as the basic unit of measurement, and energy costs are computed on the assumption that the domestic user rate is 1.8¢ per KWH.

Write a letter of transmittal that will accompany the report you are submitting to Muriel A. Compton, Vice President of Sales and Distribution. Although the report contains information about several aspects of energy consumption, use only an appropriate portion of the data presented below to develop a brief summary of your findings. This summary, which will represent a part of your letter of transmittal, should contain only that information which you feel will be of greatest interest and importance to the reader. Also, keep in mind that the information in the report will be used by the Goldfarber advertising department and by the sales force in the various departments.

Approximate Average KWH Use (Per Month)

Water Heater (family of 4)—425; Refr-Freezer (frostless)—125; Food Freezer (frostless)—125; Cooking—115; Dishwasher (1 load per day, including hot water)—115; Lighting—105; Automatic Washer (5 loads per week, including hot water)—105; Clothes Dryer (5 loads per week)—95; TV (Color, 6 hrs. per day)—65; Furnace Fan—55; Electric Blanket—30; Iron—20; Stereo-Radio—15; Coffee Maker—15; Toaster—5.

15. As Assistant Manager of Great Eastern Catalog Company, 3456 Concourse Street, Albany, NY, you have been assigned the task of developing a form letter that will be sent to all individuals who are "continuing customers." These people have all purchased from your mail order house before, and you will send the form letter along with the new catalog for the coming fall and winter seasons.

   The purpose of the letter of transmittal is to introduce the new catalog to the recipients and to encourage them to use the publication whenever they have a need to make purchases. Characteristics of the new catalog that you may wish to emphasize in your letter include:

   a. larger print for easy reading
   b. new coding system for easy ordering
   c. postage-paid envelopes for orders
   d. new billing system for all purchases

   Also include in the form letter a reference to the "referral" form that can be given to acquaintances who might like to receive a copy of the new catalog. This referral form can be found in front of the order blanks toward the end of the catalog.

16. You have just read in the local newspaper that Mr. Harry Merkle, one of your organization's best customers, has just been voted "Retailer of the Year." This is a very prestigious award and traditionally has gone to only the most highly qualified and successful business people. Write a letter of congratulations to Mr. Merkle.

17. Write a memorandum to the staff in your Accounting Department (assume that you are the department manager) informing them that the new office hours for the summer months will be from 7:30 a.m. to 3:30 p.m. The regular-year hours are from 8:00 a.m. to 4:00 p.m. Mention in the memo that the new hours are intended to allow employees to miss the heavy traffic flows in the mornings and afternoons and to provide them with additional release time for summer activities.

18. As owner of a local office furniture manufacturing company, you hire several part-time workers during the summer months of each year. For the past several years, you have hired with considerable success many of the junior and senior high school students in the community. These students have been, almost without exception,

excellent workers, and many of them have taken full-time employment with you after graduation. Write a letter to Mrs. Marge Ewing, Chairman of the Medford School Board, in which you express your satisfaction with these students. You feel that parents, teachers, and administrators are all to be commended for the leadership and education they are providing the young people in the community and that the good work some of them perform for you is a confirmation of that belief.

Application
of Writing Principles to
Special Business Messages

9

In this chapter you will learn that:

1. while the psychology of letter writing is fundamentally sound, certain messages require "special handling."

2. writing sales letters requires a knowledge of the prospect, the product or service, and the techniques of persuasion.

3. sales letters can be written using either direct or indirect format.

4. writing good collection letters requires a knowledge of debtor motivation.

5. there are many reasons why bills are not paid on time. These reasons influence the development of effective collection letters.

6. collection letters are usually written in stages of forcefulness.

In previous chapters we have discussed the logic of writing certain types of messages in either the direct or indirect format. The decision to use one approach over the other, we learned, is based primarily on the nature of the reader's response or reaction. As a general rule, following these guidelines will result in communications that best allow us to meet our objectives. On occasion, however, we have a need to develop special kinds of letters and other messages that require additional consideration and perhaps an individualized approach. Included among these special types of communications are sales letters and collection letters. Let's examine each of these types and learn why they are unique.

Sales Letters

The sales letter is a highly specialized type of communication and is frequently developed by professionals who provide this service to businesses that have a need for this technical expertise. Few organizations require their regular employees to write this type of message on a regular basis. Even though you may never be required to write a specific sales message, it will be to your advantage to know the criteria involved.

Sales letters differ from other types of communications in that they are designed to sell a particular product, idea, or service. Naturally, there will be some resistance to the product you are selling, and you will need to overcome any objections that you may encounter. Persuasion, then, becomes a key element in the writing, and you will need to use the various techniques of emphasis to develop powerful messages.

Know Your Prospect

In addition to knowing how to use techniques of emphasis to overcome resistance, you will need to know something about the prospective customer. In fact, knowing about the needs of your prospective customer will allow you to tailor your persuasive message to meet those needs. By knowing your prospect, you will be better able to anticipate some of the objections to your sales presentation. Again, the need to empathize with the receiver of your message is crucial to successful communication. Specific information about your audience includes occupation, level of income, family size, leisure-time activities, age, purchasing habits, and reasons for possibly needing what you have to offer. While not all of this information may be available to you, or even necessary for your particular needs, you should have whatever facts you can obtain. Often you can purchase through various mailing list firms the lists of names and categories of prospective buyers. On the other hand, because of your own record-keeping activities, you may already have the information you need.

Know Your Product

A knowledge of the prospective customers will help you develop a message that may have some appeal for them. This knowledge alone, however, will not guarantee that you will achieve your objectives of convincing your reader or of closing the sale. In order for the readers to be moved to respond favorably, they must be able to believe what you have told them. Source credibility becomes especially important to the reader at this point. What can you do to convince your reader that the information is correct and fairly presented? What can you do to get your reader to believe what you are saying? Apart from the requirement that we write in a believable manner, we should be able to express a thorough knowledge of the product. Probably nothing else will be so convincing as our own information base. By having a good knowledge of the products, we will be able to speak with authority. We will be able to describe the product in any degree of detail required, and we will be able to focus on the major strengths that will have particular appeal to the prospective customer. Little else can be so detrimental to a strong sales pitch as a lack of information about the product.

Another important factor in writing the sales letter is a knowledge of the competition. If you know what your competitors have to offer, including their strengths and weaknesses, you can design your messages to provide even greater impact. The writer should probably not refer to the competition in any direct way; however, this restriction does not preclude the use of tactful implication.

Use Either the Direct or Indirect Approach

Either the direct or indirect format can be used when writing sales messages. Much depends on the overall approach you use to get information to the reader. You may decide that a forceful, attention-getting opening is needed in a given situation and, therefore, will want to use the direct approach. By striking quickly you may get "on target" immediately and follow with the necessary explanatory information that will conclude the sales effort. On another occasion, you may want to "build your case" by using indirect methods. Perhaps by using a provocative question, you can stimulate the reader's curiosity and provide the motivation for continued reading. Whichever format you choose, your message must be emphatic, concise, informative, and thought provoking.

Also, note that the opening and closing paragraphs are important in sales messages because they are key positions of emphasis. Sales messages must be able to attract and hold the interest of the reader; therefore, first and last paragraphs must be developed with special care. In writing these special paragraphs, we should use concise and vivid words that identify precisely the thoughts we wish to communicate. This is no place for abstract terms that make the reader work at determining what it is we are saying.

One practical approach to the writing of sales letters is to use the opening paragraph to get the attention of the reader and the closing paragraph to suggest the action that would satisfy our primary objective. The middle paragraphs should include details or other information capable of persuading the reader to want the product our letter is trying to sell.

This indirect approach is the one most often used. Its success depends, first of all, on the writer's ability to develop an appropriate opening—a comment that not only captures the reader's attention but also flows smoothly into a presentation of ideas or facts that will persuade the reader to act positively toward the response suggested in the letter's closing remarks.

Now, consider the following letter. Does it attract your attention? Does it hold your interest? Is it informative? Is it written in the direct or indirect format? Could the opposite format have been used without diminishing the quality of the letter?

Dear xxxxxxxx:

Can we help you enjoy your summer vacation?

Perhaps you hired a young man to water your yard last summer and you spent a good part of your vacation time wondering if he would remember to water at just the right time, to close the valves tightly, and to see that all parts of the yard received the right amount of water. Chances are he did a good job; and when you paid him, you told yourself that next summer you wouldn't worry. Well, we can help you keep that promise you made to yourself.

Most people can relate to this kind of opening, especially if our timing correlates with the time that people are planning their vacations.

If we know our own business we will know that our analogy fits a great number of homeowners. It is easy for our reader to put himself into the picture.

Notice that our letter avoids scare tactics. We can help our own cause by being positive about what has happened.

You can relax if you know that Rainmaker is on the job. Rainmaker is a timing device that can be custom designed for **your** lawn. A patented timing mechanism allows you to water all or part of your lawn as often as daily or as seldom as once every ten days. The Rainmaker can be installed on your present sprinkler system or a system designed and installed by our yard-care experts.

The product is introduced by name. We explain some of the features and relate them to the reader's needs. The appeal here may be to pride, convenience, comfort, or some other emotion. Remember that most people buy to satisfy emotions rather than needs.

Just mail the enclosed card and our representative will call you to arrange for a free estimate for installing your own Rainmaker. You'll find that this summer's vacation is a lot more pleasant if you know that Rainmaker is on the job.

The desired response is made easy and natural. The closing remark names the product and reminds the reader of its desirability.

Sincerely yours,

Examine sales messages that are sent to you. Ask yourself if these messages meet the criteria suggested in this unit. Read the sales messages that are being used where you work. Are they written in a forceful manner? Do they attract and maintain attention? Based on the information contained in the communication, would you be willing to consider buying the product? If you can answer "yes" to these questions, you have been evaluating good sales messages.

Collection Letters

Credit buying plays an important part in the life of almost every business in existence today. Seldom do we find a firm that deals strictly on a cash basis anymore. The pressures on capital investments and cash flows require that astute business managers learn to use their credit opportunities wisely and that they administer their own credit extension programs with care. Both buyers and sellers of goods and services experience the need to buy and sell on credit.[1] With the decision to do business on a credit basis comes the need for a knowledge of collection procedures and collection letters.

Any discussion of credit policies and procedures should be preceded by a determination of one's own philosophy of human behavior regarding the payment of a just debt. A positive and realistic attitude in this context is that a person will want to pay and will probably pay any legitimate debts. To believe otherwise is to underestimate the goodness of people; and this belief, in turn, will lead to some very serious barriers in interpersonal and organizational relationships. To debate the presence or absence of this quality of goodness is beyond the scope of this text, but to ignore it completely would be the omission of an element essential to our discussion of credit policy and collection letters.

1. A local owner of a small furniture store prided himself in the fact that his loss on bad debts had always been less than the national average. Because of this record, he believed that he had a practical philosophy of credit and collection procedures. Upon closer analysis, however, it was noted that his criteria for extending credit to the public were so restrictive that he was missing thousands of dollars worth of business. Had he taken the time to evaluate more liberally the applications of marginal prospects, he would, undoubtedly, have increased his profits considerably simply on the basis of increased volume. It is reasonable to expect that there will be some losses from credit sales, but it is also reasonable to expect that most customers will pay their accounts if they can possibly do so.

Before we begin to examine the different types of collection letters, we should determine why it is that individuals do not pay their debts. While the reasons for nonpayment will vary with the circumstances surrounding each situation, one or more of the following elements are often predisposing factors:

1. **No job.** The debtor may have since lost his job and has no source of income.
2. **Illness.** Possibly the debtor has not been able to work because of illness. Often, illness can keep an individual out of work for extended periods of time.
3. **Error.** Maybe the individual does not owe anything. The error may be the fault of the business organization that extended the credit—poor record keeping.
4. **Overestimate of ability to pay.** Sometimes consumers overestimate their ability to pay for items bought on credit. This overextension may not be intentional, but it can and does happen to many customers.
5. **Unwillingness to pay.** For any number of reasons, a person may be unwilling to pay his debt. He may refuse because he feels he has received bad service or a bad product, or because he just wishes to avoid payment.
6. **Forgetfulness.** Finally a person may not pay a debt on time simply because he has forgotten to do so.

The person attempting to collect the money can help his own cause by finding out why payments are not being made. Knowing the reasons for the behavior often gives us a sense of direction as we attempt to collect the accounts. If the reason for nonpayment is illness, then our approach will probably be different than if the reason is simply an unwillingness to meet the obligation. Generally, initial correspondence with the customer will give us some idea regarding the reason for the overdue payment. Once this reason has been determined, we can begin our efforts to obtain satisfaction of the debt.

We will not find it unusual for a business to write several collection letters to customers who are behind in payments. Initial efforts to establish communications will often fail. This failure may be a function of the debtor's not having received the information you sent, but more likely it is because of a reluctance to communicate about a subject that reflects poorly on one's character. Some debtors may not want to correspond with you simply because they cannot meet their obligation and do not know how to deal with the problem. Whatever the reasons for not contacting you about the account balance, you must continue your attempts to make contact.

First-phase Letters

Generally, when several letters are required, they will contain varying degrees of forcefulness with respect to your appeal for payment. Collection letters written during the initial period will be relatively mild and will probably be nothing more than reminders that the bill has not been paid. In fact, many of these reminders are merely insert slips that contain information about the nature and status of the account. Subsequent letters, however, grow more forceful and the overall tone becomes more rigid and demanding. Again, knowing the circumstances of each case will allow you to develop a letter with a tone and style appropriate to the situation.

Regardless of the manner in which the first letter is written, it should convey the idea that the writer believes the debtor *is going to* pay the bill—it is simply a matter of the person's getting around to the clerical task of sending the payment. The letter should not even hint at the possibility that the account balance represents an "obligation" for which the customer is responsible. The first in a series of collection letters should never include the element of moral suasion. Give the customer every opportunity to respond to your request for payment and allow it to be done without the feeling that you are in any way questioning the person's character or intentions. Again, this letter should convey the attitude that you believe the customer *is going to* pay the debt. Examine the collection letters that follow and determine whether the tone, style, approach, and attitudes are appropriate for a first-phase or reminder message.

Howdy!

Just a reminder that your account with us for _$37.19_ is overdue. Will you please take a few moments and mail us your check?

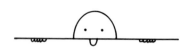

HI THERE FRIEND! REMEMBER US? We haven't seen or heard from you recently. Your account balance of _$37.19_ is a bit overdue. Please let us know if we can help in any way.

```
July 13, 19xx


Miss Mildred Holloway
547 North Cabalo Drive
Princeton, North Carolina  00000

Dear Miss Holloway:

You are now 30 days past due on your account of $37.19.  We
cannot understand why you haven't paid the amount you right-
fully owe.

When we buy goods or services on account, we expect that
we will have to pay for them at some time in the future.
Avoidance of obligations such as those you have with our
store reflects poorly on one's character and can have far-
reaching effects.

Why don't you pay us the $37.19 now and avoid the kinds of
problems that usually confront people who don't pay their
bills.

Cordially yours,


Sherry Ransome
Credit Manager

sr:bc
```

(Note to the student: Do you think the tone of this letter is appropriate for the first-phase communication with the customer?)

July 13, 19xx

Miss Mildred Holloway
547 North Cabalo Drive
Princeton, North Carolina 00000

Dear Miss Holloway:

Funny things can happen to our bills sometimes. We use
them as bookmarks, write notes on them and leave them under someone's windshield wiper, or put them under the short
table leg to keep the table from jiggling. It's very easy
to misplace or lose a bill--it can happen to anyone.

Miss Holloway, I have a feeling that something of this nature has happened to the last bill we sent you. You have
been a valued credit customer of ours for the last four
years, and this is the first time you have ever been late
with a payment. You are now 30 days past due on your balance of $37.19.

I understand how sometimes it's difficult to last from
paycheck to paycheck. Unexpected things crop up--an illness, an accident, a law suit--that can deplete our checking account prematurely. If something like this has happened to you, will you please drop me a line to let me
know why you haven't paid your bill? I'm certain we can
work something out to our mutual satisfaction.

Sincerely,

Sherry Ransome
Credit Manager

sr:bc

(Note to the student: Is this a good first-phase collection letter?
Do you think there is too much effort being made for the collection
of a debt under these circumstances and in light of the debtor's record with the store?)

These two examples attempt to communicate two primary things to the debtor.

1. The bill is overdue and needs to be paid.
2. The mailing is simply a reminder and the store has complete confidence that the account will be settled in good time.

Intermediate-phase Letters

If no response is received after the initial collection letter has been sent, additional correspondence is in order. Naturally, subsequent letters will need to be more forceful in their approach. In writing these letters, we can appeal to a person's sense of right and wrong. The prevailing attitude of the writer of the intermediate-phase letters is that the debtor *ought to* pay the bill. In a sense, the "ought-to-pay" letter raises the point of personal responsibility and fair play. Often those whose character is challenged or threatened will do whatever is necessary to resolve the situation. In the matter of unpaid bills, they may be moved to send you a check or to make arrangements whereby they can meet their obligation at a later time.

Read the examples, shown on pages 222 and 223, and determine whether the tone and degree of forcefulness are appropriate for intermediate-phase letters.

Last-phase Letters

The last-phase letters in a collection series may appear at first glance to be the easiest type to write. It would seem that there need be little concern for diplomacy or for creating the proper tone. After all, this effort will probably be the last one we will make, and the prospect of our avoiding a bad debt expense seems minimal anyway. Do not be trapped into this kind of thinking—this last-phase letter may, if well written, be just the message needed to get the job done.

One of the greatest temptations to the writer will be to express anger at the debtor. A heated letter may make the writer feel better temporarily, but it will probably diminish the effectiveness of the effort. The reader will most likely react to this letter with a reciprocating anger and then little will be accomplished. Again, as with any other writing assignment, we need to remember that our primary objective is to collect the money. In writing this final letter, our objective will be to get the money by informing the reader of the

July 13, 19xx

Mr. Harold L. Terry

325 Geckler Road

Independence, IA 00000

Dear Mr. Terry:

I have sent you two letters concerning your unpaid balance of $189.37. Neither of these letters has been answered and apparently no effort has been made to contact us by telephone. Let's make some arrangements for you to pay your overdue account balance before the situation becomes complicated even further.

We approved your application for credit on the assumption that you were sincere in your promise to meet your responsibilities. We have certainly tried to meet ours by providing you with goods and services whenever you needed them.

Please call or write to me personally so that we can resolve this problem without further delay.

Sincerely yours,

Robert L. Coston

Credit Manager

rlc:eq

(Can you identify the portion of the letter that is designed to arouse the reader's sense of responsibility? Does this letter reflect the attitude that the debtor *ought to* pay? Do you think the letter is too aggressive for the intermediate-phase?)

July 13, 19xx

Mr. Harold L. Terry

325 Geckler Road

Independence, IA 00000

Dear Mr. Terry:

Taking supplies home from the office, evading income taxes, and footfaulting in tennis are all forms of cheating. So it is with refusing to pay for credit purchases. Do you think you are cheating us, Mr. Terry?

We fail to see the difference between refusing to honor debts and any of the preceding examples of dishonesty. You are, in effect, cheating us by not sending your check for the balance shown in your overdue account. I can't believe that you would do this to us intentionally, but what else can we think?

Call me right away and make arrangements to pay us the money we have coming.

Sincerely yours,

Robert L. Coston

Credit Manager

rlc:eq

(Does this letter have the tone necessary for an intermediate-phase letter? Is it too forceful or insulting? Do you think a letter of this nature would get the desired results? How would you react to this kind of message? Does it show empathy?)

action we will be taking and, possibly, what should be done to avert the consequences. Depending on the circumstances, we may be able to repossess any merchandise that was purchased by the use of the credit, or we may be able to take the matter to court. Other alternatives include turning the entire case over to a collection agency, informing the various credit bureaus of the delinquency, and canceling all credit opportunities with our firm.

While no standard approach can be used when writing collection letters, certain key points can be stressed. These points include a specific reference to the delinquent account, a short review of the other efforts you have made to collect the money, a statement to the effect that the bill *has to* be paid, specific action you may take to obtain satisfaction in the matter, and any alternative courses of action open to the debtor. The letter should be written in the direct format, and it should include concise, concrete terms expressed in an emphatic manner.

Evaluate the following letters on the basis of the criteria referred to above. Determine whether you think the last-resort letter will be successful. Note where each approach might be strengthened if certain words or specific parts were changed.

In light of the increasing number of consumer protection laws, anyone doing business with the public will be well advised to become familiar with the full gamut of rights and restrictions. While the finer points of the law are perhaps best left to those who have been so trained, the business person can avoid much unnecessary difficulty by knowing what the "new" rights and responsibilities are.

Collection Letters—Formal Series

Many large organizations doing a considerable amount of selling on credit have a formalized program that includes a series of form letters which are periodically sent to customers who are delinquent in their payments. This procedure of sending specific letters in a series is done on a rather routine basis and often disregards any extenuating circumstances of the particular case (especially if a computer is used to process the billings). A collection-letter series has many obvious advantages, but it also has some drawbacks.

An effective collection series can be developed if certain steps are taken. First, each letter in the series must be written in the correct tone and with the right degree of forcefulness. Second, each letter

July 13, 19xx

Mr. Harold Nixer

260 West Curling

San Diego, CA 00000

Dear Mr. Nixer:

As you must know by now, your payments on the sofa and chairs you purchased from us last October are four months in arrears. Apparently you have chosen to ignore all of our collection efforts and we are now pursuing the only course of action left open to us--the filing of a law suit.

Our attorneys, Newman and King, will begin legal proceedings next Monday. I hope you realize that court costs and attorney fees that arise from this action will further obligate you and thereby increase your indebtedness beyond the present balance of $856.35. We had hoped to spare you the additional cost and the obvious embarrassment, but we have no other alternative.

If you wish to reconsider your position and stop these proceedings against you, please contact Newman and King on or before next Monday. Since the matter is no longer under our control, you will have to deal with them.

Sincerely,

Jean King

Credit Manager

jk:ms

cc: Newman and King

```
July 13, 19xx

Mr. Harold Nixer

260 West Curling

San Diego, CA  00000

Dear Mr. Nixer:

This final letter to you regarding your long-overdue ac-
count will probably be no more effective than any of the
others we have written.  However, we did want to take this
opportunity to tell you what we think of people like your-
self who apparently enjoy taking advantage of others who
try to work with them in good faith.


It is your kind of person that makes it difficult for re-
tailers like myself to really enjoy working with the pub-
lic.  Naturally we hope to make a little money in the pro-
cess, but the losers we have to deal with keep even that
possibility to a minimum.  Do us a favor next time you
need something that we carry in stock--take your business
to our competitors.

Jean King

Credit Manager

kj:ms
```

(Which of these two preceding letters has the best tone? Which do you think has the best chance of succeeding in its objective? Is it ever appropriate to get angry at someone in a situation like this? What would be your reactions to each of these letters?)

must be specific enough to be meaningful to the reader, yet general enough to cover all of the variables in the cases it is required to serve. Third, each letter must be so worded that variable information such as customer name, address, account balance, etc., can be inserted automatically. Often, letters in a collection series are prepared by professional consultants, but this procedure is not always necessary.

One example of the effective use of the collection series can be seen by examining the collection methods used by a young man who delivers a local newspaper. Ordinarily, these young men and women spend a great amount of time and money trying to collect from their customers. They make repeated calls at their customers' homes. They are asked to call back; they are told that the wife (or husband) has the checkbook and is not home now; or they find that no one is home. A few people pay their newspaper account by leaving the money or a check in an envelope in the newspaper box for the carrier to pick up on the next delivery. For the most part, though, the process of collection is long and costly, which is the reason that many of these budding young business types give up and look for other work.

Our local carrier (referred to above) started his business by sending a letter to each of the 200 customers assigned to him, explaining his delivery and collection procedure to them. This procedure starts on the last day of the month with the delivery of a newspaper to which an envelope is stapled. The envelope is rubber-stamped with the carrier's name and address for mailing and includes a notice of the month and the amount that is due for the next day (the first of each month). Most of the customers pay as a result of this initial contact by mailing their payment in the envelope provided, or by leaving the payment in the newspaper box for pickup at the time of the next delivery. The few who do not respond receive a reminder on the 6th day of the month.

> Just a reminder that your Courier account is due. Please mail your payment or leave it in the box and I will pick it up. If you have already mailed your payment, please accept my thanks.
>
> > Kurt Ryan
> > 10010 Buckhorn Dr.
> > Ph. 377-9654

This reminder is stapled to the newspaper and elicits a favorable response from nearly all of the customers. If there are some who still have not paid by the Tuesday after the 10th day of the month, they receive a second notice as follows:

SECOND NOTICE

Your payment for this month's Courier has still not been received. If there is some problem, please call me. Otherwise, will you please leave your payment in the box or get it to me by this Saturday.

Kurt Ryan
10010 Buckhorn Dr.
Ph. 377-9654

The last phase in this collection series, if necessary, is a telephone follow-up on the following Saturday. The results have been gratifying to this young man and are the envy of the other carriers who are still spending time and money trying to collect in the old way.

This young man has learned that most people *want* to pay their bills. He receives favorable comments and commendations from his customers for his businesslike methods.

Other Considerations

Anyone responsible for making decisions about credit policies or collection procedures must remember that no one set of guidelines will meet the needs of all business operations. For example, the speed with which a business uses the letters in a collection series will vary according to one or more of several factors. If the business sells high-quality merchandise to those in the top income-level groups, greater flexibility will probably be required when evaluating delinquent accounts. Consumers in high-income groups are valuable customers and will need to be treated in a manner somewhat different from that used for customers in other categories.

Another variable that can affect credit decisions is the economic situation. If money is "tight," or if inventories are low, businesses may wish to sell primarily on a cash basis. The financial position of the business will also play a role in determining credit policies. Some businesses simply cannot afford to have many accounts receivable. All of these factors will need to be considered by the astute business person who makes the decisions about credit and collections.

Summary

While good writing principles apply to all situations, specialized messages such as sales and collection letters generally require extra care. The sales letter is often developed by specialty writers outside the firm, but a knowledge of sales-letter writing is of value to anyone interested in effective expression.

In order to be able to write good sales messages, the writer must have a knowledge of the prospect and of the product. Having this knowledge allows one to tailor the words to meet specific needs. Either the direct or indirect approach can be used, depending upon the effect the writer wishes to achieve. Also, techniques of emphasis will be used by sales-letter writers.

Collection-letter writing begins with a philosophy of human behavior regarding the payment of debts. Operating on the assumption that individuals will want to pay their bills whenever they can, writers can develop communications that reflect a positive and realistic attitude. A helpful device is to become aware of the various reasons why bills are not paid. These reasons include: no job, illness, clerical error, overestimate of ability to pay, unwillingness, and forgetfulness.

Collection letters are classified as first-phase, intermediate-phase, and last-phase. Care should be taken in the writing of these letters because the elements of goodwill and the prospects of bad debts are imminent.

Chapter Exercises

1. The Student Activities Board of your school wishes to sell advertising space on 20″ x 30″ semigloss desk mats. These mats will be given to students who enroll for classes during the two-day registration period in the fall.

   Information on the mats will include a calendar for the school year, intercollegiate and intramural athletic schedules, student activities (guest lecturers, artist series, etc.) and advertisements of local businesses that cater to the college trade. Among other advantages subscribers will enjoy are the "high visibility" the ads will have and the satisfaction of having helped to support selected activities of their college. Write an appropriate form letter.

   This form letter will be sent to all businesses that are listed in the Chamber of Commerce Registry. Its objective will be to introduce the advertising program to the readers and to inform them that a student representative will be calling on them within the next two weeks.

2. Your student chapter of Administrative Management Society (AMS) wishes to sell Christmas candles as a moneymaking project. These scented candles have been designed and molded by the students themselves and are priced to compete with those sold on a national basis.

   A form letter will be sent to students, faculty, and staff members of your school informing them of the product. Prices of the candles, which will be available by November 1, range from $3.50 for the 5-inch size to $7.50 for the 9-inch decorator model. These candles are functional and can be burned on any occasion, or they can serve as decorator pieces throughout the house. Many of the candles have Christmas themes and, of course, make excellent gifts. (Note: These candles will not be new to many of the potential customers since the models you are offering were sold just three years ago.)

   Assume that you are the Project Manager and write the form letter that will be sent to the chapter's prospective customers. Use the techniques of emphasis that will make it an effective, persuasive letter. The objective of the letter will be to inform students, faculty, and staff about the product, its availability, and the procedure for obtaining the candles. Assume that the order form is attached to the bottom of your sales message. This order form will contain all the necessary information the customer needs.

3. Mary Petriken, a young artist, has just finished a series of humorous drawings depicting golfers in various awkward positions as they attempt to hit a golf ball. Each picture has an appropriate caption describing the situation. These sketches were designed to be hung

in business offices, doctors' and dentists' offices, or in just about any area where a "light touch" would be appreciated.

Develop a sales message that will appear on a brochure which shows facsimile reproductions of the many sketches that are available to choose from. Use your imagination as you write a message that will sell copies of the artist's work. Make any reasonable assumptions you wish regarding costs, deliveries, quality of work, etc.

4. You have just returned from the moon where you were sent by your employer, Interplanetary Realty, Incorporated. Your assignment was to study the terrain and other dimensions of the environment to determine how best to sell subdivision parcels to people who will be living on the moon shortly.

Use your imagination to write a forceful, effective letter that will be sent to those whose names were included on a list which was purchased by Interplanetary Realty from Space Marketing International. The names on this list represent those people who have indicated a willingness to consider relocation. This relocation program is being sponsored by the federal government in an attempt to encourage people to assist in a worldwide effort designed to identify and develop natural resources on other terrestrial bodies. Naturally, persons choosing to participate in this new adventure of the space age will receive some form of subsidy from the respective governments involved in the project.

Assume that this will be a form letter, but that it will be so reproduced as to appear to be a personal letter written to each individual on the mailing list. The variable information of names and addresses will be recorded automatically by automatic typewriter.

5. As Credit Manager of Waterloo Wholesalers, Incorporated, write a letter to Mr. Gregory Wall of Washington Square, Indianapolis, Indiana, regarding his application for a line of credit.

According to the information you have received from his references and the local credit bureau, Mr. Wall has a record of consistently late payments. Furthermore, you have learned that there is one pending court case pertaining to his delinquent accounts. Obviously, you do not wish to do business with this applicant on anything but a cash basis. In your letter to him, you may wish to stress the liberal cash terms that are available to him. Also, you may want to encourage him to reapply for credit at a later date when his repayment history would indicate a more favorable circumstance.

6. Write a letter to Ms. DiAnn Page in which you remind her that she has not made a payment on her monthly charge account for

nearly 60 days. According to the terms of the charge account agreement, she is to pay at least 10 percent of the outstanding balance every 30 days. This "delinquency" is her first in almost three years of faithful patronage, but store policy dictates that *all* delinquent accounts be treated in a similar manner.

7. Follow up on the communication to the Ms. Page referred to in the preceding problem. It is now 30 days later and you have had no response from her. You are assuming that she has received the first reminder because the letter was not returned to your department store. Write a second letter in which you review the circumstances of the case and make an appeal for payment.

8. Six months ago, as Credit Manager for Seaboard Furniture, you approved a credit sale to Mr. Dennis Wilfong for $988. Credit arrangements required a down payment of 10 percent, with the balance to be paid in three equal installments within 90 days. To date, nothing has been paid on the account and no response has been made to the first- and second-phase letters that have been mailed to Wilfong's address. In a recent telephone conversation with him, you learn that he has no intention of paying the amount due because he says he is not satisfied with the furniture; yet, he refuses to return the purchased items.

   Write a last-phase letter to him indicating that you are turning his account over to the attorneys for collection and/or court action. Point out to him the alternatives he has available: (a) making some positive effort to satisfy the debt, or (b) suffering the consequences of losing his good credit rating and paying court costs. Be persuasive and firm in your approach, but keep a positive attitude toward the situation. Give Mr. Wilfong every possible chance to "save face" if he should so desire to.

9. As Credit Manager for Davis Furniture Company, you have just been asked to approve an order for $867 worth of furniture items from Mr. Ralph Parke. Mr. Parke has been a customer of Davis Furniture for about eight months. During that time he has abused his credit privilege in several ways.

   Your store offers a 1 percent discount on accounts paid by the 10th day of each month. Mr. Parke pays his bill between the 15th and the 30th but still takes the 1 percent discount. He ignores your rebilling of the discount amount. Two months ago he did not pay his account for the month but paid in full the following month, again taking the discount to which he was not entitled.

   Mr. Parke owns several rental apartments and could be a good customer if you could get him to honor the credit arrangements. He has the money but is careless in his financial habits.

You would like to sell him this new order for furniture, but you must have the cash. You also want to collect the $420 from last month, which is past due. Write him a letter that will get the money and will keep his business and his goodwill.

Planning for a Career in Business

10

A study of information in this chapter will provide an understanding of:

1. the personal research needed to better comprehend your own needs in relation to employment for a career.

2. the importance of and techniques for developing the personal data sheet.

3. the importance of and techniques for developing the letter of application.

4. the interaction that develops during the personal interview.

5. other types of communication relating to employment.

Any activity can be best completed if there has been adequate planning for it. This statement is particularly true of career planning and management. Many aspects need to be considered by the serious student who shops the job market. Awareness of the many opportunities and problems related to career activities can help us make better plans to cope with them. For example, we should know something about ourselves, about the kinds of work available, and about the specific companies that hire people. Furthermore, we need to know how to develop data sheets and letters of application and how to conduct ourselves during an interview for a job. The intelligent applicant will do all that is possible to prepare for entry into the job market.

Know Yourself

On the surface, this advice to know yourself may seem to be an unnecessary suggestion. After all, who knows you better than you know yourself? Probably no one, but this does not mean that a little introspection is not in order. As human beings we have a tendency to deal with matters outside ourselves first. Consequently, we leave little time to think about our own needs, desires, strengths, weaknesses, and potential. Furthermore, it is especially difficult for us to be very objective about ourselves—particularly as it applies to our own strengths and weaknesses.

We need to know, for example, if we prefer to work primarily by ourselves or if we enjoy accomplishing tasks through the cooperation of others. Even though we have learned that we are expected to enjoy working with others, we may not function best under this arrangement.

Another factor we need to consider is whether we prefer to do detail work (small segments of the total effort) or whether we prefer to be involved in planning the overall project. For some people, it is difficult, if not impossible, to envision a project or plan in its entirety. For others, being required to handle detail would lead to considerable job dissatisfaction. Knowing how you would perform in each of these situations is important as you plan for a career.

As you get to know yourself, go one step further. Be honest with yourself. Refrain from applying for a job in which you know you would not be happy and for which you are not prepared. On the other hand, if a job is "just right" for you, pursue it with enthusiasm.

Know the Opportunities

Much information relative to the many different types of work performed in our country is now available. The *Occupational Outlook Handbook* is one such publication. Lists of occupational titles and requirements have been published by the various agencies of federal, state, and local governments. Some of the lists include information about levels of education required to perform the tasks, the nature of the work involved, and projected trends regarding possible employment opportunities. Public schools have, for some time, been offering formal courses that are designed to educate students about occupational information. Much of this information is made available to students at the junior high school level to enable them to begin thinking about the type of work they might enjoy doing after their formal education has been completed. Considerable effort is being made at the high school level to assist students in their career-planning decisions. A federally subsidized program of career education is one of the most recent efforts to help them. Thousands of students throughout the nation are enrolled in these programs that offer information and limited work experience in many different areas of employment.

Local newspapers and periodicals offer good information about the business outlook by a comparison of areas. Chambers of Commerce and various trade publications also provide similar information. Employment offices, both public and private, are also good sources for this kind of help. Your own college or university may have a placement office that is especially interested in helping you to find information about job opportunities and to evaluate your preparation for those jobs. The alert job seeker will become aware of current employment trends, industry outlook, and specific companies' policies by devoting some attention to radio and television broadcasts, newspaper and periodical articles, and other sources of up-to-date information.

Know Your Prospective Employer

Employers have a right to know something about the workers they hire. The company is committing many dollars in equipment, facilities, and salaries by hiring people to work for it. In a similar manner, the employee has a right—and an obligation to himself—to know something about the company he is considering working for. Only by having certain types of information about a company will a prospective employee have some assurance that the mutual efforts of employer and employee will be satisfactory.

For example, you will want to know about the stability of the company, its size and scope of operation, the labor-management relationship, opportunities for promotion, and fringe benefits. This information about specific companies can be obtained by examining literature such as company brochures, house organs, and annual reports. More specific information about company policies can be obtained during personal interviews with company representatives. This latter source of information will be considered further during our discussion of the interview process.

Another important consideration is the specific company's employment procedure. You will need to know whether you should contact the personnel department within the organization or, instead, the specific department in which you hope to work.

The Data Sheet

The expression, "Let your words do your bidding," applies to all forms of written communication, but it probably has even greater significance during the job-getting process. Perhaps at no other time will we want our messages to be so clear, concise, accurate, and appropriate to the situation.

Most business firms require some written record of all persons who apply for work with their organization. One of these records will most likely be the data sheet or resumé. Let's examine some of the major sections of this record and determine how we can use this form to present ourselves to prospective employers.

Personal Data

In this section we include such information as full name, temporary and/or permanent addresses, physical characteristics (height, weight, general condition of health), and telephone number. Some of these items may be omitted and others may be added as the applicant desires.

Education

Include here all the schools you have attended beyond the secondary level. Junior college and four-year college data should be presented in inverse chronological order (most recent listed first). By listing the latest schools attended before earlier schools, we will be emphasizing the most recent places of education, and this is precisely what we should do. The latest institutions attended will probably be the ones where you did your advanced study and where you received your certification or degree.

List the names of all the schools attended, date of graduation, specific years in attendance at each institution, major area or areas of study, and specific courses that deserve special mention. You may wish to include your grade-point average. Several options are available to you in reporting this achievement. These options include overall GPA, GPA in major field, overall GPA during the last two years (assuming you were pursuing a four-year degree), and GPA in major field during the last two years. You will have to decide which if any of these achievements you will include. You may wish to refer to grade-point average only if it is above a "B." Remember, however, that scholastic achievement may be considered an important criterion in the personnel selection process.

Reporting your high school education information may have some value under certain conditions. One opinion is that it should be reported in order to give the reader a complete picture of the applicant's formal training. Another opinion is that information of this nature is not particularly relevant. Perhaps its inclusion or exclusion will not affect the total effort one way or the other. The one factor that may influence your decision on this matter is the level of employment you are seeking. Generally, the higher the level of the position you are applying for, the less likely you will be to make any reference to high school preparation.

Work Experience

Since most of your available time will have been spent attending school, you will have relatively little work experience to report. Remember, though, that any part-time work you have had may be worth reporting. Most employers realize that young people do not have an abundance of job experiences to draw from, so they will not be expecting to see much information in this section. What they will be looking for is any indication that you have had opportunities to assume responsibilities for assigned tasks and that you have been required to work with others.

Furthermore, even though you may be applying for "white-collar" work, you should include on your data sheet any "blue-collar" jobs you have had. Reporting these may help to show how you get along with others on the job. Use your own good judgment as to which previous jobs you should include on the final report to your prospective employer.

When reporting your work experience, include the dates of employment starting with your present or more recent job and then working backwards for five or six jobs or approximately six years. Some companies ask for employment information for ten years or more, but this is usually not available nor relevant for college graduates.

List your jobs not only by job title, but also by description. The title of Office Manager may sound prestigious, but it will be more meaningful if you describe your duties, explain that you supervised five other workers, or tell how your work experience has helped to prepare you for the position you are seeking.

Usually you should explain why you left each of the jobs you list rather than let your prospective employer guess as to what the reason may have been.

Military Experience

Some job applicants have military training to report as a part of their background. Often this is valuable experience, and it is to their advantage to report it. Many times the military service provides valuable schooling opportunities that add to one's background. If you have participated in any of these schools, list them under this section of the data sheet. Additional military service information that you may wish to list includes branch of service, rank achieved, length of service, type of work, and date and type of discharge.

This section should indicate whether you belong to a reserve organization on either an active or inactive basis. Employers often look favorably upon this kind of background.

Special Awards, Offices, and Honors

The purpose of a data sheet is to highlight your qualifications and accomplishments. Therefore, the reader should be made aware of the recognition you have received for extraordinary achievement and skill. List all such information in a separate section of your data sheet. This information, so placed, will not become buried in your overall presentation.

Your having been an officer in some student government organization or fraternity will show the reader that you have been in positions of leadership among your peers. This accomplishment is generally considered to be significant.

References

Traditionally, data sheets include the names and addresses of individuals who are in a position to provide written or oral recommendations for you. Even though these references may never be consulted about your qualifications, you should make their names available. Naturally, you will want to obtain permission from the specific persons listed before you use their names. In listing the names and addresses on the data sheet, be certain to indicate the nature of your relationship with them. Giving their title is one of the best ways to show this relationship.

Probably the best reference you can list is your former employer. Character references are important, but they generally do not carry the weight of one from a person who has seen you perform in a work situation.

College professors are often good sources of references. Choose a professor who knows you well enough to provide a good, objective evaluation of you. This professor may be your major advisor, or one of the instructors you have come to know particularly well. In any event, consider including someone from your educational background to make a recommendation for you. Probably a total of three or four references will suffice for most situations.

Most colleges provide a placement credential service that allows you to have reference statements placed in a file to be copied and sent to an employer on short notice. This arrangement is a convenient way to expedite this element of the job-getting process. References from the clergy, your neighbors, or your relatives are not very helpful and probably should be excluded.

Other Considerations

As indicated earlier, the data sheet is designed to highlight qualifications; therefore, do not include information that will tend to discredit you. If you do have some background that may be difficult to explain and it is something that you feel should be brought to the attention of the prospective employer, save it for the personal interview.

Data sheets should not be presented in narrative form. Basically, the document should be a series of tabulated facts in a format that provides for easy reading. The person reading about you probably has other equally important duties to perform. Do not make it a struggle to get through information that does not have top priority—you only lessen your chances of getting the document read in its entirety.

Most certainly, do not prepare a data sheet that contains misspelled words or typing errors. These kinds of errors will represent you as a sloppy, careless person and will not promote your chances of gaining the personal interview you seek.

Variations in Data Sheet Construction

No set rule exists for the presentation of information about yourself. Figures 10.1 and 10.2 show how data sheets can vary in content and format. Try to be a little creative, but do not deviate too much from generally accepted style.

The order of presentation should be considered carefully. Data sheets should be tailored to fit the individual. If your education background is your strongest asset, you will want to emphasize it by put-

```
                        INTRODUCING
                      Mark F. Brown

PERSONAL DATA:

    Age: 22        Health: Excellent      Permanent Address:
    Height: 6' 0"  Marital Status: Single
    Weight: 165    Military: Fulfilled    102 Alden Street
                   Hobbies: Tennis and    Boise, ID 00000
                            Fishing       Ph. 208-378-5363

EDUCATION:

    1973-1975      Wartburg College, Waverly, Iowa; Major in
                   Business Administration; Graduated in
                   May, 1975, with a B.A. Degree; Overall
                   GPA 3.15 (4.0 = A)

    1971-1972      College of Southern Idaho, Twin Falls,
                   Idaho; General Studies Program

WORK EXPERIENCE:

    Dates              Employer                  Duties

    1973-1975      Shield-Johnson, Inc.    Assisted the Office
                   3876 Willow Way         Manager and supervised
                   Waverly, IA  00000      clerical work force of
                                           eight people.

    1971-1972      City of Twin Falls      Directed city tennis
                   Recreation Department   program. Supervised
                   458 No. Kingsway Dr.    seven tennis instruc-
                   Twin Falls, ID  00000   tors and coordinated
                                           activities for 250
                                           participants.

    1969-1970      The Book Shoppe         Stocked and sold books
                   9672 Jantoni Way        and supplies.  Also
                   Boise, ID  00000        assisted with periodic
                                           inventories.


MEMBERSHIP IN ORGANIZATIONS:

    Association of Young Americans, Secretary-Treasurer
    Associated Student Body of Wartburg College, Student
      Senator
    Administrative Management Society, Student Chapter
      President

REFERENCES:

    Mr. Ray R. Kent, Mgr.   Dr. Mary Tyson       Mr. John Storey
      Shield-Johnson, Inc.    Professor of          Executive Director
      3876 Willow Way         Business              AMS Associates
      Waverly, IA  00000      Wartburg College      6490 Waylon Dr.
                              Waverly, IA  00000    Boise, ID  00000
```

Figure 10.1   Example of
data sheet

```
                          DATA SHEET

                             of

Sally Jo Markell   9720 South Hemphill   Joliet, IL  00000


                         EDUCATION

1973-1975   Boise State University, Boise, ID  00000
            Associate Arts Degree, May, 1975
            Major in Secretarial Science
            Cumulative Grade Point Average 3.3 (4.0 = A)

            Specialized Courses:
              Word Processing, Machine Transcription
              Procedures of a Law Office
              Magnetic Keyboard Typewriting
              Editing for Word Processing
              Principles of Reprographics
              Technical Writing for Business
              Administrative Office Procedures

1969-1972   Jefferson High School, Joliet, IL  00000


                      WORK EXPERIENCE

1973 to     Hemper and Burgess Law Office, Boise, ID  00000
present
            Duties:  General secretarial and clerical
                     work; recording and filing deposi-
                     tions, assisting with title search
                     and preparation.

1970-1973   Central Public Library, Joliet, IL  00000

            Duties:  General office responsibilities in-
                     cluding filing, typing, and cata-
                     loguing.


                         REFERENCES

Mrs. Martha Pendergast    Mr. Willard King      Miss Susan Cole
   Head Librarian            Attorney at Law       Instructor
   Central Public Library    Hemper & Burgess Law  Boise State
   Joliet, IL  00000           Offices               University
                             Capitol 2             Boise, ID  00000
                             Boise, ID  00000


                        PERSONAL DATA

Age: 20        Health: Good          Permanent Address:
Height: 5' 4"  Marital Status: Single   1578 West 16th
Weight: 110    Hobbies: Reading and     Joliet, IL  00000
                        Golf
```

Figure 10.2   Example of
data sheet

ting it at the beginning in a position of emphasis. A weak point may be de-emphasized by giving it less space or by putting it in a less emphatic position.

The spacing and organization of the data sheet are also important factors. Use ample margins and spacing so that the data will not appear cluttered or crowded. Appropriate headings will help the reader to review the data sheet and pick up on certain highlights or areas in which he is especially interested. By all means, *keep the data sheet brief*. Generally, one page is adequate.[1]

As you prepare your data sheet, you will be wise to familiarize yourself with recent legislation affecting civil rights and equal opportunities. These laws may have an effect on what you should or should not include with your resumé. For example, you may choose to omit your age, sex, race, religion, or other factors which the law states may not be considered as employability guidelines. Remember, though, that the purpose of this data sheet is to encourage the employer to give you an interview; therefore, supply sufficient information. Omission of this information may eliminate you from consideration.

The Letter of Application

The letter of application may well be one of the most important communications you will have occasion to develop. It should represent your finest effort in writing. The time spent learning how to communicate appropriate information and attitudes about employment opportunities will certainly pay big dividends. The purpose of this unit of study, therefore, is to learn how to write letters of application which will present you in the most favorable light possible.

First of all, we should realize that the primary objective of a letter of application is *to obtain a personal interview*. Once this interview has been secured, the first major step toward actual employment has been taken. Too often, writers consider the application letter to be the vehicle used in asking for a job. You will probably not be hired outright on the strength of the letter itself. The prospective employer will probably want to meet with you in an interview, to measure you against the impression received from the data sheet and to see how you handle

---

1. Data sheets may be duplicated for mailing to more than one firm. For the letter of application, however, ALWAYS send an original.

yourself with others. Therefore, you should not ask for a job in the letter of application—ask for an interview. Asking for a position by letter places too much responsibility and to many limitations on the writer. Most of us can present a much stronger case for employment if we have an opportunity to communicate on a face-to-face basis.

The two basic types of application letters are the *solicited* and the *unsolicited.* The solicited letter is one that has been requested by someone who represents the firm you wish to work for. This letter is the easiest type to write because you have been invited to do so, and the element of persuasion does not play so important a role as it does in the unsolicited letter. Naturally, the unsolicited letter requires that you gain the attention of the reader and justify your reason for writing.

The data sheet, as the name indicates, lists data or facts. The letter of application gives you an opportunity to enlarge upon those facts and to emphasize major points that will help you secure an interview. Be careful that you do not use the letter of application merely to repeat the data sheet information. The letter will help you to explain how the facts listed on the data sheet have prepared you for the position you seek.

Perhaps in no other letter will tone and basic attitudes be so apparent to your reader. The letter will probably reflect how much confidence you have in yourself, how eager you are to start your career, the value you place on the degree you have, and other very important factors. Being aware of how these attitudes can be revealed in a letter of application will allow you to develop the "image" you wish your reader to have. Examine the sample letters below and note how attitude affects the overall message.

Personnel Director
Unicon Corporation
4678 West Harrison
Denver, CO 00000

Dear Gentlemen:

After four years of hard work in college, I am now ready to help you solve your business problems. When can we get together to discuss an employment opportunity for me?

Letter should be addressed to a specific person whenever possible. Make an attempt to learn the name of the person who is to receive the letter. Use proper salutation (Gentlemen:)

Letter begins by telling how hard he has worked. Implies that company has problems. Presumptuous to think he can solve the company's problems.

I will be available for work after graduation on May 16 of this year. I am very anxious to get to work because, as you probably know, the old bank account is rapidly approaching the disaster level.

Call me at your earliest convenience and we can get together for a chat and discuss how I can help your organization.

Cordially,
Joe Merigen

Assumes a degree of familiarity with reader that is probably not warranted. Phrase "as you probably know" could be insulting. The reader is probably not interested in the status of the bank account.

The imperative tone does not communicate the respect needed for this type of letter. Terms such as "chat" suggest that the writer is flippant about the matter.

What impression would you have of this applicant after you read this letter? Are you interested in arranging time for an interview? What is it about the letter that makes you feel the way you do about the person? Would you agree that there is a definite tone to this letter?

This same person could have written a letter that would indicate his confidence and preparation but that would also reflect seriousness and good taste. See if the following letter is an improvement upon the first one.

Mr. Herman T. Wymer
Personnel Director
Unicon Corporation
4678 West Harrison
Denver, CO 00000

Dear Mr. Wymer:

I am seeking employment with an organization like Unicon and would like to arrange for an interview with you after my graduation on May 16.

Your company has been of interest to me since I began reading your annual reports four years ago. The recent addition of the Atlanta plant should provide for even more growth than that which you have experienced during the past two years.

Note that the writer has taken the time to find out the name of the person who will read the letter.

The objective of the letter is stated in the opening paragraph. The writer does not overemphasize graduation.

Indicates a degree of preparation regarding a knowledge of the firm and a willingness to invest some personal time to learn about the firm.

The part-time experience listed on the attached data sheet should complement the work I could do for you in your accounting department. Also, my class projects involving the use of computer programming techniques should further qualify me for entry-level work with your firm. The references I have listed should be able to assist you in evaluating my qualifications. They have all indicated a willingness to provide recommendations for your use.

Data sheet information is not merely repeated but is interpreted by showing how it will be of value to the reader. The phrase "entry-level" suggests that the writer realizes that he has much more to learn.

After you have had an opportunity to review my data sheet, will you please call me to let me know when I may have a personal interview with you or your staff. You can reach me at 343-0560 any time in the evenings.

A pleasant closing which makes a specific call for action. The writer has restated his request for a personal interview.

Cordially yours,
Joe Merigen

On occasion, the spirited writer may wish to deviate from the traditional approach to securing a position. While there is always some risk in such techniques, the prospect of attracting the attention of the reader may lead applicants to try something different. One such enterprising graduate tried the method presented below.

Personnel Director
Johnsen, Incorporated
130 North Bellevue
Buffalo, NY 00000

SUBJECT: January White Sale on BA Graduate!

Due to the currently depressed job market, we are forced to reduce our inventory of slightly used graduates by one. Here is your golden opportunity to pick up one of our best models at a bargain price! He has had eight years of work experience in the lumber industry, and during the past two years at State University he has acquired the versatility and the desire to adapt to any job situation in the general business environment—**lumber or otherwise.** With a little on-the-job training, he will perform efficiently on any product from logs to widgits. Standard features include: economy of operations (over the past two years he has been conditioned to run on a "regular" salary as opposed to "ethyl"); sense of humor and fair play (developed by serving as arbiter between disgruntled loggers and righteously indignant Forest Service sales administrators); and an adaptable learning curve (as evidenced by the recent Forester-Scholar transition and 3.92 GPA).

The above was written in a somewhat jocular vein in hopes of securing the interest of your Personnel Department. If I have succeeded, I would appreciate a personal interview whereby I could further expand upon my goals and qualifications in relation to any position which you might have. I am ambitious and I desire a management position that will eventually lead to line responsibility. Thank you for your attention.

Joe Guttsy

What do you think? Would you give this young person an opportunity to further explain his position and demonstrate his abilities? Do you think some prospective employers might cast this letter aside thinking that it was a joke, or would the reader be goaded by his curiosity to find out more about this writer?

Other Letters About Employment

While the letter of application may be the most important one about employment, it is not the only kind. Other types include letters of acceptance, refusal, recommendation, and follow-up. These special letters may fill important roles while you are seeking employment.

Once you have been offered employment, you may benefit from writing a letter of acceptance confirming the arrangements. This letter thanks those who helped during the job-getting process. Remember that it takes valuable time away from the job to interview prospective employees. Also, firms usually incur some expenses during this process. Finally, a letter of appreciation is simply in good taste.

Dear Mr. Swopes:

Last week during my interview with you and your staff, you suggested that I take a few days to consider the offer of employment with your firm. I have done just that and am happy to tell you that I have accepted your offer.

The opportunity to work with a dynamic organization such as The Holton Company has been a goal of mine for some time now. I look forward to working with you in the management-trainee position we discussed so thoroughly. Even though I am slightly awed by the challenge you have given me, I am confident that I can handle the responsibilities satisfactorily. As directed earlier, I will report for work on Monday, February 3.

Thank you again for the courtesies extended to me last week.

Cordially yours,

Kenneth Wong

On some occasions you may be offered a position, the acceptance of which, you decide, is not in your best interests. Do not leave a company wondering what your decision is with respect to accepting or refusing their offer. Once you decide that you are not going to accept the offer, you should let them know as soon as possible. The company needs someone to fill the vacancy or the new position, and they will want to do so as quickly as they can. Also, while they are waiting for your response, they may miss an opportunity to hire another qualified candidate.

Dear Mr. Conklin:

The time you spent with me during my interview with your firm was very helpful in giving me a better understanding of the nature of your work and the scope of operations. The tour of the physical plant was especially informative.

Since receiving your kind offer to join your staff, I have tried to weigh the advantages of joining such a large organization against the opportunities that are available in a smaller firm. Because of my long-range goal to own my own business, I feel that employment with one of the smaller enterprises here in Freeport is more in keeping with my needs.

Thank you again for sharing your time with me last week. With the opportunities you have to offer someone with the right qualifications, I feel certain the opening you have will be filled very soon.

Cordially yours,

Mike Swopes

You are likely to be asked at some time to give a recommendation or a letter of reference in behalf of someone who is seeking a job. The person seeking this kind of help expects that the recommendation you give will be a favorable one. In writing a letter in behalf of someone, you should give specific examples that show why you feel the way you do about the person. For example, if you say that the person being recommended is highly qualified, be certain to indicate why you are in a position to say that. Do not deal only in generalities that are vague or trite. Writing a good letter of recommendation takes time and thought, but you should be willing to make the effort if you are sincere about helping the other person.

TO: DAUGHTERS OF THE AMERICAN REVOLUTION
FROM: GEORGE COX
SUBJECT: LETTER OF RECOMMENDATION FOR PATRICK ADAMS

Please accept this letter as a character reference for Patrick Adams, who is applying to your organization for a scholarship. It is my opinion that Pat is deserving of such assistance as you deem appropriate.

During the past several years that I have known this young man, he has impressed me with his positive attitude, his maturity, his high standard of excellence and self-discipline, and his leadership abilities. He has demonstrated these positive qualities many times and in many ways.

One way to determine the degree of maturity level of a young man, for example, is to observe how well he handles himself in the presence of adult audiences. On several occasions I have seen Pat interact with adults, and he has handled each situation admirably well. He seems to have the right "touch" in dealing with each opportunity. As an active member of several athletic team functions (football, basketball, and swimming) he has proved that he can accept positions of leadership or support. Even though he strives to do the best he can in all endeavors, it does not upset him if he is not always on center stage. This quality, too, is a mark of maturity.

His ability to lead his peers is perhaps best evidenced by his achievements as President of his high school's Key Club. This activity-oriented club is responsible for much of the work that is required of students to complement the larger objectives within the educational framework. Several teachers and administrators with whom I am acquainted have indicated to me how well Pat has served in his position of president.

Finally, I am especially pleased to be able to submit a recommendation on this young man's behalf because he possesses a quality that is too often missing in our young people today. He has a particularly positive attitude about all dimensions of life, and I believe this factor to be a critical requirement of effective citizenship in our society.

This letter of recommendation has been written to provide you with specific information about someone who can benefit from your efforts and support. I hope my comments are of some value to you.

Respectfully submitted,

George Cox

Generally, the follow-up letter is written to a prospective employer who is still in the process of considering your application. As the name suggests, the letter is sent following the personal interview or some previous contact with the firm. The purpose of the letter may be to determine the degree of progress that has been made regarding your application, or it could be simply to reestablish contact with the organization.

In this follow-up letter, you may wish to include an additional bit of information about yourself that was not mentioned in either the data sheet, the letter of application, or the interview. In fact, you may plan to omit some pertinent, but not critical, information that can be included in the follow-up letter. The information could pertain to some work experience you have had that would better qualify you for a particular position, or it could be about some course or activity you were involved with during your schooling. You may have completed some project or program that was in process during your interview. This kind of follow-up may also be effective in securing the personal interview after your original letter of application. Whatever your purpose in sending it, the follow-up letter may help you in obtaining the position you desire.

Dear Mr. Behling:

Last week I submitted a letter of application regarding the vacancy you advertised in the local newspaper. My interest in this position of Junior Accountant prompted me to submit my credentials right away. However, in doing so, I failed to include some work experience I had that may be of special interest to you.

Recently, I completed an audit report for a local wholesaler who is cooperating with our college in our Internship Program. Because this wholesaler's business is in many ways much like yours, I believe the on-the-job experience I gained with his firm could be of benefit to you.

I look forward to the opportunity to interview with you and your staff, and I hope to hear from you soon.

Cordially yours,

Richard Grant

One final letter about employment that will be discussed here is the letter of resignation. An employee will be showing good taste by writing such a letter setting forth the feelings, attitudes, and circumstances relating to the end of tenure with the company. Obviously, an employer cannot force an individual to write this letter, but it is a good gesture that will allow you to end the relationship on a positive note.

A positive, well-written letter of resignation can serve many purposes. It can give you an opportunity to share some final thoughts with management regarding various aspects of the work environment and your involvement with it. The letter can also be used as an opportunity to say the many things that were left unsaid due to the busy schedules and commitments that everyone seems to have. Furthermore, the letter can represent your "swan song" and give the organization a written statement of the good, mutually beneficial relationship that you have enjoyed.

Even in those situations where the parting of ways may be considered as a breath of fresh air for all persons involved, you probably should still consider writing a positive message. Psychologists tell us that it is a normal feeling to fanatasize occasionally by "telling the boss where to get off." If you are tempted by this urge, don't do it. No one gains in the long run by burning bridges. Keep your departure on a professional basis and everyone will be better for it.

Figure 10.3 incorporates many of the qualities of a good letter of resignation. Although any letter that you might write will vary insofar as the details are concerned, the attitudes will probably be similar.

The Personal Interview

The personal interview is the most important opportunity you will have to sell yourself to a prospective employer. The letter of application is important as a method of obtaining the interview, but the actual meeting determines the degree of success you will have in obtaining employment. Therefore, you should be adequately prepared to deal with this opportunity and challenge.

Chances for a successful interview are greatly enhanced if the parties involved are aware of the objectives of the meeting. Too often, the prospective employee considers the personal interview to be something the employer desires in order to obtain additional information on which to base his decision regarding the applicant. To be regarded as equally important, however, is the information the applicant obtains about the people and the organization he wishes to work for. Having specific questions in mind prior to the interview is, therefore, a requirement for a successful encounter.

February 25, 19xx

Mr. Johnathan Barness

President

Colfax, Incorporated

104 Malheur Drive

Camden, NJ 00000

Dear Mr. Barness:

As you know, I have accepted a position with KRBA Associates
effective July 1. With that in mind, it is obviously necessary for me to resign my position here at Colfax, Incorporated at the end of the current fiscal year.

I have sincerely enjoyed and appreciated the opportunity of
working with all of you, who have been very good friends
and professional associates. During the past four years,
we have had the opportunity of being in an exciting growth
environment. I am confident that we have one of the finest
micro-switch manufacturing plants in the country.

You are aware, I am sure, of the great pride and affection
I have for Colfax. My family and I have been treated
extremely well and will miss our many friends. At the
same time, however, we are all looking forward to the exciting challenges which await us in California.

Thank you for giving us the opportunity to experience the
best four years of our lives.

Sincerely yours,

Mike Margheim

Figure 10.3   Example of
letter of resignation

These specific questions should be well thought out and designed to get the information you will need to make an intelligent decision. Generally, the specific questions will pertain to the immediate and future plans of the company, growth trends, company policies regarding training programs, and opportunities for advancement. Do not raise questions about pay unless the interviewer broaches the subject. There will be time to discuss these matters later. Be certain, however, that it is discussed prior to your accepting employment. Being able to ask intelligent questions of the interviewer generally indicates that you are serious about what you are doing.

Try to anticipate the questions you will be asked. Think about the types of things a prospective employer will want to know about you. Be ready to provide good answers. Try answering the following questions that quite possibly could be asked during an employment interview.

Why do you think you want to be a (an)_____?

Why do you want to work for our company?

How long do think you will be working for us?

How long do you think you will be working for us in the job for which you are applying?

What are your intermediate and long-range goals and plans?

Do you prefer working alone or with others? Why?

What is the most common weakness you see in others?

What are your major strengths? Weaknesses?

What is the most pressing problem facing our country today?

What do you think of_____? (Often interviewers will ask questions about current events. Be prepared to respond to questions about national and international events.)

What do you do in your spare time?

What books have you read during the past six months?

Do you carry or plan to carry life insurance? What are your feelings about the concept of life insurance?

Finally, remember the importance of initial impressions. Those impressions you make during the first contact will surely contribute to the decision as to whether or not to hire you. Factors that make positive impressions include neat appearance, promptness, alertness, and general attitude. Interestingly, all of these factors can be communicated in nonverbal form.

Summary

Planning is an important ingredient in choosing and managing a career. Serious students of the job market must learn of the different opportunities available to them and of the specific requirements of each type of work. A person must also know his or her own likes, dislikes, strengths, and weaknesses. This knowledge is obtained only through carefully thinking about oneself from an objective point of view.

The data sheet and letter of application are often required by prospective employers. Knowing how to present the information on these two communications may be vital to your obtaining employment with a firm. Letters of acceptance, refusal, and follow-up are also important factors.

Obtaining a personal interview is the primary objective of a letter of application, and prospective employees should prepare for this opportunity. The personal interview provides an excellent chance for two-way communication. Be prepared to ask questions you want answered and to answer questions asked by the interviewer. Finally, note that the nonverbal clues we send are primarily the attitudes we have.

Chapter Exercises

1. Write a letter to Mr. Sam Swopes, Personnel Director of Johnston Company, refusing his job offer. You applied for work with several business organizations and had personal interviews with each of them. You have decided to take a position that has been offered by Teltron, Inc., but you at least want to thank Mr. Swopes for his time and consideration.

   Other factors related to this case include:
   a. more money at Teltron
   b. apparently more opportunities for advancement
   c. better facilities
   d. better training program for entry-level employees

2. Miss Mary Cochran, an assistant to the Administrative Services Manager of Kober Company, 911 Marshall Boulevard, in Shelby, North Carolina, has suggested that you write to the Personnel Director of her company and seek an interview for the new management-trainee position that is open. Your college background and experience, you believe, qualify you for the position and you would like to have an interview with the company to pursue the matter further.

   Your work experience, although only part time in nature, has provided you with the opportunity to learn much about management techniques, problems, and procedures. Furthermore, the various group activities in advanced college classes have given you many new ideas that you think will help the Kober Company with some of their operational problems. Write the letter, making the necessary assumptions about your abilities and the job requirements.

3. Last week you completed a series of three separate interviews with Morton Manufacturing Company. The interviews went satisfactorily and the Vice President of Finance, Ms. Mildred Byrne, offered you a position as an assistant to the Internal Auditor. She asked that you take a few days to consider the offer and let her know of your decision. You have decided to accept the offer because the opportunity is what you have been looking for. Although the assignment will require that you do considerable traveling to several branch offices, you see this as a temporary thing which poses no long-run problem for you.

   Write the letter of acceptance indicating that you will report for work on the following Monday.

4. Six weeks ago you wrote an unsolicited letter of application to Allegeheny Tool & Die Company regarding an opening they have in their sales department. One week after you sent your letter to them, they responded by saying that your application would be processed shortly. Four weeks have passed since you heard from

them and you want to know what has happened to your application.

Write a letter to them regarding the status of your application. Ask them if they can give you any information about it; also, ask them if they need any additional data from you which would help expedite matters. You do not wish to be too forceful, but you do want some action one way or the other. Direct your letter to the manager of the Sales Department—his name is William Kirtland and the mailing address is 456 Mason Line, Nashville, Tennessee.

5. Bill Maddox has applied for work as service manager of your new-car dealership. He is presently employed in a similar position with the Newton Leasing Agency located across town. His employment record, as presented on the data sheet, looks quite satisfactory, but you wish to obtain letters of reference to complete his file. Although Bill is presently employed by Newton Leasing, he has given you permission to write to his supervisor for additional information. Bill says that his supervisor knows that he is looking for a change of work and has indicated a willingness to help in any way he can.

Write a letter to Bill's supervisor, Mr. Arthur Chapin, and ask him questions about Bill's various abilities pertaining to the service end of the car business. Ask specific questions that will benefit you as you make a decision about his suitability for employment. Remember, of course, that even though Mr. Chapin has volunteered to be of assistance, the matter is probably still somewhat delicate.

6. Assume that you are working as a first-line supervisor for a small-parts factory that produces components for various automobile accessories. Yesterday you received a letter from a former employee who had worked for you for nearly two years. In her letter, Sally Hallecker asks that you write a letter of recommendation on her behalf. Sally has an opportunity to work in a similar environment in another city, but she will have considerably more responsibility. Specifically, she has never had supervisory experience, and the job she is seeking will require her to direct the work activities of approximately 10 other employees.

You remember Sally well and the work she did for you while with your firm. She was a diligent worker who had a positive attitude and she had the ability to get along well with other workers. Although you do not know that she will be able to handle the responsibilities associated with supervision, you have no reason to believe that she cannot do so. The only other factor that her performance records show is that she did have a tendency to be absent from work somewhat more often than the average worker.

As you recall, these absences were caused by some physical problem that quite probably has been resolved satisfactorily by now.

Write a letter of recommendation for Sally and address it to Mr. Harold Balliet, Personnel Manager of Dixon & Company, 444 East Washburn in Columbus, Ohio.

7. Assume that you have been working for Merchandise Mart for almost three years and that you now have a job offer to go with J-Mart, Incorporated. Your new position will offer you more money, more responsibility, a greater variety of job assignments, and better overall working conditions. Furthermore, you will be able to relocate so that you will be closer to your home town.

Write a letter to Lee Holmes, Manager of Customer Services, and communicate your decision to resign effective two weeks from today. In your letter of resignation, you may wish to summarize the experiences you have had while under his supervision and the opportunities that Merchandise Mart has provided over the several years. Add any other comments or information that you think would be appropriate under the circumstances of your employment with the firm.

Logic and Its Relationship to Writing

11

After you have studied this chapter you will be able to:

1. better understand the significance of logic and how it relates to the principles of effective expression.

2. apply your understanding of these principles to the development of your own business letters.

3. see the relationship between correct grammar and sound logic.

4. observe through letter analysis how sound logic strengthens written communication.

Many people learn letter-writing skills best by an abundant exposure to the kinds of letters they will write. Here in this chapter we will examine some of these kinds of letters. This chapter further reinforces the learning of many of the writing principles presented earlier.

In previous chapters you have looked at several examples of business letters. These examples represent some general categories of letters and have given you an opportunity to study the basic principles of letter writing as you see them applied. Even though the limitations of space make it impractical to display a sample or a "recipe" for the writing of each kind of letter you may encounter, a few examples of some of the specific kinds of letters will help you to apply your learning to a greater number of business situations. You should then be in a good position to apply these techniques to form your own letters when the need arises.

Logic

Most of us would claim to be highly logical in our thinking and acting. After all, we think things through and develop some kind of plan in our mind before most of our major activities or ventures. How do you feel about the logic exhibited by other people? And, how do THEY feel about your logic?

One dictionary defines logic as follows:

1. The study of the principles of reasoning, especially of the structure of propositions as distinguished from their content and of method and validity in deductive reasoning.
2. A system of reasoning. A mode of reasoning. The formal, guiding principles of a discipline, school, or science.

3. Valid reasoning, especially as distinguished from invalid or irrational argumentation.

4. The relationship of element to element to whole in a set of objects, individuals, principles, or events.[1]

Even though we may have little trouble accepting this definition as we think we apply it to our THINKING, we often disregard it in our writing. As a result, our writing may be ambiguous, unclear, or even insulting to the reader. One specific result of this problem may be to tell the reader too little. When we commit this error, we falsely assume that the reader knows more than he or she really knows. On the other hand, we may sound too elementary or childish if our writing contains unnecessary details or explanations. So, how can we handle this dilemma logically?

First of all, it is logical to make certain assumptions. When you drive your car down the highway on your own side of the center line, you ASSUME that oncoming cars will stay on their side. Otherwise, you would find it necessary to avoid all other cars by driving so far off the road and away from them that they could not hit you. Similarly, we must make certain assumptions when we write. We assume that the reader will attach meaning to our words similar to the meaning we intended when we used them. Even more basic, we assume that the recipient of our letter can read. But, how extensive or how brief should your message be? Which ideas will you have to explain? How will the reader respond or react to your explanation or to your message?

We considered some of these questions of logic when we discussed the order in which our messages should be presented to the reader. A pleasant or routine message should usually be written in the direct order, whereas unpleasant or persuasive messages are usually written in the indirect order. These decisions are based on logic. However, if our logical thinking stops there, we have learned only part of the lesson. Take a look at the following letter that you received in answer to your request for a price estimate and delivery date on mail-order seat covers for your seven-year-old Perkle Eight automobile.

1. *The American Heritage Dictionary of the English Language*, 1976 ed., William Morris, ed. (Boston: Houghton Mifflin Company, 1976).

Dear Miss Johnson:

This letter is in response to yours of the 16th wherein you asked for prices and delivery information on seat covers for your 1970 Perkle Eight Sport Coupe.

As you know, we carry seat covers for most newer cars and can give you immediate delivery on most of them at a price that is a pleasant surprise. However, your 1970 model is just too old, and it is not profitable for us to stock seat covers for cars of that age.

There are a few dealers who may handle this particular seat cover, but you will probably want to make your own arrangements.

Please let us know we can serve you in the future.

Sincerely yours,

Now, try to put yourself into the picture to determine how you would feel if you received this letter. How about the opening sentence? Is it informative? Helpful? Logical? Or, does it merely repeat obvious information? Could you improve on the wording about what you normally stock, your rapid delivery, and attractive prices? How do you feel when the letter writer tells you your car is "too old"? Whose viewpoint is reflected—the reader's or the writer's—in the statement "it is not profitable for us to stock seat covers for cars of that age"? Did you think that the writer was helpful in suggesting a possible source for your seat covers? Or, does the suggestion that "you will probably want to make your own arrangement" sound like a "cop-out"? Finally, how good are the chances that you will write to this company again the next time you need some help or some information?

Even though we may be able to identify these problems by some specific name such as "tone" or "viewpoint," they are very much a part of this general area of LOGIC. Notice that in this letter we may be able to find little fault with the structure or the content; the fault lies in the "principles of reasoning."

Now, let's consider the logic (or the absence of it) in the following letter. This message was written in response to a letter requesting payment by June 30 for rental of a film strip projector.

Gentlemen:

Under date of March 20, 19xx, we received billing for rental of a filmstrip projector for $5.75, and since at the time of request we had acquired a projector previously, but since you sent us one and we didn't use it we feel at this time this rental should be remitted to you.

Actually, at the time of our billing we were "out" of money for the budget year 19xx-19xx.

If you still feel that we owe this $5.75 rental please advise me, and I shall be happy to remit the amount even though the June 30th deadline you mentioned is long past.

I shall await your early reply to this explanation of our non-remittance.

Yours very truly,

Before we consider the defective logic in this letter, we should notice some other obvious defects. For instance, the old, worn-out language, as used in the opening and closing statements of this letter, should be avoided. Long, run-on sentences that result in defective punctuation should also be avoided.

Apparently, the writer must have felt considerable frustration over just how to handle the problem of paying this rental fee. That frustration is certainly passed on to the reader. A *careful* reading of the first paragraph will help us to understand certain facts about this situation. We also note the writer's agreement that the rental fee is due and payable. The second paragraph tells us why the bill was not paid—"we were 'out' of money." Now, consider the lack of logic in the rest of this letter. Is it logical for the writer to imply that perhaps we have changed our mind as to the validity of our billing? Is it logical to imply that the bill should not be paid now simply because it is past due? Again, the principles of reasoning are not sound.

The following interoffice memo was written by a supervisor to explain why a certain employee had been discharged. Does it exhibit good logic?

Bill Weston was discharged on June 17 because of the effect his employment has had on absenteeism. Before we hired Weston our absenteeism averaged two per day. However, since May 28 (the day we hired Weston), the absentee rate has climbed to eight per day. Our production output has suffered, so Bill Weston was discharged.

On the surface, this seems to indicate sound thinking on the part of the supervisor. After all, if an employee promotes any kind of bad work habits, either by his attitude or by his example, the company will be serving its best interests to discharge him. But is Bill Weston the REAL reason for the increase in absenteeism? Or did the date of his employment just happen to coincide with other events that might explain the absenteeism more logically? Did other departments have an upswing in absenteeism during this same period of time? Was the community suddenly affected by sickness or disease that would explain the higher absenteeism? Perhaps the date of Bill's employment would help to explain the problem. He was hired just before a holiday (Memorial Day). Do more workers take days off for unexplained reasons during and after holidays?

This kind of defective reasoning is sometimes described by the Latin term *post hoc, ergo propter hoc* (after this, therefore because of this). One who follows this fallacious reasoning assumes that because one event follows another, the first event caused the second. Followers of this line of defective reasoning may assume that the crowing of the rooster causes the sun to come up since the crowing precedes the rising of the sun. This is one form of a general problem with logic that is referred to as hasty generalization or jumping to conclusions.

Another kind of deviation from good logic is described by the Latin term *non sequitur*, which means "it does not follow." This line of reasoning draws a conclusion that is not necessarily related to the premise from which it is drawn. For example:

Steve Orton has eight children. Therefore, he must like children.

(This is not necessarily so. Can you think of more logical explanations?)

Beth Coleman is our best underwriter, so she will secure the account.

George was made president of the company when he was only 28 years old. Therefore, he is ambitious, hard working, and brilliant.

(Maybe! Or, perhaps, his father gave George the company.)

These kinds of problems, as well as a few others we will consider, can destroy the effectiveness of our communication. Don't be misled into thinking that you can make something so by merely stating that it is so. Any defective logic can have a negative effect on both the primary and secondary objectives of the communication.

The following examples will illustrate some of these problems and may help you to avoid them in your own writing.

Dear Mr. Gregory:

Are you looking for an alert, industrious young trainee for your Marketing Division? Well, your search is over, because I will be graduating next month.

My grade point average is 3.92 which proves that I am a hard worker. During the last semester, all my grades were A's except for one course in which I lost interest because of all the busy work. Please give me an opportunity to put my talent to work in your company.

Sincerely yours,

In our evaluation of this letter, we may be tempted to dismiss it as having been written by a braggart. By looking more closely, however, you will see some of the impurities of logic about which you have read. Is it logical for the writer to assume that his or her graduation next month *really* is the end of this company's search? Also, are all graduates alert and industrious? (This is an example of *non sequitur* reasoning discussed earlier.)

Another non sequitur problem is evident in the second paragraph. Even a high GPA of 3.92 does not "prove" that one is a hard worker. Perhaps the student is a genius and gets high grades without hard work. After claiming to show evidence of being a hard worker, the writer makes a contradictory statement by explaining a loss of interest or ambition because of *busy work*. Contradictory statements are certainly a violation of the rules of logic. The same facts could have been given to the reader in such a way that the real merits of the writer would have been evident. The following letter shows some improvements over the original.

Dear Mr. Gregory:

Is your company looking for a hard working, industrious young trainee for your Marketing Division? After my graduation next month, I will be looking for an opportunity to apply my talents and training in a company such as Westland Chemicals.

My part-time work experience gave me some good opportunities to learn about marketing procedures while completing all my course work toward a degree in marketing. The references listed will give you information about my work and character, academically and professionally.

Will you please write to me to arrange a time for an interview at your convenience.

Yours very truly,

The next example shows a letter written to refuse a request.

Dear Ms. Standish:

Thank you for giving me the opportunity of speaking at the annual convention of the Retail Credit Association. This sounds like an outstanding event and one that everyone connected with retail credit should want to attend.

Unfortunately, I shall not be able to accept your invitation. My plans for the week of August 4 call for me to represent our company at third base in the annual All-City Softball Tournament. Our team has an excellent chance to take the first-place trophy if we can hold the level of performance we have maintained during the regular season. Since this is one of the really big events, and is sure to bring favorable publicity to our company, I am sure you will understand why I am unable to accept your kind invitation.

Please keep me in mind for next year.

Cordially yours,

Some of the problems with this letter are so obvious that you can spot them immediately. However, let's take a close look at them so that you can avoid similar, but less obvious, mistakes in your writing. Having read chapter seven, you know that this kind of message should be presented in indirect format. That is, we would like the reader to understand our reasons BEFORE we present the refusal. The writer of this letter apparently made an honest effort to cushion the blow of the refusal by starting off with a somewhat neutral statement acknowledging the invitation. The next sentence, however, goes a bit too far in expressing desire and determination to attend the convention. The real problem of organization starts with the second paragraph. The first word tells the reader about the refusal. The rest of that sentence confirms the bad news before ANY reasons or details have been given. This approach represents a very common mistake by writers who seriously try to organize their letters according to the appropriate logical outline. In spite of the neutral opening, this letter is written in the DIRECT order simply because the gist of the message is presented before any details or reasons are given.

Most likely you have already noted the poor logic shown by the writer in explaining the reason he cannot attend the convention. Even if the reason is as good as the writer seems to think it is, it probably does not warrant the emphasis it receives in this letter. After all, the reader's main concern is to locate a speaker for a convention program. The writer's excitement about the softball tournament is probably of little interest and of no value to the reader. Also, the writer's interest in the softball tournament seems to contradict the interest in the convention he expresses in the first paragraph. This problem makes the closing line somewhat presumptive, since Ms. Standish is likely to assume that he is not really as dedicated to retail credit matters as she once thought.

Now let's assume a situation similar to that indicated in the last letter except that the writer decided to miss the softball tournament to speak at the convention. How will Ms. Standish respond to this letter?

Dear Ms. Standish:

I am pleased to accept your invitation to speak at the Retail Credit Association, August 6, at 10:30 a.m. My theme for this one-hour presentation will be "The Pros and Cons of Tight Credit."

In order to speak at this convention, I have had to forego participation in the All-City Softball Tournament where I was scheduled to represent our company at third base. We were expected to win this tournament, but I am willing to make this sacrifice for your convention.

Can you arrange for an overhead projector and a screen for my presentation? I will phone you after my arrival the afternoon of August 5.

I look forward to this opportunity to promote good retail credit standards.

Cordially yours,

The direct organization of this letter is certainly appropriate for a "good-news" letter. The writer gives certain information and makes a request that should help in the final arrangements for this speech. However, the second paragraph is destructive of the tone that should be conveyed by the letter. There is probably no reason for mentioning the softball tournament or the sacrifice this decision represents. The result is that the acceptance is made so grudgingly that Ms. Standish is sure to feel ill at ease for having made the request. Leave out the entire second paragraph and the letter does a reasonably good job of accomplishing its purposes. If given grudgingly, even good news is not likely to promote the desired reaction of the reader.

Remember that logic is a method of reasoning. Attention to the principles of tone, viewpoint, and empathy will help you to reason from the frame of reference of your reader.

The Relationship of Logic and Grammar

An effective letter, just as an effective sentence, must be planned and organized. When we learned earlier about the decision to write in the direct or the indirect order, this decision was based on logic. We reasoned that your reader would react in a certain way to the general nature of our message; so we planned and organized it a certain way.

Grammar should be important to your planning and organizing as an aid in promoting the logic and clarity of the sentences and letters you write. Violations of grammar rules throw the readers a "curve" which may slow them down or completely sidetrack them in their attempt to understand your letter.

If most letter writers were to develop a checklist for proofreading their letters, they would include such items as spelling, typing accuracy, punctuation, and (now that you have read the first part of this chapter) logic. But often omitted from the proofreader's checklist is the important element of good grammar.

Having studied the principles of grammar in earlier chapters, you should know the various parts of speech, the properties of verbs, and the correct case forms for pronouns. All this knowledge will be of little value, however, unless you really do put it into practice in your writing. Some students exhibit a "so what" attitude toward their study of grammar principles. Others try to convince themselves that they can just "write around their shortcomings" and still express themselves adequately. Some letter writers fail to see any effect of an "occasional grammar problem" as being serious. If you have really learned the principles you have studied thus far, you have probably overcome such faulty reasoning. Your transition to effective communication should be made even smoother if you consider these principles as they relate to logic. To help us get started, let's examine a letter that was written to a prospective secretarial school student.

Dear Miss Bryant:

To give you more information about our popular evening course, we have enclosed the booklet, "The Easy Way to Better Grammar". You will find that there is two other enclosures to help you get ready for this course.

As a student at Barclay, we are sure you will find conditions just right for a good learning experience. Each of our students have their own study carrel. The class size is limited, and they are taught by a teacher that is dedicated to student achievement. At the end of the 12-week course, you will be pleasantly surprised at your better understanding and use of grammar principles and your command of the English language.

Cordially yours,

Even though we may not know the present level of understanding of the prospective student to whom this letter is written, we can be sure the letter would fail to give any evidence to convince Miss Bryant that she could expect to learn good grammar usage by enrolling in our class. Certainly the letter is not an example of good usage. You should be able to identify six violations of the writing principles you have learned. The first one is the placement of the period outside the quotation marks. The second sentence has a subject-verb disagreement. The third sentence contains a dangling modifier. The next sentence has a subject-verb disagreement as well as a faulty pronoun reference. The fifth sentence also contains a faulty pronoun reference and an improper use of a pronoun.

The defects listed for this letter are grammatical. Now, however, consider the net effect of these problems on the reader of the letter. Is it logical to assume that our letter will persuade the prospective student to come to our school? Since logic is a method of reasoning, our writing should give evidence of the soundness of that logic.

The next letter shows another kind of problem. This is an interoffice memo explaining a new vacation policy.

To: All Employees
From: H. R. Kriswell, Plant Superintendent

Having experienced numerous scheduling problems in the past, vacations must be scheduled six months in advance. Each employee must check with their immediate supervisor to verify his planned vacation time. Once the time has been cleared at that level, you may submit your request to the Personnel Department. You will receive a notice of verification within two weeks of that time.

When this notice was distributed to the employees, two important questions were raised. The employees asked, "Does this mean we have to find out when the supervisor is planning to take *his* vacation, or does it mean we should check with him about *our* vacation?" The next question asked was "Within two weeks of *what* time—the date of our request or the date of our proposed vacation?" The "logic" of the reader should help to furnish these answers, but the wording of the memorandum is of little help.

The astute reader should also note the dangling modifier in the first sentence and the problem with logic it creates. Is it logical to assume that *vacations* have experienced numerous scheduling problems? The verbal phrase, *Having experienced numerous scheduling problems in the past,* dangles because it does not logically modify the subject of the main clause. Dangling modifiers are good examples of meaning one thing and saying another. Since that should never be your intention, be certain that you avoid this common writing fault.

This next letter was written to promote the sale of a new adhesive product to be used on plastic and other synthetic fabrics. Try to put yourself in the position of the production manager who is interested in locating an adhesive for use in the production of chairs, bar stools, and other upholstered furniture.

Dear Mr. Compton:

A sample of our new Kordo Tex adhesive is enclosed. This adhesive is more durable, and yet more flexible, than any product you can buy. You will find that it contains less of those ingredients which have a tendency to discolor many synthetics on which it may be used.

Kordo Tex is available for $6.90 per pound. Just send the enclosed card to indicate the quantity you would like us to send.

Sincerely yours,

The problem in this particular letter is identified specifically as *incomplete comparison.* The writer tells us that his product is "more durable, and yet more flexible," than ANY product we can buy. According to this comparison, we cannot buy Kordo Tex. The writer means that this product is better than any OTHER product we can buy, since Kordo Tex is one of the products that is being compared.

The writer states that Kordo Tex contains "less" of certain ingredients. What does "less" mean? Does it mean less than is necessary? Less than the old Kordo Tex contained? Less than any other adhesive? We need some standard of comparison that tells us what "less" really means.

Perhaps an even greater weakness of this letter is the reference to a potential problem of discoloration of the material on which this adhesive is used. The writer apparently intended to alleviate such fears by telling us that this product would have LESS tendency to discolor than would certain other adhesives.

Whether you represent a secretarial school writing to a prospective student or a manufacturer writing to a prospective user of your product, the grammar you use in expressing your ideas will have an effect on the way in which your reader will reason through your message. Remember the "hidden messages" that are a part of every communication, and write to EXpress rather than to IMpress.

Someone coined the word "gobbledygook" to identify a verbal vice that has a negative effect.

Dear Mrs. Dixon:

Enclosed will you please find our invoice in the amount of $54.80 which is being sent to you for the purpose of identifying and describing the articles of merchandise which you purchased during the month of June. The aforementioned amount brings the sum total of your account to the sum of $476.93, a substantial portion of which is presently past due.

Reduction of your account is imperative and can be accomplished by the remittance of checks periodically in accordance with the terms which were mutually agreed upon. Your account should then be kept current.

Cordially yours,

In addition to being cold, mechanical, and tactless, this letter is so wordy that the reader is likely to lose the main idea of its message. This type of language is sometimes referred to as *gobbledygook*. Gobbledygook is a term used to describe the pompous, stilted language used by some writers and speakers. This kind of writer is not likely to say "your check for $20" when he can say "your remittance in the amount of $20." He is not likely to say "use" when he can say "utilization." Users of gobbledygook exemplify the theory that if one word is good, two are better.

Use visit	instead of	visitation
" done	" "	accomplished
" now	" "	presently (or at the present time)
" if	" "	in the event that
" because	" "	due to the fact that

Be on guard against the use of these words and phrases as well as many others that detract from the clarity and simplicity of your writing. Most of the language of gobbledygook is in the passive voice. This hides the real subject and weakens the verbs we use to express meaning. Gobbledygook words are usually abstract generalizations instead of the concrete, crisp words with which we should write.

Although the use of gobbledygook is not necessarily a principle of grammar, we have discussed it here because of its relationship to grammar and logic. Your own good logic should tell you to seek for the best words and blend them to form clear, sharp sentences, paragraphs, and letters. A review of the ideas you studied in chapters 3 and 4 will help you avoid the verbal vice of gobbledygook and to use care in choosing words that will assist your readers in their method of reasoning (logic).

Certainly your readers are going to form opinions, either consciously or subconsciously, about you or your company from your correspondence. If they see errors, you will be categorized as a person or a company that makes errors. Some of the most costly errors, however, are those which may not be recognized as errors. Defective grammar and logic often result in incorrect decisions or actions that may be destructive to the economy or the goodwill of those involved. A dangling or misplaced modifier may change the meaning of our message. A defect in our method of reasoning may cause us to eliminate a step in the explanation that is vital to the decision-making process of the reader.

Techniques of Logic Applied

In chapter 3 we studied the relationship between clarity and logic. At that time we learned that impurities of logic can result from any one of several weaknesses in writing. Let's examine each of these weaknesses now in our final effort to bring together all the methods of effective expression.

The first factor that adversely affects the quality of logic is *poor word choice*. Obviously if the writer chooses words that are too far removed from the intended meaning, the reader may well miss the essence of the message. This possibility of misinterpretation stresses again the importance of empathizing with the receiver to determine which words will be assigned meaning that most closely conforms to that of the sender.

Poor word placement within the sentence affects the quality of logic. As we have already learned, meanings of sentences can be changed drastically simply by changing the relative location of certain words. Words, particularly modifiers, tend to associate most readily with those words that are closest to them. We must, therefore, take care to place words in their correct sequence. Poor location can result in misplaced modification, vague meaning, and/or impure logic.

The quality of logic can also be affected by *inappropriate use of techniques of emphasis or de-emphasis.* Good writing requires that readers be assisted in identifying the main points which are being communicated. If, for example, we de-emphasize a main point in a sentence by placing it in the dependent clause, we have told the reader something other than that which we intended. Similarly, if we place important information in relatively insignificant positions (such as in the middle of a paragraph, rather than at the beginning or end), we have told the reader the wrong thing about the worth of the idea so expressed.

Another detractor to good logic is the *loose arrangement of ideas* within the message. Good organization is important to just about anything we do, and it is especially important in written communication wherein the reader must attempt to follow the reasoning of the writer without any assistance. If ideas are sprinkled indiscriminately throughout the message without thought having been given to the relationship of other ideas, the reader will not have the sense of direction needed to understand what is being said.

Inappropriate tone or attitude affects the logic of the writer in a very subtle way. If the writer is attempting to develop a message that communicates an attitude of compliance or conformity but uses certain words which suggest the contrary, the logic will appear to be weak or defective. Writers need to examine their efforts carefully to determine whether there is a consistency of attitude throughout the message. Words that have connotative values that are inconsistent with the expressed attitude of the overall message should be avoided. We studied this problem earlier when we considered the topic of para-language—*how* something is said rather than *what* is said.

Insensitivity to the emotional dimension of the situation is another important consideration that relates to logic. This factor points again to the need to empathize with the intended receiver. Naturally, no two persons will have the same degree of emotional involvement with a given situation. Writers must, then, develop a feeling for how the other person will be reacting to what is being said. Failure to be sensitive to this aspect of communication will impair the quality of logic.

Let us now move to several examples of written communication that possess the qualities of good logic (figs. 11.1, 11.2, 11.3, 11.4, 11.5). As you consider each letter, apply a mental checklist of good writing techniques. Ask yourself that very important question, "Is the message logical?"

Summary

In this chapter we have considered the role logic plays in the effective expression of ideas. We have examined several different pitfalls that cause impurities of logic, and we have learned ways to avoid these problems.

The relationship between good logic and good grammar is evident when we note the various ways correctness in word choice and sentence structure strengthen our reasoning that appears in written form. In fact, we see how many of the rules of grammar are actually based on the principle of logic.

Logic can be impaired through a poor choice of words. The words we choose must do the job they were intended to do—nothing less will be satisfactory. Once the correct or appropriate words are chosen, they must be placed in their most effective positions relative to the other words they must work with to express an idea. Poor location causes logic problems and serves only to confuse the reader. Correct use must be made of techniques of emphasis and de-emphasis if we are to have logical and powerful messages. Main points must be emphasized and supporting information must be subordinated.

Our ideas must be logically arranged so as to enable the reader to follow what we are saying. Loose arrangement of ideas detracts from message effectiveness. Proper tone and attitude can be especially helpful to business writers. Furthermore, consistency of tone and attitude are requirements of good writing. Finally, good writers will be sensitive to the emotional dimension of the situation about which they are writing. To be able to have this sensitivity, one needs to empathize with the reader.

```
                              2839 15th Avenue
                              Portland, Oregon  00000
                              April 17, 19xx


     Mrs. Marilyn Straight, Chairperson
     Macon County School District
     439 East Fort Avenue
     Newport Beach, California  00000

     Dear Mrs. Straight:

     The local newspaper has been carrying reports concerning
     various actions taken by our Macon County School Board.
     As a recent graduate of Macon High School, and as an in-
     terested citizen of this community, I am taking this op-
     portunity to share with you my views on one very important
     topic you are presently considering.

     You, and most of the other members of the Board, have come
     out in support of a relatively new approach to public edu-
     cation often referred to as the "Alternative School."  I
     am urging you to take a second look at the product this new
     approach is turning out.  Although this concept has been
     in existence for only about four years, we are beginning
     to see how detrimental it really is to the youth of our
     community.

     This pedagogy which permits our elementary school children
     to study what they want and only when they want to is
     causing serious problems in our junior high schools.  I
     firmly believe that this excess of permissiveness is
     cheating both the student and the community out of a legit-
     imate education.

     Those of us whom you represent are vitally interested in
     the quality of our educational programs and believe that a
     return to the basics would be to the advantage of every-
     one involved.

                              Sincerely yours,



                              Max Z. Rafferty
                              A Concerned Citizen
```

Figure 11.1 Example of
good logic in letter writing
—from a concerned citizen

```
WESTERN ASSOCIATION OF AUDIO-VISUAL DISTRIBUTORS

April 17, 19xx


Mr. Jarold Porter
Sales Manager
Panavision Corporation
387 North Lakeshore Drive
Chicago, Illinois  00000

Dear Mr. Porter:

This letter is an invitation for you to join us during the
19xx regional convention we are having in March.  Your or-
ganization has been particularly supportive of our efforts
to grow professionally, and your presence will be appreciated
by all those in attendance.

The enclosed information provides you with the dates, lo-
cation, and program theme for this important event.  If
you need additional information, please call me right away.
We are expecting a record setting number of participants,
and we want you to be with us.

Very sincerely yours,



Mary Ann Bamrick
Convention Coordinator

MAB/RC

Enclosures: Information Sheet
            City Brochure

P.S. Also let us know if you would like to have space re-
     served for your exhibits--we will have plenty of room
     for everyone.
```

Figure 11.2   Example of
good logic in letter writing
—an invitation

```
                    L E T T E R H E A D



April 22, 19xx



Ms. Melva Montgomery
867 Grieser Way
Southport, LA  00000

Dear Ms. Montgomery

Congratulations for having been selected as "Outstanding
Graduate of the Year."  Your contributions in the areas of
scholarship, leadership, and cooperation have been signifi-
cant, and Central High School will surely miss you in the
years to come.

One of the many ways students and faculty will remember you
is by having your picture on display in the Honors Cabinet
alongside those who have been similarly distinguished in
previous years.  Be sure to stop by to see your picture and
to visit with us when you have time.

Please let us know if we can be of any assistance to you in
sending transcripts or letters of recommendation to colleges
and universities you are presently considering attending.

Sincerely yours



John C. Craven
Principal

jcc:mh
```

Figure 11.3   Example of
good logic in letter writing
—congratulatory

```
                    L E T T E R H E A D


                    January 11, 19xx


Thrifty Wholesalers, Inc.
6908 Fairview Avenue
Brookline, MA  00000

Gentlemen:

    Our latest shipment from you (P.O. 3968A) arrived in
plenty of time for our Parking Lot Sale which we concluded
last Monday.  Because of the success of this three-day
promotion, we are enclosing our Purchase Order for more
merchandise to replenish our inventory.

    In addition to the items listed on our order, will you
please send promotional literature on the following prod-
ucts.  Apparently this information was not included in our
last order, and we need these brochures to complete our
various displays.

                    1. B & D Work Table (foldaway model)
                    2. Router Kit--3/4 HP
                    3. Gemini Automatic Door Opener
                    4. Belt Sander No. 4576

    Please send this shipment by Freightways, Inc.  We
seem to have the best service from them, and they are very
pleasant to work with.

                         Cordially yours,



                         Phomia Slymin
                         Manager


PS:dc

Enclosure
```

Figure 11.4   Example of
good logic in letter writing
—regarding an order

```
                    L E T T E R H E A D

June 22, 19xx


EasyRider Furniture Company
138 Dewars Avenue
Grand Rapids, Michigan  00000

Gentlemen:

The new Wallhugger Reclinolounger that you developed to
compete with the medium-priced lines sold by our competi-
tion has been faring well in our area.  Our store has sold
nearly every chair you have sent us since last January.
We are now receiving several complaints from our customers,
however, and we need your assistance in solving the prob-
lem.

Far too many of these chairs are being returned to us for
repair of the arms and side panels.  Apparently the new
design does not provide for any reinforcement of this part
of the frame.  Our customers have reported that the sides
are coming loose, even with the slightest use of the chair.

Our repairmen are adding supplemental bracing to the defec-
tive areas, but this procedure appears to be only a tem-
porary solution.  Will you please have your designers re-
check the plans for these units and tell us how to deal
with the problem.  We must be able to satisfy our customers
in every respect, and we feel that we must act quickly.
Hopefully, we will be able to repair the units and return
them to their owners on the same day that we receive them.

Please call us as soon as you have been able to determine
how to correct the problem.

Cordially yours,



Tobin Conners
General Manager

tc:ms
```

Figure 11.5   Example of
good logic in letter writing
—to present a problem

Several case problems are presented below. Each case is concerned with a different topic, but all require that you use sound logic in your response. In some instances, the cases contain more information than you need to develop an adequate or satisfactory response. It will be up to you to determine what information is needed and relate it to the case solution. Some of the data, for example, may be helpful to you in solving the problem, but it would not necessarily be appropriate to include it or to refer to it in your written assignment.

As you prepare to write responses to these case situations, consider the various aspects of logic that have been presented in the chapter material. Check your work carefully to determine that it has all the qualities of effective expression. Think of these assignments as culminating activities that relate to the creation of various types of business communication.

Letter Problems

1. As the owner of a 16-unit motel, The Colonial Inn, you have recently discovered that the water bill for last month's usage is three times as much as the preceding bill. Your volume of business has remained relatively stable for the past four months, and you believe that an error has been made somewhere.

   New construction next to your motel has required that your water main be modified to allow a "hook up" for the new facility. You suspect that part of the problem may be the result of an improper connection in the pipeline. Whatever the reason for the increased cost being charged to your account, you are convinced that you are being charged for more water than you are using.

   Three telephone calls to the Tri-County Water Corporation have failed to produce any action that could help solve the problem. Write a letter to the Manager of Customer Service of the Corporation asking that appropriate action be taken.

   Other background information includes:
   a. You have been in business at the Colonial for fourteen years.
   b. You have never been late in making your monthly payments for water service.
   c. The individual units in your motel have only recently been redecorated.
   d. The motel is located near downtown businesses.
   e. A new shopping center is being constructed directly across the street from your motel.
   f. Sometimes water billings are made on the basis of estimates. (Meters are not read every month—especially during the winter months or during peak periods.)
   g. You don't want to be late in paying for the water you have

used; however, you don't feel you should pay the amount shown on the billing.

h. Occasionally service lines break and considerable water is lost before the problem is identified and corrected.

i. It is possible that an error was made in the "hook up" for the new construction next to your business and someone else is using water that is being charged to your account.

2. Write a letter to Mother's Drive Inns, Incorporated, located at 984 N. Mill Avenue in St. Louis, Missouri. Ask them for information regarding their franchise operations. Assume that you are interested in establishing a franchise in your community, but at this point have little knowledge of how or where to start. The following information pertains to this situation.

a. You are 25 years old and have had two years of college study in retail sales and management.

b. Your work experience is quite limited, although you have been employed by a Mother's Drive Inn for the past two summers as a part-time fry cook. Furthermore, you are ambitious and desirous of going into business for yourself.

c. Your mother and father have indicated that they will stake you to an initial down payment or investment of $10,000. This money would be considered a loan which would have to be paid back; however, it would be an interest-free loan.

d. You have two possible locations already identified; however, one of them, according to a reliable source, may not be available for long.

e. You are interested in getting started in your new business as soon as possible.

3. As supervisor of the Word Processing Center of Cascade, Incorporated, write a memorandum discussing the problem of coffee break abuse, directed to the employees in your department. Your staff members are spending too much time on their rest periods and you feel that corrective action is in order.

Background relating to this situation is as follows:

a. You have been working for Cascade for the past eight years—as supervisor for the last three.

b. Your staff is composed of 18 workers—13 women and 5 men. The average length of service of the workers in your department is approximately three years.

c. Although a few of the employees have less than a high school education, most have one or two years of post-secondary training.

d. You seem to be fairly well accepted by the employees, although two or three apparently resent your being promoted ahead of them.

e. Company policy provides for a morning and afternoon break of 15 minutes each. These breaks are being "stretched" by nearly everyone and the situation is now almost out of hand. Many employees take as much as 40 minutes for each break.

f. No coffee or beverages of any kind are allowed at work stations.

g. A previous memo, written and distributed about four months ago, had almost no effect. You believe that it was not worded as strongly as it should have been.

4. Assume that you have been asked to participate in a panel debate at your school in which the subject of "speed limits" will be discussed. The basic question to be considered is: "Should the present 55-mile-per-hour speed limit be retained, or should the limit be raised to a higher speed?"

Further, assume that you will accept the invitation to be on the panel and that you must submit a brief statement of your feelings on the debate question. Write a letter to Ms. Maureen Walker, Chairperson of Intracampus Debates, indicating that you would like to be a member of the panel. Include in your letter your basic thoughts regarding the debate topic. In your responses to the question, be specific enough to make her aware of your position on the topic, but do not attempt to include your entire presentation in the letter.

Additional background in this situation is as follows:

a. This is one of a series of debates on topics of interest to the students on your campus. The debates are held approximately three times each school year and are attended primarily by college students, although a few townspeople are usually in the audience.

b. Usually there are about a hundred people who attend the debates.

c. Your allotted time for presentation of your viewpoint is ten minutes.

d. Ms. Walker's address is the Speech Department of your college.

e. You may take any position you wish on the subject of speed limits.

5. Write a letter to the Editor of your local newspaper in which you express your views on a current problem or situation in your community. Be certain to give your reasons for the particular point of view or position you take.

6. Assume that you are the Office Administrator of Dooley Construction Company and that it is your responsibility to process claims for

Workmen's Compensation Insurance. You are presently processing the claim of James T. Carpen, who has submitted a report saying that he broke a rib on his right side in the course of picking up a heavy plank while at work.

Background information on this case is as follows:

a. The accident is reported to have happened last week. Mr. Carpen has been unable to work since the accident.

b. His personal physician has submitted a report to your office indicating the nature and extent of injury. His report also shows that Mr. Carpen suffered abrasions about the head and that he showed evidence of teeth marks (apparently human) on his arms and back. This additional information about Mr. Carpen's injury suggests strongly that he was involved in a personal fight with another person, in which case he would not, of course, be eligible for benefits.

c. If the facts of the case are that Carpen did not hurt himself as he reported (on the job during the course of his assigned duties), the doctor would not be paid for his services through Workmen's Compensation. He would be billing Mr. Carpen directly. Because of Mr. Carpen's work history, it is likely that the doctor who treated him might not get paid for his services if Mr. Carpen is required to pay the bill.

Write a letter to Mr. Carpen's doctor, Dr. Harold Slinger, 149 Broken Bow Drive, Memphis, Tennessee, and explain the situation to him. Ask him for his professional opinion regarding the likelihood of such bodily injury being caused by merely picking up a plank.

7. Assume that you are home from college for the summer and you wish to take one summer-school class at the local university. Before you take the course, however, you want to be assured that it will count toward graduation at your regular school. Write a letter to the Registrar's Office of the school that you are attending full time and ask them whether the course you are proposing to take during the summer will meet the requirements for your major.

Additional background information about this case follows.

a. Because of personal reasons, you had to withdraw from the second semester of Freshman Mathematics. You now wish to take the class during the summer while you are living and working in your home town.

b. You have obtained a copy of the proposed course syllabus which fairly well outlines the content of the material to be covered. You are to include a copy of this syllabus with the letter you send to the Registrar's Office.

c. In your letter, you should ask specifically whether the school will accept as transfer credit the course you wish to take during the summer. Make any other reasonable assumptions you wish that pertain to this case problem.

PART 5

Oral Communication

Oral Communication of Business Messages

12

A study of the information in this chapter will allow the reader to:

1. relate the principles of communication to the topic of oral communication.

2. see the relationship between an outline and an oral report.

3. determine the relationship between the instructions given to employees and the nature of the message.

4. realize the importance of an appropriate communication environment.

5. learn the guidelines for effective and efficient dictation.

6. appreciate the significance of the boss/secretary working relationship.

7. to relate the word processing function to existing communication systems.

In chapter 1 we studied the various steps in the communication process. This theory of communication is important to us whether we are concerned with transmitting messages in writing or through speech channels. Regardless of the form it takes, a message must be conceived, encoded, transmitted, received, and decoded. And, of course, adequate feedback must be provided to the initiator of the transaction. Subtle differences do exist, however, between written and spoken communication.

Comparing the Differences

One of the major differences between written and oral communication is the quality of creativity. When we develop ideas and produce them in written form, we tend to reflect more on their content than we do when we speak our thoughts. Assuming a minimum level of proficiency in the use of the language, this tendency to reflect usually results in communication that is relatively precise, well planned, and accurate. We are generally more creative in our writing than in our speaking because we simply have more time to think. Furthermore, we seem to feel that there is a permanence about information that appears in printed form—and that anything permanent should be correct.

Another difference between these two forms of communication is the quality of spontaneity. Spontaneity is a positive factor in communication that can enhance the effectiveness of speaking. Because of the time it takes to develop written communication, we often lose this quality of quickness of thought and originality that we can have in our speech. We should try to incorporate the quality of creativity in oral communication without losing the benefits of spontaneity. Incorporating both in our communication, regardless of the form, requires considerable attention to technique and a high degree of criticalness.

Oral communication in business can take place while presenting report information, giving instructions to workers, and dictating to a secretary or through a dictation machine. Each of these important opportunities for oral transmission requires special consideration, but all can be handled best if the proper business environment is created. Let's consider this environment and how we can create it before examining the separate areas of reporting, instructing, and dictating.

You will recall from our earlier discussion of communication theory that we are influenced more by our perception of reality than by reality itself. We must make this distinction once again because it relates specifically to the present topic. Many factors can influence this environment and certainly one of the most important ones is the prevailing attitude of the participants in the transaction. Good communicators will be sensitive to these attitudes and will strive to create conditions that are favorable to a successful encounter.

A positive attitude is most beneficial to business transactions; in fact, without it, chances for complete success are minimal. Anger, for example, inhibits rational thought processes and permits decisions that are based on anything less than objectivity. Clear thinking is best achieved in the absence of anger or other forms of emotional involvement. A proper business environment, then, is one which exists within the framework of positive attitudes. This attitude will allow us to think in terms of what *can* be done rather than what *cannot* be done, and what benefits will accrue to us rather than what obstacles confront us.

Presenting Report Information Orally

The effective presentation of report information includes knowing your audience, knowing your material, and knowing how to deliver it. Each of these components is vital to your success and each deserves special consideration at this time.

Knowing Your Audience

Knowing the audience requires first of all that you know the background information needed to make a reasonable and understandable presentation. For some audiences, little if any updating will be required; in fact, your audience may be the very people who gave you the assignment in the first place. They may know more about the general subject than you do and will need only a presentation of your findings relative to the problem. Other audiences may know little, if anything, about your report subject and will need considerable information from the beginning. Meeting this need, knowing your audience, is critical to the successful presentation of report information.

Knowing the audience also requires that you know *what kind* of information they need and desire. Some will want only the essence of your findings, the generalities; others will want specific details of operational data or procedures. Not knowing the kind of information needed or desired by your audience will surely diminish the effectiveness of the overall presentation. Of course, empathy assumes that we can psychologically project ourselves into the role of the other person. As speakers, then, we must view the situation from the perspective of those in the audience. We must ask ourselves what will be needed to best permit understanding by those who are listening to us.

Knowing Your Material

Probably, you will know more about your report than will anyone else. This probability is only reasonable to expect, because you will have been working very closely with the problem. Merely working with a problem, though, does not assure you of complete knowledge of all its dimensions. Be certain that you have a clear understanding of the problem that you were assigned to resolve, that you have made a thorough examination of all the relative data, that you have considered all the possible alternatives to the problem, and that you have tested your final solution in a thorough manner.

While working closely on a business problem generally provides you with more knowledge of the subject than most other people will have, it does not assure you of the complete objectivity you will need in order to make intelligent decisions about your total effort. In fact, you may lose some of your objectivity as it relates to the problem for the simple reason that you have been working too closely with it. Try to maintain a certain independence of attitude that will allow you to keep the perspective so necessary for the correct judgment which should accompany your report effort.

A thorough knowledge of your subject matter is by far the most important requirement for effective presentation. Anyone who does not know the subject matter well is doomed from the start. In addition to knowing the subject well, the reporter should know how to organize the material into logical units that can be easily understood by an audience. One should consider first of all whether to use the direct or indirect approach for presenting the ideas. Although the direct approach is generally appropriate for most business needs, there may be times when the indirect format will achieve better results.

Regardless of the presentation format, the ideas must be logically structured into major and minor components. This organization will accommodate those who are listening to the report. Members of the audience will be expecting to hear information presented in some logical sequence, and any deviation will be disruptive and result in confusion or lack of clarity. Know what your major outline should be in order to achieve your objective and stay with it throughout. Study the partial outlines below and note how the subject matter is organized in a logical sequence to generate maximum understanding.

Example 1:

AUDIT REPORT

STATE OF IDAHO

DEPARTMENT OF EDUCATION

I. Introduction
    B. History
    A. Statutory Authority for Existence of the Department
    C. Internal Organization of the Department
    D. General Functions and Responsibilities
        1. Regulatory Functions
        2. Leadership Functions
        3. Service Functions
II. Purpose, Scope, and Summary
    A. Purpose of Audit
    B. Scope of Review
    C. Summary and Conclusions

III. Review of Programs and Procedures
   A. State Superintendent of Public Instruction
   B. Programs Initiated to Correct Deficiencies in Service to Districts
   C. Administrative Assistant
   Z. . . . .

Example 2:

HITTING THE BASIC GROUNDSTROKES OF TENNIS

I. General Considerations
   A. Physical Conditioning
   B. Concentration
   C. Coordination
   D. Anticipation
II. The Forehand
   A. The Grip
   B. The Backswing
   C. The Stroke
   D. The Follow-through
III. The Backhand
   A. The Grip
   B. The Backswing
   C. The Stroke
   D. The Follow-through

Regardless of the nature of the information, organization is a desirable quality in communication efforts. Your audience will expect the information to be presented in a logical sequence and you should accommodate them. Material presented out of sequence will serve only as a distraction which, in turn, will diminish your effectiveness.

Other factors of effective speaking besides knowledge of subject matter, knowledge of the audience, and logical organization include rapport with the audience, methods of delivery, and use of visual aids. Of course, basic to all communication efforts, whether writing or speaking, is the element of confidence—and confidence comes with knowledge and experience.

Rapport with the audience must begin with the proper attitude toward the assignment. If a speaker has a positive feeling toward the report, enthusiasm will probably be imparted to the audience. They, too, will feel that the subject is important and that their time is not being wasted. Although some report assignments will have greater appeal to you than will others, most will be significant to the organization's objectives and deserving of your best efforts.

The methods of delivery are also important considerations in presenting an oral report. In fact, they may be the most important variable of all those mentioned so far. For it is through the delivery itself that one communicates ideas to others. Specific components of delivery include rate of speech, voice qualities and general articulation, kinesic behavior (body language), and facial expressions.

The rate of one's speech pattern can tell an audience something about the significance of the topic, the speaker's interest in and concern for the problem, and perhaps something about the level of confidence. Generally, a fast rate of delivery is associated with high levels of interest, anxiety, or a high degree of confidence. Conversely, a slow or hesitant delivery may point to low levels of interest and confidence. Note, though, that any of these nonverbal characteristics must be interpreted within the context of the situation. For example, in a given situation, a fast rate of delivery may be the result of speaker disinterest—it may have absolutely nothing to do with his enthusiasm for the topic. In another situation, this high rate of delivery could be the result of an enthusiastic attitude.

Voice qualities and general articulation such as smoothness of speech patterns and enunciation also communicate information to the audience. The effective speaker should develop the positive qualities that will enhance the overall presentation. Most speakers can change and/or control these variables so that they work to the speaker's advantage.

Kinesic behavior (body postures and gestures) is particularly important because it is so highly visible to others. As we learned in our earlier study of nonverbal communication, body language often reveals much more than we think it does. Speaker posture can communicate attitudes at almost any moment. Contrast the attitude of one who stands with feet apart, elbows pointed outward, and chest protruded with that of one who stands with feet together, elbows to the sides, and shoulders sloped forward. Quite possibly, the latter speaker will convey a picture of something less than total confidence, interest, and control. Similarly, certain gestures with arms and hands at strategic times during the presentation of information will strengthen the overall performance.

The face is the most dynamic part of one's body. Facial expressions are the focal point for most audiences and, therefore, deserve special attention as we consider speech behavior and delivery. The eyelids, eyes, and eyebrows can communicate many different meanings, so it is little wonder that the face is considered to be so important a communicating medium. Smiles, frowns, and expressions of surprise (or happiness, sadness, shock, humor, etc.) all provide the speaker with additional reenforcement as he seeks to emphasize or de-emphasize a point in the delivery. Good speakers will learn to use all of these techniques in support of their presentation of business information.

Advances in audiovisual equipment technology provide us with almost limitless degrees of sophistication that can supplement an oral presentation. Many of these aids are relatively inexpensive and most businesses are able to afford at least a minimum inventory of such items.

Copy machines come in many sizes and most are capable of reproducing quality work that is often as good as the original document. These machines can generate copies of charts, graphs, pictures, and other facsimiles that can be used when presenting a report. In many organizations, copy machines have virtually replaced the carbon copy as the basis for file copies.

Overhead projectors allow the user to reflect information on a screen or other white background such as a smooth wall. By using transparencies one can, in effect, control the attention of audiences much more readily than by depending solely upon verbalizations. Another method of getting information to the audience is to provide handouts of material for each person. This method, however, can cause temporary distraction from your presentation. Too often listeners spend their time referring to the handouts when they should be listening to what is being said.

Whatever the form of audiovisual aid used, graphs, charts, pictures, or other drawings and sketches should be applied to illustrate the data. The expression, "a picture is worth a thousand words," is never more true than when referring to situations in which technical or otherwise complex information must be communicated. Of course, different colors can be used to emphasize selected factors in the presentation. Kits are now available that make it relatively easy to construct attractive transparencies, and overlays can be made to show the progression or degrees of a concept.

Giving Instructions to Others

Oral communication in business is extensive and it generally involves supervisors and subordinates who are respectively giving and receiving instructions and information. Because of the imprecision of our communicative skills, it is little wonder that we experience difficulties in making our meaning clear or our instructions complete. Let us consider two of the major barriers to effective oral communication.

Mistaken Assumptions About Agreement of Meaning

Too often, a manager will mistakenly assume that the words he uses will be interpreted exactly as they were intended to be. We know that words of themselves do not have meaning—we assign meaning to them. Naturally these meanings will vary between sender and receiver, and frequently the disparity of meaning is so great that communication problems arise. Effective communicators will seek a verification of the accuracy of their transmission. This verification can be accomplished by getting feedback from the receiver. Any misinterpretations can then be corrected immediately. From a practical point of view, however, too many supervisors fail to obtain any verification whatsoever. Similarly, too few subordinates ask enough questions about instructions they receive to assure them that they understand precisely what it is they are supposed to do or how they are supposed to do it. While it is the responsibility of both parties to ascertain the accuracy and completeness of the information, it is primarily the job of the supervisor. Unfortunately, the communication climate in most organizations is too restrictive or intimidating to allow the employee the freedom to ask questions about oral communications.

Variations in Superior/Subordinate Perceptions

We have already learned that as individuals we tend to perceive the real world from our own frame of reference and from our own background and experiences. This perceptual orientation applies to superiors and subordinates in a work environment as well. This fact, that we have different bases for perceiving things, probably accounts for the differences that exist between the way a superior views a situation and the way a subordinate sees it. One would be unrealistic to expect that all individuals in an organization would see all situations in the same way, but we would hope that common goals (mutual goals) would make for a lessening of differences in perception.

These variations in perception must be considered by the person who is to communicate in an organizational environment. This individual must be willing and able to empathize with the receivers to the extent that their reactions are anticipated. Translated into actual behavior, then, a supervisor must be certain that the subordinates have all the information necessary to understand the message they receive. All too often a supervisor will edit the information before passing it on to subordinates, without making important facts available to those who need them. This editing can be either intentional or unintentional, but in either case it hampers effective communication. If the supervisor is passing on data from someone higher up in the organization, certain information will be deleted, other elements will be added, and finally that which remains will be somewhat distorted. This type of communication, called *serial transmission of organizational information*, represents a significant barrier to oral instructions. A final suggestion at this point: supervisors should realize that subordinates will perceive a situation differently, and that these differences will need to be allowed for.

Dictating Business Information

Up to this point in our discussions of written communication we have concentrated on grammar, sentence structure, word choice, viewpoint, letter tone, etc. We have assumed that a business writer would have ample time to reflect on the composition and would be able to make the necessary adjustments to the writing in order to achieve the objectives. We generally do have this time to refine our communications; however, when we begin dictating our thoughts to a secretary or through a dictating machine, we have a new set of requirements. The novice dictator may feel, in many instances, that he or she is having to relearn everything learned previously. While it is true that all of the principles and practices we have studied thus far still apply, regardless

Figure 12.1   The modern secretary can be of great help to a boss.

of the medium, other factors come into play that vitally affect the overall quality of the message. Knowing how to deal with these new requirements will assist us in our efforts to become effective business writers.

The modern secretary can be of great help to a boss. In many instances the secretary can supplement the superior's strengths. Similarly, a good boss can provide valuable assistance to the secretary. This good working relationship can develop a strong and effective team that can, in turn, make the work easier and do it more efficiently.

The good secretary can help a boss best by knowing as much as possible about the business organization, the work that is performed, and the people who do it. Being informed about these various factors will allow the secretary to do assigned work more efficiently. In a sense, the boss's work is the secretary's work. A secretary should know about work schedules, personnel requirements, purchasing procedures, and federal, state, and local laws pertaining to business operations. By knowing the needs of the business, the secretary will be in a good position to provide valuable assistance.

The business man or woman can be of help to the secretary by knowing something about the specific skills required for that position. Among the many skills may be the ability to take dictation and/or transcribe information that has been recorded on dictation machines. In many offices, the dictation and transcription functions make up a substantial portion of the secretary's work day. Anything that the boss can do to make the task easier will benefit everyone. Let's consider at this point the secretarial skill of writing manual shorthand and determine how a dictator of business messages can be of help to the writer.

Shorthand is generally learned under ideal conditions and taught by professional educators who are also professional dictators. Manual shorthand is written by using certain symbols (outlines) that represent the sound of words. These symbols, once learned, can be made with considerably greater speed than can their longhand counterpart. Because of this and other technical factors, shorthand writers can record material as much as ten times faster than by the use of longhand methods.

This greater writing speed permits dictators to speak in a conversational manner that facilitates the composition of letters and reports. The secretary who is taking the dictation must listen to what is spoken and convert it to shorthand symbols on paper. Dictators can make the task easier by speaking in natural phrases and maintaining a relatively constant rate of delivery. Most trained secretaries will be able to record information that is spoken at speeds of up to 120 words per minute. Naturally, the dictator must speak clearly so that the correct words are recorded. Sometimes, because of unclear enunciation, the wrong word or words appear in the completed transcript. This type of error can be costly and embarrassing to an organization.

If there is a substantial amount of dictation to be done on a regular basis, it may be advisable to set aside a certain time period for this work. Generally the early part of the day is best suited for dictation. Having the correspondence dictated early in the day will allow the secretary time to prepare the material in mailable form for same-day mailing or disposition. Outside interruptions should not be tolerated during the dictation period. Telephone calls can be delayed for a short time as can personal interviews and other appointments.

All related information needed to dictate the communication should be readily available. Having to retrieve information from the files can inhibit the process and create but another form of interruption. Good dictators will also have some form of outline—mental or written—that will make the work easier. Thinking through the situation before the material is dictated will make for more intelligent communication. Also, the secretary should be given specific names and addresses at some time during the dictation process. Many names sound alike, and errors involving their spelling can adversely affect the final copy.

Most of the same guidelines that pertain to dictation involving a shorthand writer also apply when using a dictation machine. Related information should be readily available, interruptions should be minimized, the message should be planned, and specific dates, addresses, and spelling should be noted. Remember that the material recorded on an intermediate medium such as magnetic tape or plastic disc must still be transcribed by another person. By keeping the needs of the transcriber in mind, the dictator will make everyone's job easier and more efficient. Also, the dictator should be responsible for punctuation, paragraphing, and correct grammar usage in dictating the material. Furthermore, by using the mechanical features of the dictation machines to indicate the length of the communication or special instructions to the secretary, total costs can be reduced considerably.

Some business organizations that use dictation machines have centralized secretarial or stenographic pools that are staffed by workers trained specifically to transcribe the information sent to them. In other circumstances, perhaps where the amount of dictation and transcription cannot justify the existence of such a pool, individual secretaries prepare the typewritten copy.

Advantages of using the manual shorthand method include having confidential material exposed to fewer personnel, having transcripts prepared according to your own priorities of time, and having the personal touch of someone who is probably familiar with the circumstances of each case. Use of a dictation machine provides the advantages of saving the secretary's time involved in recording the information, being able to do the dictating whenever you wish, and having the actual recording serve as a file copy.

Recognizing the need for practice in order to develop efficient and effective dictation skills, the wise student will take advantage of every opportunity to obtain experience in this area. Even though most young business men and women who are in entry-level positions may not even have a secretary or dictation duties, they stand to benefit from any practice they can obtain. Beginning dictators may encounter one or both of the two major barriers to effective dictation.

One of these barriers is the tendency to develop mental blocks at some time during the dictation process. When this happens it is best simply to review the dictated material up to that point. Often this review will provide the stimulus needed to formulate the next unit of information. Also, these mental blocks may be minimized by planning a good outline of the material you wish to communicate. In no instance

---

CHECKSHEET FOR DICTATION

1. Dictate in natural, conversational phrases.
2. Use a constant rate of delivery.
3. Speak clearly so as to avoid inaccuracies and embarrassing errors.
4. Set aside a block of time for dictation that occurs on a regular basis.
5. Control interruptions during dictation periods.
6. Dictate information in the mornings to allow the typed messages to be mailed or distributed.
7. Have all necessary materials and information at hand before dictation is begun.
8. Develop a written or mental outline of the material to be dictated.
9. Spell out names and addresses to avoid costly errors.
10. Provide punctuation, paragraphing, and correct grammar when dictating. (Don't depend upon the secretary to "clean it up.")
11. Give all specific instructions regarding special mailing, number of copies, distribution, etc.
12. Avoid mental blocks and rambling on by sticking to your dictation outline and objectives.

---

should dictation ever be started before the primary objective of the message has been determined.

The second barrier is almost the reverse of the first one. On occasion, a dictator will develop the tendency to "ramble on." This refers to the inclusion of unnecessary information. This barrier detracts from the quality of conciseness that we have already identified as inherent in all good communications. Another disadvantage of the tendency to ramble is the increased cost of preparing the transcript. With the cost of many business letters running in excess of $5.00 each, it is simply not practical to develop long, unnecessary messages. The suggestions given for overcoming the barrier of the blocked mind apply here also. Think about what you are writing, what your objective is, and what you have said earlier in the letter or report.

In many of the larger organizations *word processing centers* are being created, which puts increased emphasis on efficient dictation techniques. These centers, which are sophisticated extensions of the "pool" concept, are designed to improve the efficiency of internal and external communication programs. Basic to all operations within these centers is the dictated message, and those who use the services will need to know how to communicate through appropriate channels.

Word Processing

One of the most important developments of the paper explosion is the communication concept known as *word processing*. To understand what word processing really means, we need to review briefly the evolution of letter writing.

Business technology has helped us to advance from the time when a business discussed its letter output in terms of a dozen or so letters per month. As the need for more communication swelled the number of these letters to hundreds and even to thousands, businesses sought more efficient methods of producing letters. The demand for more letters exceeded the ability of one secretary, so another was added, then another, and another. By taking dictation in shorthand and transcribing with typewriters, these secretaries were able to produce many times more letters than were previously possible through the use of longhand.

But, even with these newer and better methods, the demand for more communication soon exceeded the physical capabilities under the existing systems. Time was the all-important factor. The dictation of a letter required that two busy people work together for a few (or many) minutes. The length of this time period depended on the ability of the one to dictate efficiently and in a well-organized manner, and of the other to take shorthand quickly and legibly. This process also required a work station convenient to both workers for the dictation and transcription process.

Again, technology came to the rescue with the dictation machine. Now, the busy executive could dictate messages more conveniently—while traveling in a car or plane with the battery-operated dictation machine—and at times other than the regular working hours. By means of the dictation disc, belt, or tape, the secretary could take the recorded words of the dictator to the typewriter. There the secretary transcribed the message with the help of the stop-start playback feature of the dictation machine.

The dictation machine opened up a whole new dimension in communication. One development was the "stenographic pool." Originally, each executive was assigned one secretary who performed all the duties of a stenographer and typist in addition to other secretarial duties of the office. These duties were often performed with varying degrees of skill and proficiency. Under the "pooling" concept, four or five expert typists may be assigned to a specially equipped work station to perform the stenographic duties for perhaps a dozen executives. The dictated messages were delivered to the pool by messenger, by automatic transporters, or by direct telephone dictation. One of the available steno-typists transcribed the message and returned it to the office of the dictator for signature. Meanwhile, an executive secretary had time available to do other kinds of work. For most companies, this conversion to the pooling concept has not reduced the number of personnel but has significantly increased the work output.

In a sense, the pooling concept is a step toward word processing. In fact, many companies refer to their steno pool as a word processing center. Some schools teach courses that they call word processing even though they are little more than machine dictation courses designed to prepare students for the pooling concept used by many companies.

Word processing has become a reality with the development of sophisticated electronic equipment. One such item of equipment displays the transcribed message on a screen for editing and revision. With this system, the message is received by telephone dictation or some other method and can be stored for playback and transcription.

As the word-processing operator transcribes, the message appears on a visual screen. The message can then be edited or changed to result in error-free copy ready for mailing.

Another feature of the word-processing systems permits the storage and retrieval of previously recorded material. Because of the speed with which this equipment can function, the operator can locate letters, paragraphs, or other information in a matter of seconds. These can be displayed and revised, then retyped at speeds greater than that of the secretary. This speed and potential for error-free copy results in greater productivity and efficiency in business writing.

As more and more companies convert their communication centers to word-processing systems, business students, trainees, and business executives will find an increasing need to become familiar with the concept of word processing. The development of even more sophisticated equipment is continuing.

Summary

Communication theory applies to all methods by which communication is transmitted. As long as there are senders and receivers involved in the transaction, there exists a need to consider all the steps in the basic process. The differences between written and oral communication are significant, however, and we will profit from learning what they are. Creativity and spontaneity are the major differences that influence the quality of these forms of communication. Another factor that affects our exchange of information is the business environment that we create. The best environment is, of course, one that is based on a positive attitude toward both the situation and the people involved.

When we present report information orally, we need to know the audience and the material. We must also have a thorough knowledge of the report information, and we have to be able to organize the presentation in a logical and understandable manner. Rapport with the audience, methods of delivery, and use of visual aids further enhance the quality of our communication.

Giving instructions to others in our employ requires that we do not assume that all people will assign the same meanings to the words we use. Too often it is mistakenly assumed that there is an agreement of meaning. Furthermore, we should remember that the perceptions of superior and subordinate are at variance. Each will view a situation from his or her own frame of reference and these differing viewpoints may well be the basis for additional communication problems.

Dictation is a specialized skill that requires a considerable amount of thought and practice. Business men and women can increase their communication efficiency by learning how to work with the secretary in developing written messages. A good working relationship between boss and secretary will benefit both. Many businesses use the dictation machine rather than the services of a secretary to dictate their business messages. A knowledge of how to use it is required of the modern business person.

More and more business messages are being handled through word processing centers. In these centers, specialists receive dictated or prerecorded messages that are viewed and edited electronically and prepared for mailing at significantly higher speeds than were previously possible.

1. Discuss the major differences between written and oral communication. What is the significance of these differences as they relate to our responsibilities as business writers?
2. Discuss the importance of knowing your audience when presenting report information.
3. Why is it reasonable to expect that the person giving the oral report will know more about the topic under consideration than will anyone else?
4. Discuss how organization contributes to the communication of ideas through oral transmission. Do you think it is any more important to have good organization when presenting ideas in oral form than when presenting them in written form? Why?
5. What do the authors mean when they refer to "rapport with the audience"?
6. Discuss the variables that can influence the method of delivery.
7. What factors of nonverbal communication are important parts of an oral presentation?
8. In the nonverbal context, what part of one's body is the most dynamic?
9. What specific audiovisual equipment can aid in the presentation of report information?
10. What is meant by the phrase, "A mistaken assumption about agreement of meaning"?
11. How can the variations in superior/subordinate perceptions contribute to communication problems?
12. Identify the two major barriers to correct dictation and tell how they can be overcome.
13. Outline the various steps required to enable one to give efficient dictation.
14. In what ways is machine dictation different from the traditional method of having the spoken word recorded in manual shorthand form?
15. Check an article found in a current publication that contains information about the concept of word processing. Develop a one-page abstract that contains the essence of the article.

Bernstein, Theodore M. *The Careful Writer*. New York: Atheneum, 1973.

Fruehling, Rosemary T., and Bouchard, Sharon. *Business Correspondence/30*. New York: Gregg Division, McGraw-Hill Book Co., 1971.

Hemphill, P. D. *Business Communications: With Writing Improvement Exercises*. Englewood Cliffs, N.J.: Prentice-Hall, 1976.

Himstreet, William C., and Baty, Wayne Murlin. *Business Communications*. Belmont, Calif.: Wadsworth Publishing Co., 1973.

Krey, Isabelle A., and Metzler, Bernadette V. *Principles and Techniques of Effective Business Communication.* New York: Harcourt Brace Jovanovich, 1976.

Lawrence, Nelda R. *Writing Communications in Business and Industry.* 2d ed. Englewood Cliffs, N.J.: Prentice-Hall, 1974.

Liedlich, Raymond D. *Coming to Terms With Language: An Anthology.* New York: John Wiley & Sons, 1973.

Linton, Calvin D. *Effective Revenue Writing 2.* Washington D.C.: Superintendent of Documents, U.S. Government Printing Office, 1962.

McIntosh, Donal W. *Techniques of Business Communication.* Boston: Holbrook Press, 1972.

Menning, J. H.; Wilkinson, C. W.; and Clarke, Peter B. *Communicating Through Letters and Reports.* Homewood, Ill.: Richard D. Irwin, Inc., 1976.

Murphy, Herta A., and Peck, Charles E. *Effective Business Communications.* New York: McGraw-Hill Book Company, 1972.

Pei, Mario. *The Story of Language.* Rev. ed. Philadelphia: J. B. Lippincott Co., 1965.

Pickett, Nell Ann. *Practical Communication.* New York: Harper's College Press, 1975.

Poe, Roy W., and Fruehling, Rosemary T. *Business Communication: A Problem-solving Approach.* New York: Gregg Division, McGraw-Hill Book Company, 1973.

Shurter, Robert L. *Written Communication in Business.* 3d ed. New York: McGraw-Hill Book Co., 1971.

Sigband, Norman B. *Communication for Management.* Glenview, Ill.: Scott, Foresman and Co., 1969.

Vardaman, George T., and Vardaman, Patricia Black. *Communication in Modern Organizations.* New York: John Wiley & Sons, 1973.

Wolf, Morris Philip, and Aurner, Robert R. *Effective Communication in Business.* 6th ed. Cincinnati: South-Western Publishing Co., 1974.

Report Writing

PART 6

Preparing to Write
Business Reports

13

A study of the information in this chapter will provide you with:

1. an awareness of the role report writing plays in organizational communication.

2. an understanding of the reasons for business reports.

3. guidelines for the classification of reports.

4. the ability to identify various types of business problems.

5. a knowledge of the methods used in gathering data.

Report writing is a professional skill. The success of many professional workers may be determined by their ability to communicate ideas and information through reports. A report is any oral or written message that transmits objective, factual information in response to a problem. Effective reports assist businesses in their decision-making functions.

Ineffective reports waste time and, therefore, money. Worst of all, they waste ideas—ideas that are never fully developed because they remain only in the mind of the originator. Many business workers have ideas, but the men and women who get promoted or who get salary increases are those who can present those ideas to others through effective written and oral reports. Only then can those ideas be acted upon.

Many reports are prepared with the help of other people. The one who receives credit for the report may have done little more than conduct the research. Because of this involvement with others, you may often find a need to coordinate the efforts of researchers, typists, computer analysts, and co-workers to produce your finished report within the limits of your time frame. Since the report will bear your name, you will be responsible for the quality of each of these phases of the report preparation.

The various kinds of business letters that have been described do an adequate job of taking care of most correspondence in business, and letters represent an important kind of business report. These letters travel in all directions within the company and outside the company. Sometimes, however, a need arises for a special kind of correspondence. A company, or a department within the company, may recognize a need for information to help in making decisions for the future. The need may be for an analysis of previous events or a projection of expectations for the company. Top management may request information about the progress on a project or an assignment. A planning committee may be asked to prepare a recommendation for the location of a proposed sales office. Or a manufacturing company may assign the research department to experiment and report on the development of a new product.

Each of these business situations could result in a need for a business report. Reports are a part of the routine activity as well as the special activity of nearly all businesses. Even though business reports may be either written or oral, our attention here will be directed toward the written report and its importance to business.

Classification of Reports

We may classify reports in a variety of ways. For example, a report may be formal or informal; it may be long, short, or medium in length; its function may be to present information or to analyze data; it may be one of a series of monthly reports, or it may be a once-in-a-lifetime special report. These possibilities suggest that reports can be classified according to style, length, function, or frequency of occurrence. Numerous other classifications are possible, but these, generally, will serve our purposes.

The formality of a report is determined by the writing style that may, in turn, be determined by the audience for which the report is prepared. The *informal report* may be anything from a handwritten memo on a note pad to a neatly typed report of several pages. The informal report may use an abundance of personal pronouns, and the writing style may be casual. (See figure 13.1.)

The *formal report* is "dressed up" for a special occasion. The language, writing style, and format are appropriate for this special occasion. The use of first-person pronouns is usually avoided. However, the writing need not appear to be stilted or pompous. Whether the report is formal or informal, there should be no sacrifice of good grammar, clarity, or any of the other elements of effective writing.

The dividing line between formal and informal reports may be very difficult to determine. The distinction is often made only in the mind of the report writer.

The length of the report should always be determined by need. The elements of conciseness and completeness, so important in business letters, are of similar importance in reports. A report written within an organization may be as short as the informal penciled mes-

Interoffice Memo	
To:	Date:
From:	
Subject:	

Joe,
The invoice numbers you asked about are:
L 481, L 492, and L 504.
Don

Figure 13.1 Examples of Informal Reports

sage on a note pad, or as long as dozens of pages reporting research and recommendations for plant expansion. Every report should be only long enough to cover the subject clearly. As reports become longer, their length is increased to an even greater extent by a need for additional parts that may be required for clarity. For example, a lengthy report may be made even lengthier by its need for a table of contents, an index, or an appendix.

Reports may also be classified according to their purpose or function. One kind of report may be intended merely to give information. The monthly balance sheet prepared by the accounting department may be an example of an informational report. Other reports may take basic information, analyze it, and make recommendations for its application in a given situation. The determination of the function of many reports is often made by the agency or the person authorizing the preparation of the report.

Some reports are *periodic* in occurrence. Monthly reports, year-end reports, and semiannual reports to stockholders are all examples of periodic reports. By contrast, a special report may be originated to serve a single purpose, and therefore may never be repeated.

Regardless of the classification of the report, the report writer should observe all the elements of effective communication. Careful, logical presentation of information and objective interpretation and recommendations will assure the effectiveness of the report. Most reports are based on factual information; therefore, personal opinions or projections outside the scope of the facts should be avoided. These expressions may weaken the objectivity and the validity of a report as will hasty conclusions based on incomplete or incorrect information.

Reasons for Reports

Consider the events described here as they affect a medium-sized manufacturing firm. Ten salesmen sell the firm's products in a large area of the Midwest. Weekly reports from the sales staff indicate that sales are increasing in six of the ten areas; however, sales in the other four areas have not shown any growth over the past two years. The sales manager asks for and receives from each of the sales staff an informal report, which indicates that the company's products are not competitively priced in the problem areas because of the cost of shipping the products the long distance from the factory. One salesman recommends that the company consider establishing a warehouse within the affected area from which shipments to customers could be made. He thinks that the cost of making truckload and trainload shipments to the warehouse for distribution within his sales territory would be considerably less than present costs for individual shipments.

The idea could have some merit. However, before the decision can be made, management needs some information. The following chapters will show how that information can be gathered and presented in logical order so that the decision can be made. At this point, the information is presented only to show the need for reports as possible solutions to business problems.

In our hypothetical problem, various kinds of reports will be needed. Obviously, several short memorandum reports will be used to send and request information from one person or department to another within the company. These reports may authorize or generate more reports, both formal and informal, as the research continues. Letter reports may be written by manufacturers, builders, and freight companies quoting prices, rates, and building costs that may have an effect in determining the feasibility of the venture. Of course, many telephone calls and other kinds of oral communications will take place during the course of the research. However, the need for permanent records, evidence of quotations, and interim decisions indicates the need for written reports over the oral transmission of the data.

The result of all the research and paperwork will likely be a formal report of many pages addressed to the president for his presentation to the board of directors. The report will probably include recommendations for or against certain parts of the proposal. In chapter 14 we will take a closer look at these elements of the report.

We can better understand the need for reports by considering the kinds of problems that business must face and find answers to. These problems may be routine or special. Routine problems are those that the company expects to encounter as a natural result of its day-to-day business. For example, the sales department knows that it must submit a periodic report of sales volume; management knows that regular reports must be sent to stockholders and that reports of income and taxes withheld must be submitted regularly to the government. Quite a number of statistical reports may originate with the accounting department. These informational reports may serve as a basis for analytical reports by some other department.

In addition to the many routine reports that may be required, most companies have need for special reports. These describe any of the nonroutine problems or requests for information that may occur. Our hypothetical situation describes the need for a special report.

Identification of Business Problems

Before a wise person will attempt to answer a question, he will be certain that he understands the questions. Even so, the wise report writer will not attempt to write a report in answer to a business problem unless he first understands what that problem is. This idea may seem so universally acceptable that it would not be worthy of much of our time in the study of report writing. However, let us consider some of the difficulties entailed in identifying business problems both broadly enough and narrowly enough as to enable us to pursue a course for their solution.

Some business problems may be rather clear cut. The writer may be thoroughly familiar with the problem—he may have already recognized the problem and decided to tackle the task of finding a solution. However, other business problems may be vaguely defined or stated in such general terms that the real problem is not clear. This may be especially true if the problem is assigned in writing and the instructions and information are not clear or complete to begin with. In this case, the writer will need to find more information or seek a more clear-cut statement of the assignment.

As a report writer, once you clearly understand the problem, you state that problem in writing. This statement of the problem then serves as the foundation for the entire report. Because of the importance of the problem statement, we should devote some time here in studying how to write it. To do so will help us to avoid unclear statements that may cloud the mind of the report reader. A clear statement of the problem will also help to keep the report writer "on track" throughout the research and writing of the report.

The problem statement can generally be made in one of three ways. These are the infinitive phrase, the question, and the declarative statement.

The infinitive phrase is so named because it contains an infinitive in stating the nature of the problem. The following are examples of problems stated in this way.

Problem statement: To determine the feasibility of constructing a new warehouse at Farmington.

Problem statement: To compare the sales results of marketing plans A, B, and C.

The purpose of this report is to present the effects of increased competition in the Central Region.

The third example shows an effective way of stating the problem or the purpose of the study or report. Although it is in the form of a statement, it contains an infinitive phrase that states the purpose or the objective of the writer in responding to the specific problem.

The following examples represent problem statements written as questions.

Problem statement: Does the color of the wrapper have an effect on the marketability of Argo soap?

Problem statement: Should the new sales office be
                     located at Site A, Site B, or Site C?

The purpose of this study is to find an answer to the following
question: What should be done to improve the working relations
in the Layout Department?

Notice that the root of the third example is stated in the form of
an infinitive phrase followed by the question. This form would probably not be used to introduce a single question. However, if our study
seeks answers to several questions, this kind of root statement may be
helpful in introducing the list of questions.

The declarative statement, while not as popular, may also be
used to state the problem or the purpose of the report. Following are
some examples.

Problem statement: The Personnel Department wants
                     a report of vacation costs over
                     the past three years.

Problem statement: Management wants a time-
                     analysis study conducted detail-
                     ing the letter-writing costs of the
                     stenographers' pool.

With the declarative statement, the specific problem is often implied rather than stated clearly. That is one reason why this form of
problem statement is not regularly used.

Regardless of the method you select for stating the problem
for which your report is being written, you should be sure that
the statement expresses clearly what the problem is. Each of the
following problem statements exhibits a possible weakness. See how
you could improve upon these statements to correct the weakness that
is indicated for each.

What can be done to improve the efficiency of the tax commission office?

(Lacks clarity. Efficiency of whom? Secretaries? Custodians? Is
there a problem with paperwork buildup or runaway utilities
expenses?)

Why are tuition costs so much higher at Applebury State College?

(Begs the question. What does the writer mean by "so much higher"? Is this just a gripe, or is it a legitimate problem? Does it mean that tuition costs are higher than ever before or just higher than at similar state colleges?)

Problem statement: To determine the effect of coal-fired power plants.

(Stated too broadly. Do you mean the environmental effect? The effect on energy costs? Does it mean increased employment in Appalachia? Would the effect be the same for a small town in Arizona as for a large industrial center in Michigan?)

By now you should realize that you must of necessity state your problem clearly. You should state it narrowly enough that you can handle the problem within the scope of the report but not so narrowly that you will overlook certain elements of the problem.

Another important quality of the problem statement is that it should include the objective of the study. Proper identification and statement of the problem will indicate how the study will help to solve the problem.

A process called *factoring* is helpful in identifying all the "subparts" of the problem. The factors of a problem may include all the subtopics that make up the total problem. Or, the factors may include a number of statements of explanation or possible solutions to the problem. Regardless of the method you choose, the factoring process will help you to examine more carefully the nature of the problem and to assure the examination of all those elements that may have some bearing on the report purpose.

Methods of Gathering Data

Once you have recognized the need for the report and clearly identified the problem and its factors, you are ready to begin the gathering of data that will help meet the objectives of the report. You may refer to this important step as research, as gathering of data, or as investigating the problem. You can best accomplish this stage of report preparation in three steps. First, formulate your plan. Second, gather the material you will need to support your plan and to assure that you will meet the objectives of the report. Third, evaluate the material you have gathered. Discard extraneous material.

To a certain extent, you formed your plan in the steps already discussed—recognizing the need for the report and the audience to be served and assuring a clear identification of the problem. Your plan will now include a look at some of the methods of gathering data and the sources of that information.

Careful, thoughtful planning will help to shorten what might otherwise be a long and complex process. For many business problems, information has already been gathered and may be available in company publications, libraries, newspapers, or other sources. Reference to these sources may often lead to others through the use of bibliographies and references to companion articles. In some cases, however, the researcher will need to develop the data through experiments, questionnaires, interviews, or surveys. These two approaches are referred to as secondary research and primary research.

Secondary Research

Secondary research refers to the gathering of data from any source that did not originate with the researcher. This includes all information from books, periodicals, other reports, or almost any printed source. In these instances, someone else, or some other agency, has gathered data, drawn conclusions, and made recommendations that may have some bearing on the problem we are investigating. This is valuable information and you should use it if it is applicable to your problem and providing you give credit to the original researcher. The use of someone else's material without proper credit is plagiarism. This literary theft is not only ethically wrong but also legally wrong. Chapter 15 explains how this credit should be shown.

The library is one of the best sources of secondary research information. Here, books, periodicals, and indexes are categorized for the researcher's use. A few hints on library use and specific sources of information may save hours of frustration. For example, most libraries catalog their books according to the Dewey Decimal System. This system provides for classification of all books into one of ten categories. Each major category is identified by a three-digit number. The first digit identifies the major classification, the second digit is a division within that category, and the third digit is a section within the division.

	000	General Works
	100	Philosophy
DEWEY DECIMAL	200	Religion
SYSTEM	300	Social Sciences
First-digit	400	Philology
classification	500	Pure Science
	600	Useful Arts—Applied Science
	700	Fine Arts
	800	Literature
	900	History

The first stop for most library researchers should be the card catalog. The card catalog contains a three-way listing of all books, films, and reference works that can be found in the library. The material is listed alphabetically according to author, title, and subject matter. In addition to the author and the title, the card lists certain descriptive information about the book that may help the researcher to determine whether that particular work contains the right kind of information.

A number of libraries, especially larger ones, use a file system developed by the Library of Congress. This system uses the letters of the alphabet, rather than numbers, for the main classification of books. The Library of Congress system permits the classification of a greater number of books because it is not limited to the ten categories of the Dewey Decimal System.

The following shows a sample from the card catalog of a book listed according to the Library of Congress system.

HF   Business Correspondence for Colleges
5726   Hunsinger, Marjorie
H8   Business correspondence for colleges. New York,
        Gregg Publishing Division, McGraw-Hill (1960).
        250 p. illus.
        1. Communication. Correspondence.

The call number is in the upper left-hand corner, the title is on the first line, and the author is listed next. This is followed by a brief annotation about the book, name of the publisher, and the date of publication. This book contains 250 pages and is illustrated. A cross-reference of topic information is also shown. Many cards include with their information a cross-reference to show the call number by the system not used in that particular library. For example, this same book, under the Dewey Decimal System, would be given a call number of 651.750711. The other information shown on the card would be similar under either system.

The card catalog is only one source of information for library material. Current information, in journals and other periodicals, is often best found by consulting one of the many indexes published for that purpose. *The Business Education Index* lists, by subject and author, all the recent articles and publications about business education. *The Education Index* similarly lists information in the field of Teacher Education. The *Business Periodicals Index, The Wall Street Journal Index,* and others list current information on a variety of business subjects. These indexes list the names of authors, titles of articles, names and publication dates of the journals and periodicals where the information may be found, and other information that may be helpful to the researcher. Often one can save considerable time by referring to these indexes.

Organization before and during the research will save hours of time and will simplify the task of gathering information. Failure to organize may result in fruitless search, a conglomeration of unorganized data, and an omission of the best and most timely information for the subject being considered.

Include in your system some method for cross-referencing of information. A separate bibliography card should be prepared for each book or article from which information is gathered. These cards can then be arranged alphabetically and numbered. Separate cards should then be used to list information from these sources. The information on the note cards can then be numbered to correspond to the bibliography card identifying the source. This kind of cross-reference is helpful in organizing the data for typing the results, for the preparation of footnotes, and for bibliographies. The use of almost any system of cross-referencing of information is superior to a haphazard, unorganized approach to the research problem.

Other good sources of information, in addition to the library, are company publications, dictionaries, encyclopedias, and almanacs. Some kinds of service organizations have accumulated files of information on their area of service and are usually willing to share that information.

Primary Research

Sometimes the researcher may find that information is unavailable or is insufficient to answer the purposes of the study. If this is so, you may need to generate the necessary data through interviews, questionnaires, direct observation, or from an experiment.

The *personal interview* is an effective way of gathering information from other people. Its success, however, depends on the preparation and the expertise of the interviewer. All the elements of tact, courtesy, and empathy must be used to obtain correct and useful information. The interviewer should make an appointment and identify the reason for the interview. A good knowledge of the subject and of the person being interviewed will help to assure the interviewee that the time is being well spent. This will also help the interviewer to control the flow of the questions and answers. Prepare the questions ahead of time, giving careful attention to see that they progress naturally, with each question getting support from the previous question. Don't talk any more than is necessary, and never argue. Remember that you are there to gather information. Argument will disclose your own prejudice and will stifle the free flow of information. Be prepared to receive inaccurate answers (given unintentionally or even intentionally) and answers that may be totally different from what you expected.

Remember the objectivity of your report. The interview must also be objective. Avoid personal questions that are not pertinent to your report. Keep the interview short. The person you are interviewing is likely to be busy. The cost of imposing on a busy time schedule will not help your interview.

Get permission to write down the interview information. Trying to rely on your memory will cause you to overlook or unintentionally distort some of the information. Getting permission ahead of time to write down the results of the interview will put the interviewee at ease as you make notes during the conversation. Be sure to include all the details that may be needed later to document your reporting of the interview.

While the interview offers some distinct advantages in gathering information, it has some limitations. The data gathered is often difficult to tabulate because it includes opinions, explanations, and other lengthy answers. Also, the time required for an interview seriously limits the number of people that can be included in the survey.

The *questionnaire* is an effective and often-used method of obtaining information. Many of the same guidelines for the interview apply for the questionnaire. That important quality called empathy was never more important than in the preparation of questionnaires.

The questionnaire is really in two parts. The first part (although not the first to be prepared) is the cover letter. This letter presents the questionnaire and solicits a response from the recipient. This cover letter may be the closest you will ever get to writing a sales letter. It requires *the* finest effort. Reader viewpoint must be evident. The letter should explain how the reader will ultimately or immediately be benefited by completing the questionnaire. Refrain from apologizing for intruding on the recipient's busy schedule or explaining what a "nuisance" questionnaires are. While these suggestions may seem too elementary, they point out the reason for many questionnaires ending up in the waste basket.

If the letter is well done, the reader will take a closer look at the questionnaire. What will he see? Perhaps *you* should take a close look at your questionnaire. Some questionnaires get discarded simply because they are so cluttered or so tightly grouped that they look formidable. Others contain long paragraphs of explanation or have large lined areas indicating that an excessive amount of writing and time may be needed. Examine *the* questionnaire for eye appeal.

The following checklist may help to solve some of the problems of the mechanics of questionnaire preparation.

Don't ask personal questions. Even if they are answered, the responses are not likely to be reliable.

Example: How often do you use deodorant?

Be certain that the wording is clear. Try to be sure that the reader will know what you mean.

Analyze your subject matter. Is a questionnaire the best method of getting the information you need?

Practice tabulating and evaluating the possible answers to your questions. Are the questions really pertinent to your study? Can the responses to your questions be tabulated or summarized in a meaningful way?

Prepare your questions in such a way that they are easy to answer. Some questions can be answered with a check mark in the appropriate place, others with a number, others by circling the correct answer. Questions that require sentences or paragraphs should be avoided. Even if they are answered, they are hard to tabulate.

Avoid wording that suggests the answer you want. Don't give the impression that you have an ax to grind or that you are expressing a gripe.

Arrange your questions in logical sequence. This will help the reader to see the value of the questionnaire.

Keep your questionnaire short but complete. A short questionnaire looks easy to complete and will invite the respondent to get started. However, be sure that you ask enough questions to get all the information you need.

Try out the questionnaire before you actually use it. Some feedback from a pilot sample, a few friends, or a class of students will help to get the bugs out of your questions. Then, revise it and try again before you use it on your sample.

An important part of the planning for your questionnaire will include some thought as to the makeup for your sample. To whom will you send the questionnaire? Why? How many people should receive it; and how will you select the names and addresses?

At this point, our communication of ideas will be helped with some mutual understanding of the common terms that may be associated with primary research—questionnaires, experiments, or observations. Since many of these terms will be used in explaining this kind of research, learning their meaning will be helpful to you.

Population or universe is the complete set of individuals or measurements that has some common characteristic. This represents the total group about which we are interested in gaining information. For example, all students at Michigan State University may constitute a population. All housewives or all car owners may also be our population.

Sample is a subset of the population. Our sample may be 10 percent of the students at Michigan State University. *Random sample* refers to a selection process by which every individual in the population has an equal opportunity of selection. Selection by reference to numbers from a table of random digits is a common method of random sampling. A decision to send a questionnaire to every tenth name on an alphabetical list of the population is also an example of random sampling.

Variable is a property or characteristic that is subject to change. An *independent variable* (also called the experimental variable) is one that is fixed by the limits of the study or experiment. Sex, school grade, and color of eyes are examples of independent variables. *Dependent variables* are those characteristics that are being measured as a part of the study. Test scores, production rate, and number of errors are examples of dependent variables. A *constant* is a fixed value. It does not change. Pi (3.14159) is a constant; one hour is a constant.

Measures of central tendency refer to three kinds of "averages" about which the scores or observations in a test may be grouped. The most common measure of central tendency is the arithmetic mean, or simply *mean*. The mean is determined by summing the scores or observations of each individual in the sample and then dividing the total by the number of observations. The *median* is the midpoint of all the scores when they are arranged in ascending or descending order. The median score is literally at the 50th percentile, which means that 50 percent of the scores are higher and 50 percent are lower. The *mode* describes the score that occurs with greatest frequency. We may say that it is the most "fashionable" score.

Validity refers to the quality of a test to measure what it claims to measure. Even though validity is not absolute, it can be measured comparatively by statistical means.

Reliability is the quality of a test to measure consistently what it does measure. If a test is reliable, a student taking the same test twice within a short period of time will achieve the same score each time.

A *hypothesis* is a tentative explanation or solution to the problem that is being studied. The researcher may hypothesize that students using calculators will achieve significantly higher scores than those students who do not use calculators. This is a hypothesis. Or, he may assume that there will be no difference in the score of these two groups of students. This is a *null* hypothesis, or a hypothesis of no difference.

The definitions of these terms will not give you an in-depth understanding of the statistics involved in experimental studies. However, you will have an opportunity to apply these terms in further reading and as you pursue the writing of reports. For now, let us consider some of the other methods of gathering information by means of primary research.

Observation

Many kinds of information can be gathered simply by observing what is being done. If, for example, we want to determine whether brown or black shoes are more popular on our campus, we need only to post ourselves at some point where a representative sample of the population may pass by, and tally the number of black shoes and the number of brown shoes.

While this procedure may sound rather simple, we will need to exercise care to be sure that our results are valid. For example, we may not necessarily be correct in saying that more men on campus wear black shoes if our observation took place at a formal dance.

The observation method may be used to perform a time-analysis study in a classroom or a business office. This method is often used to measure traffic flow patterns and attendance at games or similar events.

Experimentation

Experimentation is one of the most important methods of scientific research. A well-planned experiment is effective in the gathering of information for many kinds of studies, since it measures changes that are brought about by certain variables.

An *experiment* is a test or series of tests to determine the validity of a hypothesis or to measure the effect of certain variables as they are applied in an otherwise controlled situation. A scientist may conduct an experiment to measure the effect of adding increasing amounts of a chemical to some known substance. A teacher may conduct an experiment to determine which textbook promotes the most rapid learning of some academic principle. A manufacturer may conduct an experiment to determine the best method of packaging a product to promote marketability. We are finding many more ways to use the experimental method in solving business problems.

Because most experiments are designed to measure change, the researcher must consider some method of testing. Since there are so many kinds of tests, both written and performance-oriented, some very special attention should be given to the design of the testing procedure you will use.

Assume that a manufacturer wants to measure the effect of various kinds of background music played in a room where workers are assembling electronic components. This experiment would likely start with some measure of the output of the workers without any kind of music. Then, by introducing soft, classical music followed by a test of worker output, then loud, hard rock music followed by a test, and other qualities and intensities of music, each followed by a test, the researcher might be able to determine that a certain kind of music, or no music at all, produces the best results from workers in the assembly room.

This describes a simple pretest-posttest design. Note that the variable here is the music. Bear in mind that the experiment should be conducted with every effort made to control all the other elements of the surroundings so that to all intents the only variable is the music.

Assuming that our design and controls are flawless, we have a valid test and the results are reliable. However, other variables may have an effect on our study. For example, what is the effect of time? Suppose that production increases significantly for one hour with a certain kind of music, then decreases steadily as that music continues. Then time becomes a variable that should be considered. The workers may increase their output, regardless of the kind of music, simply because they realize they are part of an experiment. This is referred to as the Hawthorne Effect as the result of a classic experiment in the 1920s.[1] Careful attention to our design will help to eliminate this kind of problem.

1. The Hawthorne studies were conducted at the Hawthorne plant of Western Electric Company. The output of workers was measured at varying degrees of light intensity. Regardless of the direction of change in light intensity, production increased for the experimental group and also for the control group. The conclusion was that social forces rather than the experimental variable of light intensity accounted for the change. Many worthwhile side effects resulted from this study, including a change in understanding of human relations and the importance of worker attitude. These studies were conducted by Elton Mayo and others. The following books are among those that give a detailed account of this experiment.

Elton Mayo, *The Human Problems of an Industrial Civilization*, 2d ed. Division of Research, Harvard Business School (New York: Macmillan Co., 1946).

F. J. Roethlisberger and W. J. Dickson, *Management and the Worker* (Cambridge, Mass.: Harvard University Press, 1939).

As with the other methods of gathering information, the experiment must be carefully planned. The researcher must understand the problem and be able to state it clearly. The possible results of the experiment should be formulated. These can be stated as hypotheses, which can then be tested to see whether they are true. Some guidelines will help the researcher to make this determination. For example, in the testing of individuals or groups, some change is likely to occur just as a matter of chance. Some understanding of statistics will help to assign this area of change to chance. Any change beyond this limit can then be attributed to the experimental variable that is being measured. The researcher must also determine how much change is significant for that particular experiment. The following hypothesis illustrates this point.

> Hypothesis: There will be no significant difference in the performance of assembly workers regardless of the kind of music played during working hours.

This hypothesis, which is stated in null terms (hypothesis of no difference), can then be tested as a part of the experiment. The researcher must determine beforehand what is meant by *significant* and will likely qualify this hypothesis by stating that the variable will be tested at some statistical "level of confidence." If the decision is made to test this at the .05 level of confidence, this means that the researcher is willing to assume that the measured change could be the result of chance 5 percent of the time. By applying a rather simple statistical test of the data, the researcher can determine whether the hypothesis can be accepted. The details of such a test and the statistical formulas that are available can be found in most introductory statistics textbooks. The researcher who gets involved in this type of experiment should become familiar with such a text or seek the help of a statistician. For our purposes here, an understanding of these terms and some of the ways in which the experiments may be used will help in gathering the information needed for many kinds of reports.

Summary

Reports are an important method of presenting business information and are written in response to many kinds of problems for which answers are needed.

Reports are classified according to the style in which they are written, the length, the function or purpose, and the frequency of their occurrence. The dividing line for the various kinds of reports is not always clear. The report writer should develop the report on the basis of a clear understanding of the problem, the audience for whom the report is prepared, and the purpose for which it is prepared.

Research is vital to the preparation of most reports. The research may be based on source material compiled by others (secondary), or the material may be originally developed by the report writer (primary). The library, or some other collection of books, periodicals, or other reports, is the most common source of secondary research. Primary research may be conducted through personal or group interviews, questionnaires mailed or delivered to a representative sample of individuals, or through some kind of experiment. By these methods the report writer will gather facts, determine present conditions, and measure change as the bases for arriving at conclusions on which business decisions can be made.

Many kinds of report problems will require a combination of primary and secondary research. Whatever method is used, careful planning and a clear understanding of the problem will help to get one started toward gathering the necessary data for making intelligent decisions. In the next two chapters, we will see how this information can be used to produce the final report.

1. Explain the relationship between the ability to organize the report and the ability to communicate effectively.
2. How does the note from Don to Joe (fig. 13.1) qualify as a report?
3. What are some basic differences between formal and informal reports?
4. Decide on some problem associated with registration on your campus and write a concise, clear statement of that problem. Compare your statement with those of other students.
5. How would you go about gathering data for the following situations? Explain whether your methods would be primary or secondary research.
   a) You need to know how your school's registration process compares with that of a similar school.
   b) Should beginning shorthand students spend more time reading shorthand than writing shorthand, or vice versa?
   c) Should your company support unionization?
   d) Outline historical trends in business education.
   e) Recommend an inventory control plan for Company X.
6. Explain the difference between reliability and validity.
7. Explain how a knowledge of the Hawthorne Effect would be helpful in setting up a design for an experimental study.
8. For your problem in Question 4, state a hypothesis that could be tested. Then state the same idea as a null hypothesis.
9. For the following scores, find the mean, median, and mode. 51, 57, 36, 39, 37, 49, 45, 66, 55, 51, 45, 51, 45, 51, 42, 44, 45, 34, 69. If our sample were larger, would the mean and the median tend to be further apart or closer together? Explain why.
10. Is it possible to get a truly representative sample by using the names listed in the telephone directory? Explain.
11. As a research analyst for XYZ Company, you have been asked to gather information and report on the advisability of switching to the use of credit cards for your charge customers. Using your imagination for this research and the report you will develop, supply the following information:
    a) Develop a problem statement or statement of the purpose of the study.
    b) What will be your population? Will you need a sample?
    c) Will you develop a questionnaire? use interviews? or rely on secondary research?
    d) How many possible factors can you identify for this problem? List them.
    e) Develop a title that would adequately describe your report.
    f) How would you classify your report according to the guidelines listed in this chapter?

Interpreting and Organizing Report Information

14

The study of information in this chapter will aid the reader to:

1. interpret business data. Included are:
   a) Barriers to Interpretation
   b) Methods of Interpretation
   c) Use of Visual Aids

2. develop the report outline through the application of empathy and by the sorting of the report information.

3. apply writing fundamentals to the reporting process.
Emphasis is placed on the factors of readability and parallelism.

The gathering of information from the primary and secondary sources may produce a sizable stack of unorganized bits of data. Before this mixture of facts can be turned into an effective report, it must be interpreted and organized into logical sequence. Only when these steps have been completed can one proceed with the final typing of the report.

Interpreting Business Data

The report writer must have a clear understanding of what the data really mean before making a decision as to their value to the report. Even as we considered the necessity for getting a complete understanding of the problem before we started our research, so must we now understand how our information relates to our original problem as background, as explanation, or as a solution. The facts themselves may be of little value until the writer gives them meaning.

Barriers to Interpretation

To help in the task of interpreting information, let us examine some of the barriers to objective interpretation. One of these barriers is the mental attitude or the mind preset of the writer. This problem was alluded to in the guidelines for the preparation of the questionnaire. Few problems can be so destructive of report effectiveness as evidence of writer bias. This problem may be revealed in the title of the report, in the statement of the problem, or in the interpretation of the data. As the writer, you may be unaware that your attitude is showing. Consider the following example of a report title:

A STUDY OF SEX DISCRIMINATION PRACTICED BY THE PERSON-NEL DEPARTMENT OF THOROX INDUSTRIES

—or this example of a problem statement from another report:

The purpose of this study was to show that the Baramco Plant should be built at Site C.

In each of these examples, the reader would likely to get the impression that the report may be presenting a one-sided view of the issue. The title in the example appears to assume that sex discrimination does exist, and the problem statement indicates that the writer is already convinced that the plant should be built in a certain place. Evidence of this kind of prejudice may seriously stifle the objectivity of the report.

Suppose that we obtained identical mean scores for an experimental group which had been exposed to a new teaching principle (the experimental variable) and a control group. An unbiased writer might simply state that there was no difference in the scores. However, a biased writer might explain that, while there was no difference in the scores, the "expressed opinions of many of the participants indicate that Method C is better."

Some errors in interpretation may be caused by the inability of the writer to analyze the data correctly. This shortcoming can often be remedied by consulting with others who may be more knowledgeable in some of the areas covered by the data. Statisticians, students, teachers, business executives, and others may be willing to share their knowledge and point out aspects of the data that would otherwise go unnoticed.

Another problem in interpretation may be caused by an attempt to compare data that are not really comparable. Our data may show that the majority of high achievers at a college in Wisconsin are blue-eyed. A careless researcher may interpret this to mean that blue-eyed people are high achievers. A wiser researcher may find that the majority of ALL students at that college—including the low achievers—are blue-eyed.

Closely related to this problem is a fallacious cause-effect relationship. A high positive correlation may exist between the length of women's hemlines and the water level in the Great Lakes. Shall we assume that one causes the other; and if so, which is the cause and which is the effect? After extensive tests showed a high correlation between smoking and lung cancer, the researchers concluded that smokers have a greater tendency to incur lung cancer. However, some die-hard, habitual smokers concluded that those people who are susceptible to lung cancer have a tendency to smoke.

Extensive and careful testing is an aid to objective, accurate interpretation. Perhaps even more important than careful testing, however, is the cultivation of a proper attitude toward the problem. Exercise care to avoid trying to prove that some preconceived notion is correct or jumping to conclusions that have not been carefully thought out. Conducting a negative test will often help avoid this pitfall. In this test, the researcher tests an interpretation that is directly opposite to one which has been reached. Each conclusion is then analyzed carefully and logically to see which, if either, should be retained.

Methods of Interpretation

The writer has the responsibility of interpreting the information for the reader. The reader relies on this interpretation and uses it to follow the flow of communication in the report. For this reason, the writer's narrative of the interpretation should follow closely the data to which it applies. The reader can then more easily relate the data to the overall message of the report. An explanation of the relevance of certain information will help the reader to understand the data and to tie everything together in a smooth flow of the discourse.

Statistical techniques are often helpful in interpreting data. The mean, median, and mode represent certain kinds of "averages" or indications of midpoints in the observations of individual scores. You have learned from chapter 4 that words do not, of themselves, have meaning. Equally true is the statement that a score, by itself, does not have meaning. It takes on meaning only when it is compared with other scores or with some other statistic referring to other scores. A look at some facts relating to the following scores from Groups A and B may help to picture this.

GROUP	SCORES
A	59, 77, 78, 80, 82, 82, 84, 87, 88, 90, 90, 94, 99
B	59, 62, 70, 80, 80, 84, 84, 90, 94, 95, 95, 98, 99

Consider first the similarities for each of these groups of scores. For example, the mean in each of these groups is 84.30. The range of scores (41) is also identical for each of the groups, and the number of scores in each group is 13. The median score is 84 for each of the groups. However, when we compare a score of 94 with the other scores in Group A, the comparison is different from the same comparison in Group B. In Group A, only one score is higher, whereas in Group B, four scores are higher. This should serve as a word of caution to induce a careful and accurate interpretation of this kind of data.

One of the most-used methods of comparison is to relate a certain score to the mean of the scores for that group. We can then express that score as being a certain value above or below the mean. A problem arises, however, when the array of scores includes a few very high or very low scores. Assume that in checking the I.Q. of 12 mentally retarded students we find that one has a surprisingly high I.Q. of 120. Our scores may look like this: 120, 80, 70, 70, 68, 66, 64, 64, 64, 64, 62, and 60. The mean for these scores is 71, which is higher than all except two of the scores of the group. Obviously, the mean is not really representative of the group.

This problem can be handled by excluding the lowest 25 percent and the highest 25 percent of the scores. When these two *quartiles* are eliminated, the middle 50 percent *(the interquartile range)* remains. The scores in this interquartile range are usually grouped more closely about the measures of central tendency. The interquartile range for our I.Q. scores would include 70, 68, 66, 64, 64, and 64, with a mean of 66.

This comparison has a serious limitation, however, in that it cannot be used to express any mathematical relationships that may be basic to our final interpretation of the data.

Still another method used for interpreting data is to compare by reference to a *ratio*. A ratio is an expression of the relationship between two values and is shown as the quotient of one value being divided by the other. If we find that of 105 people, 21 have the same opinion, we can say that the opinion is shared by a ratio of 1:4. Notice that our comparison here is between the 21 people who share the opinion and the 84 who do not. If we state the same idea as a percentage, we would say that 20 percent of those sampled were of this same opinion. Exercise care to see that the wording correctly indicates what is being compared.

Other statistical models and formulas will help in the interpretation of data. Before getting involved in areas that may be unfamiliar to you, seek the help of a qualified statistician. This will help you not only to avoid erroneous interpretation but also to find meaning for information and conclusions that might otherwise be overlooked.

Use of Visual Aids

The saying "A picture is worth a thousand words" is certainly true in the interpretation of research data. For the researcher as well as the reader, some kind of visual aid often will explain more than many pages of words.

Since the general purpose of the report is to communicate, this objective should receive our highest consideration in the selection and use of the pictures, charts, graphs, and tables we use. Many kinds of visual aids are possible. Most report writers will need to develop their own to fit the specific requirements of their report.

Various kinds of bar graphs are often helpful in portraying data. The reader can interpret the information at a glance and can see the visual display of *differences* that may not otherwise be obvious.

Figure 14.1 shows a simple bar graph with captions to indicate the nature of the parts of the graph.

Other kinds of bar graphs are helpful in pointing up differences and relationships. This kind of chart can be adapted to show changes in both directions from the central point. A multiple-bar chart can be used to show rather complex comparisons. Such charts are easy for the reader to interpret and will save many pages of explanation if carefully prepared. Figures 14.2 and 14.3 are some examples of bar graphs. Depending on the kind of information being depicted, the bars may be shown either vertically or horizontally.

A very popular and useful kind of visual aid is the pie chart (fig. 14.4). The round figure is divided into sections representing individual pieces of pie. The size of each section represents the proportionate share of the whole "pie."

The pie chart should always include figures (usually percentages) to represent the real value of each of the sections. One drawback to this kind of visual aid is the difficulty the viewer has in assigning relative values to the individual sections.

Another kind of visual aid that is interesting but of limited real value is the picture graph or pictograph. This kind of aid may, for

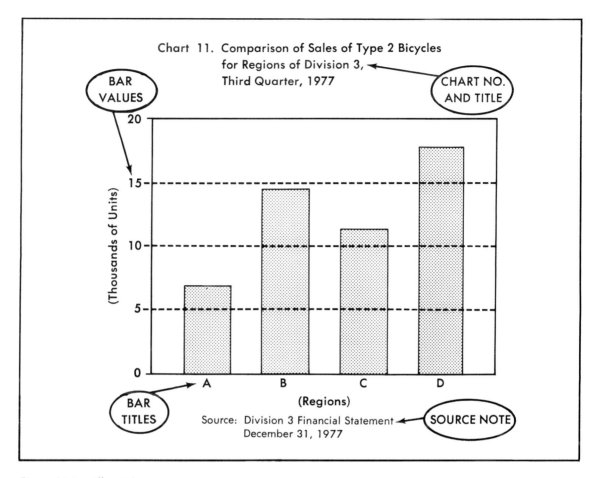

Figure 14.1 Illustration or chart preparation and identification

example, use pictures of ships of different sizes to represent the tonnage of imported merchandise. A ship of a certain size for the year 1966 may represent 50,000 tons of a certain product. If the tonnage for 1978 was 75,000 tons, the ship depicted for that year would be 50 percent larger. A serious limitation is that the human eye cannot discern the real value of these differences in size.

Another use of the picture graph involves objects of the same size, each having a fixed value. The changing values then are shown by the addition or omission of a certain number of the objects. This is often used for showing the population density or population changes.

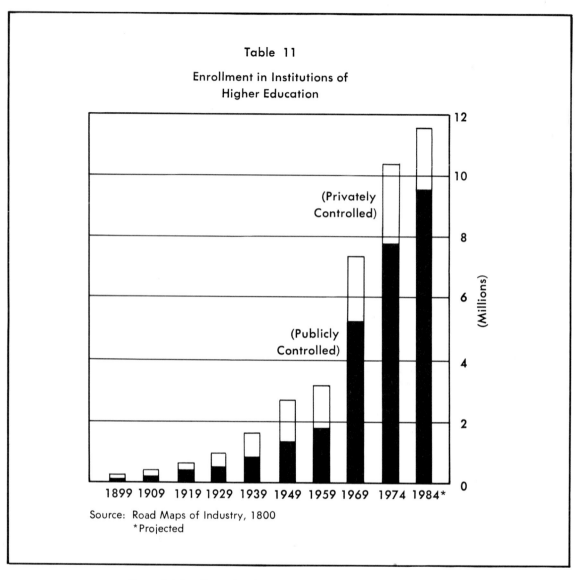

Table 11

Enrollment in Institutions of
Higher Education

(Privately
Controlled)

(Publicly
Controlled)

1899	1909	1919	1929	1939	1949	1959	1969	1974	1984*		

(Millions)

12

10

8

6

4

2

0

Source: Road Maps of Industry, 1800
  *Projected

Figure 14.2   Example of
bar graph

A small figure of a man or woman, for example, may represent 100,000 people. Ten such figures would represent one million people. To show a population change to 850,000, the writer would show eight full figures and one half-figure. While this may be very interesting, other kinds of charts would probably do a more practical job of depicting this kind of information.

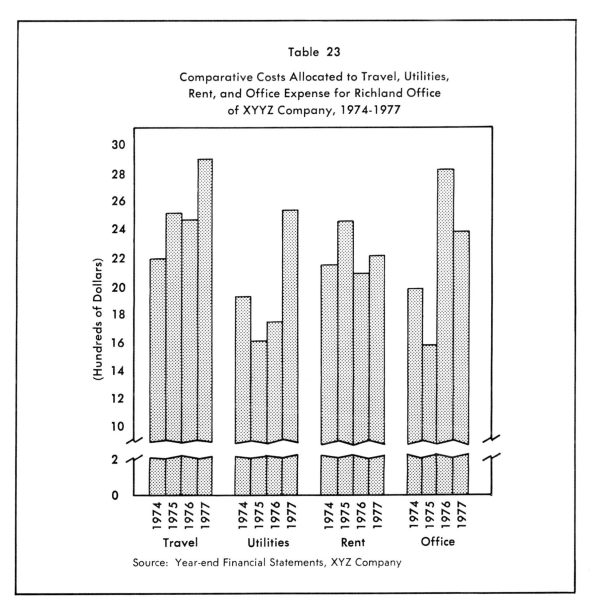

Table 23

Comparative Costs Allocated to Travel, Utilities,
Rent, and Office Expense for Richland Office
of XYYZ Company, 1974-1977

Source: Year-end Financial Statements, XYZ Company

Figure 14.3   Example of
multiple-bar chart with
scale break

Perhaps the most used of these statistical visual aids is the line
chart (figure 14.5), one of the best ways of showing change over the
passage of time. This change is shown by a solid line drawn from some
beginning to some other point on a grid. The grid shows the time

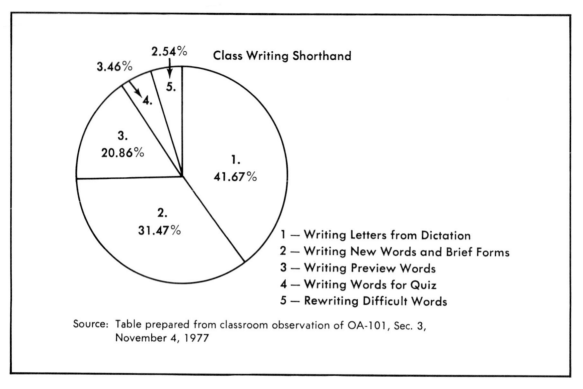

Figure 14.4   Illustration
of pie chart

series plotted along the horizontal (X) axis while the element to be measured is plotted along the vertical (Y) axis.

The line chart is also useful for showing two or more series by adding more lines to the grid (fig. 14.6). This multiple-line chart is usually limited to four or five series because of the need to distinguish between the lines. The differences in the lines can be shown by colors or by a difference in the makeup of the various lines.

Other kinds of visual aids may include flow charts, diagrams, or photographs. Whatever kind you may choose, design it to help the reader to understand your report data.

Developing the Report Outline

In addition to the actual interpretation of our data, we will probably engage simultaneously in some process of classifying and sorting the findings into usable categories. This classifying will reveal certain

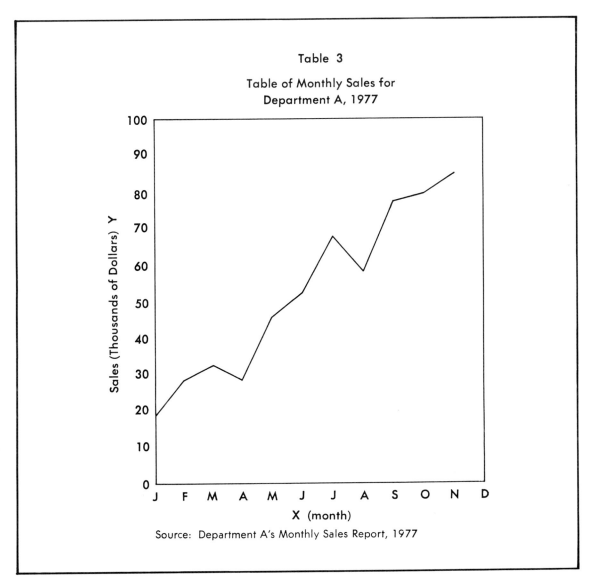

Table 3

Table of Monthly Sales for
Department A, 1977

Source: Department A's Monthly Sales Report, 1977

Figure 14.5   Example of
single-line chart

relationships about the data and will help you to visualize its contribution to the total plan. The overall process will be helped if we
formulate some plan for the outline of the report.

A thorough understanding of the communication process is at
least as important in report writing as in any other kind of writing.
Because of the time required to research and prepare a worthwhile

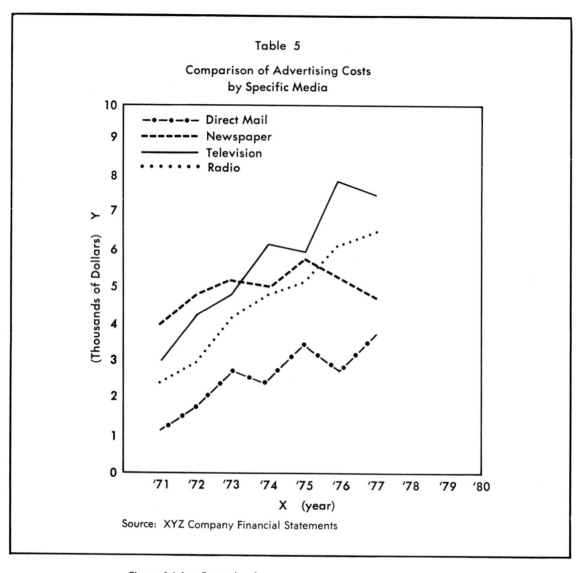

Table 5

Comparison of Advertising Costs
by Specific Media

—•—•—•— Direct Mail
– – – – – – Newspaper
———— Television
• • • • • • Radio

(Thousands of Dollars) Y

X (year)

Source: XYZ Company Financial Statements

Figure 14.6   Example of
multiple-line chart

report, all the elements of effective writing must be evident in our first attempt. As a report writer, you will seldom be in a position to rely on more than a single communication cycle to complete the transfer of meaning. For this reason, you will want to be sure that the report will do its job.

Applying Empathy to Report Writing

From your understanding of the psychology of letter writing, you remember that certain messages tend to be received more favorably than others. For this reason, some letters are written in the direct order while others are written in the indirect order. The same procedure will work as you plan your report.

As you interpret your data, you will probably find that your study points toward certain conclusions. How will those conclusions be received and understood by your readers? This question is similar to the question you asked before you formulated the message of your letter. If the reader is likely to receive the message of your report with an unfavorable reaction or needs a carefully presented foundation of facts to understand the main theme of the report, you will do better to present your information in the indirect order. On the other hand, information and conclusions that will be easily understood or favorably received should be presented in the direct order.

Assume that a study is made regarding the feasibility of purchasing a competitive company that would be operated as a subsidiary of your company. The information you have gathered indicates that the move would in the long run be a wise one. However, the present outlay of funds is not likely to receive vigorous support from those members of management who will make the decision. So you will most likely want to present your report in the indirect order. A premature disclosure of the recommendation to make such a purchase may establish barriers to an objective reading of the balance of the report. Your ability to empathize with the reader will help you to determine the psychological outline that should do the best job.

Having made your decision as to the format for your report, you will now want to study your data to determine how best to use it to contribute to your plan. Two important reminders here will help. Remember the objective nature of the report. Empathize with your reader. Any evidence of bias or attempts to manipulate the data will destroy the effectiveness and the credibility of the report.

The following examples show the variation in the direct and indirect approach to a common report topic. Only the briefest outline of ideas is shown to illustrate this comparison.

Clara Mitchell should be dismissed from her service as a secretary in the Marketing Department.

Clara's abrasive nature is a source of constant conflict with and among the other employees in the Marketing Department. Furthermore, her misuse of the company's sick-leave policy makes her undependable during times of greatest secretarial need. She was absent fifteen days during the last three months and claimed sickness as the reason each time. Eight of the absences were confirmed to be due to causes other than sickness. Therefore, Clara Mitchell should be given notice of dismissal.

Now compare this direct approach with the following indirect approach to the same problem.

Clara Mitchell has been a secretary in the Marketing Department for four months. During the past three months, she has been absent from work fifteen times. Sickness was listed as the cause each time. However, reasons other than sickness were found to be the cause for eight of these absences. Clara is often absent during the times when her secretarial services are sorely needed by others in the Marketing Department.

Clara is uncooperative and unfriendly with others in the Marketing Department. This has had a negative effect on other employees ever since Clara was hired four months ago.

For the good of the company and the Marketing Department, Clara Mitchell should be given notice of dismissal at once.

Sorting the Information

Once you have developed the outline by which you will present your report data, you are ready to sort your information according to that outline. Perhaps if we assume that each item of our information is contained on the separate note cards described under "Secondary Research" in chapter 13, we can visualize this process. The information on this stack of cards could probably be categorized according to that part of the report to which it contributes.

Some of this information may be secondary research data that will help to establish the basis for the report. You will want to use this in your introduction. Some of your note cards will contain details of the methods you used to conduct your study. Others will summarize data or contain the conclusions.

For the initial sorting of your information you will probably be guided by the outline (direct or indirect) you decided upon. So, for the direct approach you will arrange your packages of data to fit the conclusion-to-details outline. For the indirect approach your arrangement will be from details to conclusion. While this is certainly an over-simplification of the outlining process, it will illustrate the mental procedure by which we can begin the sorting of our information.

To categorize printed material more accurately and to assist the reader to follow the patterns of thought, most writers will include headings and subheadings throughout the copy. These serve to introduce packages of information and to tell the reader what he is about to learn. These helps are of special importance to the report. The most important heading of all is, of course, *the title*. When you look for research information in the library, you are most likely guided by the titles of books and articles. The title should tell you what you will read about. For this reason, the title to your report should be chosen with special care. To the extent necessary, it should answer the questions who? what? where? why? when? and how? Notice that many of these questions are answered in the following title:

Audit Report for State of Oregon TREASURY DEPARTMENT, Salem, Oregon, January 1, 1977, to December 31, 1977.

and in the following:

Job Entry Requirements for Typists, Stenographers, and Secretaries in the Salt Lake City Area, 1968.

Special care in the selection of the title for your report may also serve to help you avoid subjects that are too broad or too narrow in scope.

This same degree of care should be exercised in the selection of additional headings and subheadings. Several systems of numerical and alphabetical outlining help to divide printed material into convenient units. The most common of these includes a combination of Arabic and Roman numerals, as well as alphabetic symbols.

I. (First degree)
    A. (Second degree)
        1. (Third degree)
            a) (Fourth degree)

(1) (Fifth degree)

(a) (Sixth degree)

II. (Second level of first degree)

Other systems, including a straight numerical system, are equally acceptable. The numerical system uses only numbers and decimals to designate each degree in the division of the chapter outlines. However, for most of our writing, the divisions can be adequately shown simply by a change in the placement or style of the typed heading or subheading. The following examples may serve to identify the parts of the report.

MAJOR HEADING OR CHAPTER TITLE

The major heading is centered and typed in all capital letters. It is triple-spaced above and below. For long major headings, use the inverted pyramid style and single space between the lines of the heading. The inverted pyramid style means that each typed line is shorter than the line above it.

SECOND DEGREE OF DIVISION

The first order subheading or second degree of division is typed flush with the left margin, and is in all capital letters. The caption is triple-spaced above and double-spaced below. For long captions, use an underhung indentation with single-spacing between the lines.

Third Degree of Division

This level of subheading is indented to align with the first line of the paragraph. It is triple-spaced above and double-spaced below. The major words are capitalized.

One drawback to the above system is that it is, for most practical purposes, limited to three orders of subdivision. If more subdivisions are needed, one of the previously described systems should be used.

An important matter of logic will help here as we consider the various possibilities for subdividing a report chapter. Within every level of subdivision, we must have at least two headings. Your logic will tell you that if anything is divided, the result will be at least two parts. Therefore, if you have identified a first degree of division of a chapter as Roman numeral I, you must later have also a Roman numeral II; a fifth degree identified as (1) must be followed by (2). This practice, of course, holds true for the three degrees in between.

Applying Writing Fundamentals

With your data having been interpreted and sorted into logical sequence, you are now ready to give some attention to the methods you will use to communicate that information to your audience. The writing fundamentals that you apply to letter writing are no less appropriate for the business report. Two of these elements seem to deserve special attention here because of the nature of reports. Because a great many reports are lengthy, and technical in nature, their readability should be such that the message is not obscured by excess verbiage or any other writing defect. And, because of the potential for listings, headings, and comparisons of ideas, the need for parallel structure increases in importance as we write our report. A look at these two elements will help us to smooth out our writing.

Readability

Before you wrote your business letter, you gave special consideration to your reader—you wrote to the reader's level of understanding and interest. This practice becomes even more important in the writing of reports. Whereas the letter was written for a single reader, the report may be for any number of people—from one to thousands. Furthermore, this audience may represent various levels of ability in reading skills.

A review of the communication process will remind you that one of the drawbacks to written communication is the limited number of cycles possible because of the time required for feedback. The time required to research and write the report usually limits the opportunity for meaningful feedback to one cycle. So you will want to be sure that your message is understood by as many members of your audience as possible. One method of accomplishing this is to match the readability of your report to the level of the lowest ability among the members of your audience.

From chapter 3 you learned that readability is generally determined according to sentence length and the number of difficult words. Special attention to these two elements will help you to write at a level appropriate to the understanding of nearly all who may read your report. This does not mean that the wording "talks down" to the reader; nor is the writing chopped into so many short simple sentences that the reader is left breathless as a result of hopping from sentence to sentence. The writing will, however, show the use of concrete words, sharp comparisons, and a smooth flow of ideas. Compound and complex sentences should not be ruled out but should be used wisely and sparingly, with appropriate transitional words and phrases to show similarity and contrast of ideas. This kind of writing will lead the reader from one idea to another and will build the foundation for understanding the analysis, conclusions, and recommendations in the report.

The use of personal pronouns is often an aid to readability. Unless you are limited by instructions and by a specific need for formality, consider using the personal writing style for the report. Some writers avoid the personal pronouns and attempt to meet the requirement for formality by substituting such words as *writer* or *author*. This results in a stilted writing style. Compare the following examples:

Personal:	I compared the three sets of scores.
Substitute:	The writer compared the three sets of scores.
Impersonal:	The three sets of scores were compared.
	or
	Comparison of the three sets of scores showed . . . . (Active voice)

Even though the use of personal language may aid in readability, there is, however, some risk that the report will lose its objectivity through a careless use of first person pronouns.

If you remember that you are writing to EXpress rather than to IMpress, you will be more likely to write from the reader's viewpoint. The facts of the report will be more easily understood when they are expressed in sharp, concise sentences. For some reason, many writers take on a different personality when they attempt to write. The desire to impress causes us to seek out pompous, vague words. These words are often referred to as "buzzwords." Users of buzzwords may casually drop an expression such as "functional logistical capability" into the conversation or into the report. The phrase, which means little or nothing, is intended to impress the listener or the reader who is not likely to admit that he doesn't know what it means.

Readability will generally be improved if we remember to think "short." Use short words, short sentences, and short paragraphs. Avoid phrases such as "In view of the fact that . . ." when "Because" will serve our purpose better. Why say "at the present time" when we mean "now"? Why tell a reader to "scrutinize the gratuitous specimen" when we mean "look at the free sample"?

Parallelism

Another factor that should be considered at this point is the need for parallel structure. Having learned from chapter 5 about the need for parallelism within sentences, we can now apply this principle to the report.

This need for parallelism may become more clear if we remember that the lack of parallelism results in a problem of grammatical structure often referred to as a *shift*. The reader's attention is shifted from one straight flow of thought because of some dissimilar structure in the sentence parts. Certainly we should avoid this kind of problem in the report.

Similar problems with parallelism occur in writing captions for the subdivisions of the chapters. Perhaps this can be seen more clearly if we examine the methods by which we can identify the captions we will use.

Just as the title must be chosen carefully to assure that it tells the reader what the report is really about, so must the captions be clear and descriptive of the sections they introduce. The captions used most often are noun phrases, sentences, participial phrases, and "decapitated" sentences. The following examples of subheadings show the use of these caption styles.

Noun phrase:	Changes in Unemployment National Distribution of Income
Sentence:	Unemployment Has Risen National Income Is Distributed Unevenly
Participial phrase:	Rising Level of Unemployment Balancing the Distribution of Income

Decapitated sentence:	Unemployment Rising During 1970s
	National Income Distributed Unevenly

Similar levels of subdivision within a chapter should use the same grammatical structure for the captions. The following captions lack parallelism.

1. Discount Accumulation
2. Premium Amortization
3. Expenses Should be Reimbursed

Items 1 and 2 are noun phrases, but item 3 is a sentence. The problem can be corrected by changing item 3 to a noun phrase—Expense Reimbursement—or by changing items 1 and 2 to complete sentences. Either is satisfactory providing the structure is the same for all the captions.

The problem with nonparallel structure may not always be grammatical. Failure to state captions according to logical groupings may also result in nonparallelism.

A. Increasing Cost of Education
B. Rising Food Costs
C. Problems of Unemployment

The first two captions talk about rising prices, but the third shifts to a different idea. Even though unemployment may be related to the other two headings, the relationship is not clear; the caption reflects an inconsistency in the expression of the ideas. Perhaps item C should be in a different section of the report or the title should be changed to show a relationship with the other two captions.

Summary

Once the report information has been gathered, the writer must commence the task of interpreting the information for the report readers. By understanding the barriers to effective interpretation, the writer can objectively present the report data in an interesting and understandable manner. Visual aids of various kinds will help the reader to get the most meaning from the data.

The report outline will generally follow the inductive approach. Regardless of the specific approach, the outline should be arranged in a logical sequence to lead the reader to the best understanding of the data. A well-organized method for identifying headings and subheadings will be especially helpful.

Since many reports deal with technical information, the writer has the added responsibility of presenting the information at a level of readability that is compatible with the reading ability of the reader(s).

Smoothness of the flow of information is promoted by good grammatical structure, effective use of transitional words and phrases, and by consistency in our word patterns. Failure to observe these guidelines results in awkward shifts in viewpoint and language that create barriers to understanding.

With the report information gathered, interpreted, and organized we are now ready to assemble it into final form so that it can be presented to our readers.

Chapter Exercises

1. Discuss the importance of charts, graphs, or other visual aids in reports. Include some guidelines for determining titles for graphs, their placement within the text, and the writer's responsibility for their interpretation.
2. Explain the relationship between objectivity and impersonal writing style as applied to report writing. What are some writing problems associated with impersonal style?
3. "It is impossible to interpret data for a report reader without showing some kind of bias." Discuss this statement.
4. What additional information would you need to interpret a score of 92?
5. Explain the difference in comparing by ratio and by percentage.
6. What kind of chart or graph would you use to depict the 1976 and 1977 sales of the nine sales offices covering the United States?
7. An analytical report that fails to come to some definite conclusions and recommendations is obviously based on a defective design. Discuss this statement.
8. Discuss the logic in having two or more subdivisions of a section or none at all.
9. Because some reports contain very technical information, we cannot be concerned about the readability level of our writing. Discuss.
10. Can you see any defect in the following captions listed under a major heading? Explain.

    a) Findings Regarding Preemployment Testing of Applicants
    b) Policies of Businessmen in Screening Applicants
    c) Findings Show Higher Regard for Personal Characteristics

Presenting the Report

15

As a result of reading this chapter, you will get an understanding of the physical properties of the report as it is put into final form for presentation to your audience. Specifically you will be able to:

1. identify the parts of the report and the logic of their order of appearance in the report.

2. recognize the function of each of the report parts.

3. determine methods and reasons for proper documentation of the report data.

4. understand the importance of the appearance of the report and receive some guidelines to assure a good first impression of the report.

Putting the report into its final form may require the finest efforts of the report writer. Even the best job of researching, interpreting, and organizing of report information may be for nothing if the final package is so poorly presented that it fails in its bid for recognition.

This final package must meet certain basic requirements to accomplish its purpose. Here, in this chapter, we will consider the parts that will make the report complete and the appearance of the final package that will set the stage for the appropriate relationship between the writer and the reader.

Parts of the Report

You will remember that the short, informal report may consist of nothing more than a penciled note giving information to a co-worker. A long, formal, research report may consist of hundreds of pages with the necessary supplementary parts for guiding the reader through its complexities. Between these two extremes we may have any number of variations and any number of report parts. For our purposes here, let us consider the long report to describe the many possible parts and to explain their functions. Then we will see how certain parts can be eliminated for the shorter reports. This explanation will present the report parts in order of their appearance in the completed report.

The Title Fly

The title fly (or flyleaf) will be used in only the most formal reports. This is a page containing only the title of the report. The report title is typed in solid capital letters and is usually underscored. The title should be slightly above center vertically and centered horizontally.

If the title is so long that it takes up more than one line, it should be typed with the longest line at the top and each succeeding line shorter than the preceding line. This is referred to as the inverted-pyramid style.

Even though most reports will not require the use of the title fly, its use will enhance the formal reports where it is used.

The Title Page

The title page contains the title and other factual information which will help to introduce the report to the reader. Many universities and businesses have their own style of format for this page, so it would be inappropriate to describe the ideal title page layout.

In addition to the title, the title page will generally disclose the name of the person or agency for whom the report was prepared, the name of the writer, and the report date. Sometimes additional information—the purpose or the authorization of the report—may be shown. This information is generally shown in either a three-part or a four-part display with appropriate spacing to enhance the appearance of this page.

Letter of Transmittal

The letter of transmittal is an actual letter from the report writer to the recipient of the report. This letter is a means by which the writer presents the report to the reader and acknowledges the authorization for the report. The letter of transmittal (usually written in personal language) is also an appropriate place for the writer to express any personal feelings regarding the report and its use. In effect, the letter of transmittal says, "Here is the report you asked for." Although this letter may contain some writer's comments about the report, it is usually kept quite brief.

The letter of transmittal may take the place of, or be replaced by, a foreword or a preface. Their purpose is to help the reader to understand the report. They may contain suggestions about the background of the report and its use. No special format is required for the preface or foreword. Usually, they will be shown with the one-word heading to identify them and will contain a brief statement introducing the elements of the report.

Table of Contents

As the name implies, the table of contents is a listing of the contents of the report by page number. The same typing style and placement of captions is generally used in the table of contents as is used throughout the report. This table lists the major headings and subheadings, and gives the number of the page on which each appears, to aid the reader in finding sections of the report that are of special interest. Sometimes the subheadings may be grouped in a paragraph of captions listed under the major heading. These two variations are shown here.

Alternate method:

Notice that "leaders" are used between the caption and the page number. These leaders are made by typing the space-period-space period combinations across the line. The periods should be aligned vertically to add to the readability and neat appearance of the table.

List of Tables

Closely related to the table of contents and similar in appearance is the list of tables. This is a listing of the tables, charts, or graphs that appear in the report. A report with few or none of these aids would have no use for a list of tables. On the other hand, a report with numerous visual aids may have separate lists of tables, charts, figures, etc. Where used, the list of tables would show the table number, the title of the table, and the page number on which the table is located.

Synopsis

The synopsis may be one of the most important of the report parts because it contains the report body in miniature. For that reason, a great deal of attention will go into its preparation. Synopses may vary in length, but they should be products of conciseness. Your synopsis should represent your best effort at writing with directness and clarity.

Because the reader of your report is likely to be a busy person, the synopsis will help to gather together the essential facts and conclusions, so give a "thumbnail sketch" of the entire report.

One weakness commonly observed in synopses is the tendency of the writer to summarize only the findings or conclusions. Remember that the synopsis is the report in miniature. Each major part of the report proper should be represented proportionately in the synopsis. In condensed form you will present your introduction, review of literature (if applicable), methods, findings, and conclusions. With the best planning, this can often be done in one or two pages.

Since the purpose of the synopsis is to save time for the busy reader, it will serve little or no purpose in a short report. Consider the length and nature of your report in determining whether a synopsis would be of value.

The Body of the Report

All of the foregoing may be referred to as prefatory or preliminary parts of the report. With these parts having served to introduce the report, the reader is now ready for the body of the report, or the report proper.

To a great extent, the order of the arrangement of the parts of the report will be determined by your decision to write in the direct or the indirect order. Since most reports are written in the indirect order, that order is shown in the following outline. Remember, however, that the direct approach is used for reports, as for letters, on subjects that your logic indicates will be favorably received.

Typically, the research report will include an introduction, a review of related literature or historical background, the findings of the study, and a summary. Some of these topics may be combined with other topics, some may be eliminated, and others may be added, depending on the scope and the nature of the report. For example, a review of related literature would be inappropriate if the study involves a problem on which no previous literature has been compiled. For some studies, the methods and procedures would be included in the introduction; for other reports, a separate section or chapter may be added to include these topics. Our purpose here is to show some guidelines for a long, formal, research report. As the length, formality, and extent of research decrease, parts may be combined or eliminated to suit the needs of the researcher and the situation.

The INTRODUCTION, as the name implies, introduces the reader to the problem that will be discussed in the report. The purpose of the study is explained and tentative solutions or answers to problems (hypotheses) may be given. This section of the report should also include some information as to the reason for the study, the methods that will be used to achieve the objective(s) of the report, and other information that will help to set the stage for the report reader. The following shows an outline of subheadings that may be used in the introduction to an experimental study which involves students in classroom situations.

INTRODUCTION

THE PROBLEM
    Purpose of the Study
    Hypotheses
    Questions
    Definitions
    Delimitations
METHODS AND PROCEDURES
    Variables
    Registration Procedures
    Orientation and Assignment to Sections
    Pretest
    Presentation of Course Material
    Posttest and Evaluation

Some explanation here will help to visualize the use and importance of some of these topics. The *purpose of the study* would include our statement of the problem or a statement indicating the purpose or the objectives of the study. *Hypotheses* were explained earlier. They are included in this section to acquaint the reader with the possible solutions or tentative explanations of the problem with which the study is involved. These should be carefully stated so as to show no prejudice. Many reports are strengthened by the writer's asking of certain *questions* as though they were being asked by the reader. The assumption is, then, that the report will reveal answers to those questions.

The report writer has certain freedoms as well as obligations in the writing of the report. Since there may be occasion to use some words or phrases in a special way, there is often a need to include a section that offers *definitions* for those words and phrases. This helps the reader to know that the term means a certain thing when it is encountered in that report.

The *delimitations* of a study establish the boundaries or limits within which the study is concerned. The delimitations may list specifically the groups that are involved in the study, the time frame within which the study is concerned, or the specific location for the study.

The heading METHODS AND PROCEDURES indicates the inclusion of information describing how the study, research, or experiment was conducted. One important value of this section is that it makes possible a replication of the study by future researchers. This is often helpful as a means of testing certain other variables that may appear to be present but untested in the existing study. An immediate benefit of a good description of the methods and procedures is the credibility that it gives to the study. The reader is shown how certain variables were controlled or tested. An explanation of the selection of experimental and control groups assures the objectivity of the report.

The REVIEW OF RELATED LITERATURE section reports the gist of previous studies, articles, or books about the subject of your report. Some of this literature may offer partial answers to narrow your field of research, or in some other way may help in the establishing of guidelines for your study. If previous research is scarce or nonexistent, there is no reason to include this section.

This seems to be an appropriate place to discuss documentation. Library research, interviews, and some other kinds of research results in data that originated with someone other than the writer. The originator of the information should be given credit or recognition for the information. To fail to do so is an act of plagiarism or literary theft. While this was alluded to in chapter 12, you will need some guidelines here for the physical presentation of this documentation. The methods most used involve footnotes, an explanation within the narrative, or a bibliography. Often there is a combination of these methods. The use of explanation within the narrative is effective for only very limited references to outside sources. Too frequent or extensive references would break up the narrative and interrupt the flow of the message to the reader.

Perhaps the best method of documenting is to use the *footnote*. As the name implies, the footnote is a reference note at the foot of the page wherein mention is made of some information for which the writer is indebted to someone else. General information or common knowledge is not, of course, subject to this requirement. For other kinds of information, however, the documentation should include the name of the individual or source from which the information was taken, the name of the publication or details of the interview, the publisher's name (where applicable), date of publication, and the location of the material within the publication.

The examples in figure 15.1 show the format for footnotes documenting information from several kinds of sources. This list is only representative and not all-inclusive. Many colleges and universities have their own format, or base their recommendations on one of the numerous style manuals that furnish guidelines for the preparation of reports and term papers.

The footnote is indicated by superposing an identifying number immediately following the reference to material that should be documented.

He states that "grammar and spelling and punctuation are about as important as remembering to wear a tie to make a presentation to the Board of Directors, and for the same reasons."[33]

---

33. Richard A. Hatch, "Towards Some Behavioral Objectives for an MBA Business Communications Course," **The ABCA Bulletin** 35 (March 1972): 24.

The footnote explaining this notation would be typed at the bottom of this same page. The footnotes should be separated from the tex-

(Article in Periodical)

23. James M. Lahiff, "Motivators, Hygiene Factors, and Empathic Communication," *The Journal of Business Communication* 13 (Spring 1976): 15.

(Book)

42. Richard M. Hodgetts, *Management Theory, Process and Practice* (Philadelphia: W. B. Saunders Co., 1975), p. 296.

(Newspaper)

34. *San Francisco Examiner & Chronicle*, June 26, 1966.

(Unpublished Works)

14. W. L. Hutchinson, "Creative and Productive Thinking in the Classroom" (Ph.D. diss., University of Utah, 1963), p. 7

(Interview)

15. Statement by Robert T. Malgren, personal interview, March 12, 1977.

(Dictionary)

29. *The American Heritage Dictionary of the English Language*, 1976 ed., s.v. "computers." ["s.v." *sub verbo* "under the word"]

Note: While this is not a complete list of all possible references, it will serve as a guideline for most footnotes. Consult a style manual for types of sources not shown.

Figure 15.1
Examples of footnotes

tual material by a solid line one and one-half inches long. Use the same pattern for margins and indenting as used in the text and single-space within the footnote.

When this method of footnoting is used, the footnotes for all documented material should be typed on the same page as the one on which the reference is made. This requires some careful planning to assure ample room at the bottom of the typed material. Some suggestions are given later in this chapter that will help in this procedure.

Complete information should be shown in the footnote documenting the first reference to any particular work. However, two systems of abbreviations are used to refer to subsequent references to the same work. One long-used system uses the abbreviations for the Latin terms *ibidem, loco citato,* and *opere citato.* Even though these are Latin terms, their abbreviations are usually not italicized or underlined when used as part of footnotes.

Ibid. is used to refer to consecutive references to the same source. If the page number is the same for the second reference, the abbreviation alone is used. If the page number is different, indicate this by showing the page number of the second reference.

[23]Ibid.   [24]Ibid., p. 47.

Since this term means "in the same place," its use is restricted to *consecutive* references to the same author AND the same work. For nonconsecutive references, the term *"op. cit."* ("the work cited") may be used along with the last name of the author and the page numbers. If the nonconsecutive reference is to the same page number and the same volume, the term *"loc. cit."* ("the place cited") should be used instead of *op. cit.* Page numbers are unnecessary with *loc. cit.*

A method that is coming into greater use refers to the author by listing only the last name followed by an abbreviated title for the work and the page number(s) where the reference is found. This method replaces the Latin abbreviations *op. cit.* and *loc. cit.* and is used only *after the first reference has listed the complete information.*

Under certain guidelines, footnotes may be numbered within the text but grouped at the end of each chapter or at the end of the report. This method is convenient for the writer but has some drawbacks for the reader.

Footnotes may be needed in any part of the report and are discussed here only because of the greater likelihood of their need in a section dealing with previous research and literature that is related to the present study.

Exercise care in quoting or paraphrasing the words or ideas of another person. The precision to be used here goes so far as to include the quoting of unusual words or even mistakes attributed to the original writer. This can be shown by the use of brackets inclosing the Latin word *sic* immediately following the error, misspelled word or unusual expression. *Sic* means "thus, or so," and indicates that the word or phrase should be read as stated.

"He said that he judged a company by the tone of its correspondance [sic] and that he was no longer interested in doing business with them."

This explains to the reader that the misspelled word is quoted precisely and is not the typing error of the present writer.

Quotations of four or more words should be enclosed in quotation marks. Quotations longer than four typewritten lines should be single-spaced and indented.

The FINDINGS OF THE STUDY section or chapter includes the data or other facts that result from the methods and procedures used in the study. This is the part of the report wherein you will likely use graphs, charts, or tables that depict the scores or other values to be interpreted as a part of the study. Remember that this information is factual. Avoid any expressions of opinion that may disclose a bias. You should, however, interpret the data for the reader. After all, you are probably the most knowledgeable person anywhere as far as your report is concerned. You can help the reader by including meaningful visual aids, complete and accurate interpretations, and an explanation of the findings of the study. In this and the other parts of the report, use appropriate subheadings that will help the reader follow the report narrative.

The concluding part of the report body may have any one of a variety of names. Some possibilities are SUMMARY, CONCLUSIONS, or RECOMMENDATIONS. Or, the title for this section may include all of these names. The title should appropriately describe what the reader will encounter in this section. For example, if the report is analytical in nature, you will be making certain recommendations. The title should tell the reader that such is the case.

Some special attention should be given here to helping you preserve the objectivity of your report. Even though such terms as *conclusions* and *recommendations* may suggest that you can take special liberties to express opinions, stick to the facts. If you feel that an opinion is appropriate, be sure to state that it is an opinion. Otherwise, a skeptical reader may question the objectivity of your entire report.

Here, in the concluding section of your report, you will want to bring everything together for your reader. This is the "so what?" section of the report where you will tell the reader what the report has done to meet the stated objectives or to answer the problem that served as the basis for the report.

The conclusion of the report may simply state certain alternatives disclosed by the research. Or it may pull all the thoughts of the report together to help the reader see the relationship of the various parts of the report.

Typically, the final part of the report will be the recommendations. Here you will state what should be done as shown by the research findings. If the research has been conducted carefully and if the analysis was accurate, you are in a position to recommend some course of action to your reader. Vague language such as "It would probably be a good idea to try . . ." is inappropriate and shows the writer's lack of confidence in the research.

Many reports include a *summary* at the end of each section or chapter. These are helpful in bringing the ideas of that chapter together and setting the stage for the next chapter. A final summary that brings together all chapter summaries is also helpful. This would, of course, be unnecessary in a short report.

The parts of the body of the report have been referred to as parts, sections, or chapters. In the long, formal report, the parts may be classified as chapters with chapter titles identified as INTRODUCTION, REVIEW OF RELATED LITERATURE, etc. For other reports, these sections may be identified only as subheadings under two or more major headings. The writer should determine the method and designations that would be most helpful to the reader.

The Appendix

The part that follows the body of a major report is the APPENDIX. As the name indicates, this is a supplement that is added to the body of the report or book. Many items, such as charts or tables, may be so long that to include them in the body of the report would pose a barrier to the flow of the narrative. One of the guidelines given for the placement of the visual aids was that they should follow as closely as possible the first place they are mentioned. This helps the reader to refer to them for clarification. However, if the length or the nature of the material is such that to include it would cause too wide a gap in the wording of the report, we can help the reader more by including it in an appendix.

The appendix also includes other kinds of supplementary material such as technical data or other material that supports the research. If the appendix is long, or contains several kinds of information, it should

These entries correspond to the examples of footnotes already shown. They are listed in alphabetical order as though they applied to the same report.

American Heritage Dictionary of the English Language, 1976 ed.

Hodgetts, Richard M. *Management Theory, Process and Practice.* Philadelphia: W. B. Saunders Co., 1975.

Hutchinson, W. L. "Creative and Productive Thinking in the Classroom." Ph.D. dissertation, University of Utah, 1963.

Lahiff, James M. "Motivators, Hygiene Factors, and Empathic Communication." *The Journal of Business Communication* 13 (Spring 1976): 15-23.

Malgren, Robert T. Personal interview. March 12, 1977.

San Francisco Sunday Examiner & Chronicle, June 26, 1966.

Figure 15.2 Examples of bibliography entries

be separated into parts to help the reader. Usually a division such as Appendix A, Appendix B, etc. is appropriate to designate the appendix categories.

For most reports, the final part is the BIBLIOGRAPHY (see fig. 15.2). The bibliography consists of an alphabetical listing of all the references that contributed to the report. Other names for this section of the report include REFERENCES, REFERENCES CITED, or LITERATURE CITED.

The format suggested by some style manuals lists the bibliography entries by number according to the sequence of their citation within the text. The alphabetical listing is used most often and is the one described here.

Since both footnotes and bibliography entries are used to document the sources of material for the report, let us compare these two kinds of references. The first example below shows a footnote entry and is followed by a bibliography entry for the same reference.

45. George T. Vardaman and Patricia Black Vardaman, **Communication in Modern Organizations** (New York: John Wiley and Sons, Inc., 1973), pp. 357-381.

Vardaman, George T., and Vardaman, Patricia Black. **Communication in Modern Organizations.** New York: John Wiley and Sons, Inc., 1973.

Even though these entries list the same kind of information, some differences should be noted. For example, the footnote is numbered and lists the name in the usual sequence, whereas the bibliography lists the surname first as a means of alphabetizing. The example shown depicts the footnote format which would be used for printed manuscripts such as books and other published works. For typewritten manuscripts the first line of the footnote would be indented, and the reference number would be superposed with no space between it and the first word of the footnote. Successive lines would be single spaced, even though the manuscript would be double spaced. The first line of the bibliographic entry begins even with the left margin, but the succeeding lines are indented or *underhung*. Also note that the footnote shows the location of the reference within the work cited by listing the page numbers. The page numbers are not necessary in the bibliographic entry since we are referring to the work in its entirety.

Successive bibliographic entries for works by the same author need not repeat the name of the author. For the second entry, the name is depicted by a solid underline ten spaces in length, as for example:

Bacharach, Bert. **Book for Men.** New York: A. S. Barnes & Co., Inc., 1953.

————. **Right Dress—Success Through Better Grooming.** New York: A. S. Barnes & Co., Inc., 1955.

For reports with a great number and many kinds of references, the bibliography may be separated into categories identified as Books, Periodicals, Newspapers, and Other Sources. These separate listings help the reader to identify and locate specific references.

Some reports and many books may require an INDEX. This is an alphabetical listing of the important or key words and the numbers of the pages wherein the words are used in the text. The index is very helpful to the reader when used to seek out specific information.

Appearance of the Report

Even though this topic is considered in the final position of our discussion of reports, appearance is probably that factor which will make the first (and often the most lasting) impression on the reader.

For that reason, you will want to give some attention to those factors that affect the appearance of your report as it is presented to your readers. Two of these factors are the selection of the paper and the mechanics of the typing.

Choice of Paper

The choice of stationery was explained in chapter 7 as one of the factors that promote the effectiveness of our letters. This same guideline applies to reports. Choose a good quality of white bond paper. Paper in the 20-pound weight is usually superior to lighter weight paper. The corners are not so likely to curl, and the heavier paper is easier to handle.

Many universities and other agencies require a certain kind and quality of paper for reports, theses, and dissertations. A typical requirement may specify that paper of a certain rag content be used. The rag used in the production of paper improves the durability. Erasures are also easier on this kind of paper as there is less danger of rubbing a hole or otherwise marring the surface of the paper. Most paper of this quality contains a watermark. If you insert this paper so that you are typing on the same surface and in the same position as the watermark, you can be sure of adding a slight additional quality to the sharpness of the appearance of your report.

Typing

Attention to several mechanical factors will help to assure the best appearance for the presentation of your report. Be certain that the typewriter keys are clean to avoid a smudged appearance (caused by certain letters being filled in with debris that tends to build up on the keys). If you use a manual typewriter, type with smooth, even stroking to give your typing a uniform appearance. A good quality fabric ribbon or a polyethylene ribbon will also help to sharpen the appearance of the typing.

Typing-error corrections may be made in a number of ways. One of the most accepted methods involves the use of correction fluid. Several good brands are available with either a water base or a chemical base. These fluids consist of an opaque, white liquid (other colors are available for colored stationery) that is applied with a brush to cover the error. The correction can be typed as soon as the fluid is dry. This kind of correction is almost unnoticeable.

A good quality correction tape is often acceptable. This method requires restriking the error over a tape, which is covered with a chalk-like substance. This substance is deposited on the paper in place of the error, and the correction is then typed in the same place.

Of course, erasing is also generally acceptable. Follow a recommended technique for erasing to avoid smudging or wearing holes in the paper. Be sure the error is erased cleanly before typing the correction.

The appearance of your report will be enhanced if the typed material is arranged with some regard for eye appeal. Major headings should be carefully centered between the margins. The inverted pyramid style will improve the appearance of headings that are too long to be typed on one line.

Since most reports will be bound or stapled on the left, the margins should generally be established as follows: Top margin for the first page of a report and for the first page of each major section should be 1 1/2 inches or 2 inches. For other pages, use a 1-inch top margin. The side and bottom margins for all pages should be:

Left side—1 1/2 inches
Right side—1 inch
Bottom—1 inch

Most typists prepare a page-end indicator as a guide for determining the bottom margin. This is made from a standard sheet of paper, 8 1/2 by 11 inches. The numbers 1 to 33 are typed vertically line by line down the right edge of the paper to the center line, and the numbers 33 down to 1 are typed similarly on the lower half. This sheet can then be inserted behind the sheet on which you are typing so that the right edge with the numbers is visible. As you type down the page, a glance at this indicator will tell you when to stop typing the textual material, including footnotes and page numbers, to allow for the appropriate bottom margin.

An accepted method for typing the page numbers in a report is to type the number centered at the bottom 1 inch from the bottom edge of the paper and a double space below the last line of type for all pages that have major headings. For all other pages, type the page number on line 5 from the top and aligned with the right margin.

Two series of page numbers are used for reports. The first series consists of small Roman numerals used to number the preliminary pages of the report. The first page to be assigned a number is the title page. Its number is "i" (lowercase Roman numeral), but the number is not shown on this page nor on the page containing the letter of transmittal. All the other preliminary pages are numbered consecutively with small Roman numerals.

The first page of the report body is numbered with Arabic numeral "1" centered at the bottom of the page as indicated. This numbering continues through the body of the report, appendix, bibliography, and index.

Consistency and care in the preparation of the report will assure that the hours spent in gathering and organizing the data will not be wasted in a report that loses its effectiveness because of appearance. Even though your job may be finished with the writing of the report, remember that your reputation as a report writer will endure as long as the report itself endures.

Summary

The manner in which your report is presented to your audience may be as important as the methods by which you gathered and organized your data. The report parts should be organized in a logical manner so that the information flows smoothly for the reader.

The preliminary parts of the report will help to explain the organization of the report and to set the stage for the reader. The report body and the supplementary parts will give the reader the facts and documentation to supply the information necessary to understand and to act upon the message of the report.

The appearance of the report creates the first impression on the reader. Attention to the selection of the paper and the mechanics of typing will result in a report with good eye appeal.

Discussion Exercises

1. Explain some of the guidelines that should be considered in determining how many parts should be used in a report.
2. Discuss the value of beginning each chapter or section of a report with an introduction and ending with a summary. Are these examples of transitional aids?
3. Explain the logic in using two sets of numerals, Arabic and Roman, for the report parts. Why not use a single set and continuous numbering?
4. Discuss the value of using abbreviations to identify succeeding footnotes referring to the same source. Do you think it would be better to write out each footnote completely?
5. In your report, you are quoting part of a paragraph from another writer. You wish to omit an internal sentence which does not contribute to your report. How can you show this omission?
6. There is some variation in the recommendations for listing footnotes and bibliography entries. Regardless of the plan followed, what are some guidelines which should always be part of your plan?
7. What are some advantages and disadvantages of listing footnotes at the bottom of each page? at the end of each chapter? at the end of the report?

Chapter Exercises

1. Write a report recommending that a company (make up a name) publish a monthly employee newsletter.
2. Your Student Affairs office wants to know whether the student body would support an Art Exhibit. Income from tickets at $2 each would go to a charity. Make your recommendations.
3. Your university is considering dropping shorthand from the curriculum because "businesses just don't need secretaries with shorthand ability any more owing to the availability of dictation machines." Make your recommendations with appropriate support to the Curriculum Committee.
4. The Artworth Company employs twelve outside sales personnel, each of whom travels about 30,000 miles per year. The company furnishes them a new car every other year. Leasing of cars has been recommended, but the company owner—a very conservative, successful businessman—is concerned about the restrictions that could be caused by his not owning the cars outright. Of course, the cost of leasing is also a concern. Prepare a report in which you recommend for or against leasing, and substantiate your recommendations.
5. Recommend the use of an accelerated method of reporting depreciation in preference to the straight-line method presently used by

your company. Explain how this changeover would be made, legal restrictions on changing the method for existing assets, and any other problems management should know about.

6. Recommend alternative methods of evaluating and grading students.

7. Describe the ideal course content for students majoring in general business (or some other subject).

8. Report as to how the company stands to benefit from retirement programs, health and accident insurance programs, or some other fringe benefit.

9. Compare the attitudes of individuals, both as students in a business communications course and as the same person in administrative positions five years later.

10. Present a program for improvement of employee morale at Judson, Inc.

11. Write a report explaining the trend of unions during the past ten years. Relate this trend to its effect on white-collar workers.

12. Describe the effect of "right-to-work" laws in your state.

13. Report to Decker Sales on the cost and procedure for incorporating within your state.

14. Recommend an incentive pay program for the sales personnel (inside and outside sales) of the Artis Company.

15. Jaybar Company wants to know the effect of packaging on the sales of a beauty soap. Using your imagination or real data gathered through research, explain your findings and make some recommendations.

Report Writing Case

The bases for writing reports are as numerous as the problems that confront the thousands of business organizations every day of every year. The following case is adapted from one of these problems and is included as a basis for your report writing experience.

Since most report problems require that the writer make certain assumptions, you will need to use your imagination to fill in some details in this case in order to get enough information to form a foundation for your report. You may also need to make certain sound business decisions as you apply the principles of report writing organization and logic. However, these are not the main objectives of this case. The main objective is, rather, to furnish you with certain data that you can use as a foundation for practice in the writing of a report without having to resort to the time-consuming research necessitated by a real business problem.

An insulation installer, ABC Insulation Company, is interested in establishing a service outlet in Rockford, Nebraska. You have been asked to research the feasibility of such a venture. As a result of your research, you have accumulated the following facts:

ABC specializes in insulating residences, both new and old.

Recent concerns over energy costs and energy availability have prompted considerable interest in insulation as an economically sound investment.

Success in Rockford will depend, to a certain extent, on the competition and performance of existing insulation companies.

The range of costs for insulating 3- to 5-bedroom homes is $400 to $1,000.

ABC would need about 360 jobs to break even. Traditionally, about 50 percent of ABC's business is in the reinsulation of older homes. In addition to residences, ABC expects to do some multiple-unit dwellings and commercial buildings.

Data you have collected show the following insulation companies operating in Rockford, with insulation jobs completed as indicated for the previous three years. Figures show insulation of new residences only. Multiple-unit dwellings would add approximately 20 percent to these figures.

Company	Year Established	Number of New Residences Served		
		1975	1976	1977
Carlson Heating	1961	350	400	450
Comfort, Inc.	1974	300	300	220
Hallmark Insul. Co.	1969	250	410	480
Maylan Insulation	1949	390	500	560
Detweiler & Sons	1973	310	305	210
Johnson Brothers	1973	250	290	390
(Four other small companies)	1951 to 1975	425	490	550

Supplying or assuming any other information that may be necessary, prepare your report for Mr. R. M. Balsford, of ABC Insulation Company of Omaha, Nebraska. Decide whether your report should be written in the direct or the indirect order. Your report should include a recommendation as to the feasibility of establishing an insulation business in Rockford. Include a letter of transmittal and other parts that would be helpful in a report of this scope.

Appendix A

Even though chapter 4 defines pronouns and the chart in chapter 5 lists the personal pronouns, we need to understand certain other rules about pronouns before we can use them with complete confidence.

In addition to the personal pronouns, our language includes *relative pronouns* (who, whom, which, that, whoever, whomever, whichever, whatever); *interrogative pronouns* (who, whom, which, what); *indefinite pronouns* (another, anyone, each, either, everyone, no one, nothing); *demonstrative pronouns* (these, those); and the *intensive* and *reflexive pronouns* (myself, yourself, himself, themselves, ourselves, herself). Some general guidelines for the use of these pronouns may help you to use them correctly and to apply the proper pronoun required in your writing.

The *relative pronoun* takes the place of the noun in the clause it introduces and connects that clause with the rest of the sentence. This pronoun changes form to indicate number, person, and case. The number and person of relative pronouns may be seen in the following sentence.

The request came from Mr. Perkins who is in Seat 5.
The request came from the three students who are in Row 3.

In these two sentences, we have the same relative pronoun, *who,* but different verbs. In the first sentence, *who* is singular since its antecedent is *Mr. Perkins.* In the second sentence, *who* is plural since its antecedent is *students.*

One of the employees who are on vacation is supposed to call the office on Wednesday morning.

This kind of sentence requires that we look carefully to see the relationship between the words. The relative pronoun *who* is plural since its antecedent is *employees;* therefore, the verb is *are.* The second verb, *is,* is singular because its subject is *one.* Your logic will help you to see that we are saying many employees *are* on vacation, and one *is* supposed to call.

More About Pronouns

Now notice the difference in the number of the relative pronoun when we insert the word *only* before *one*.

> Mary is one of the employees who are going on vacation.
> Mary is the only one of the employees who is going on vacation.

In this last example, the singular pronoun *one* is considered to be the antecedent.

Interrogative pronouns ask questions. They are in the same form as the relative pronouns (who, whom, which, what) but differ in their function.

> Who will volunteer for the assignment?
> What is the name of the book you returned?

The interrogative pronouns do not determine the number or person of the verb. For sentences beginning with these pronouns, find the real subject and make the verb agree with it. Or, determine the number and person of the pronoun by referring to its antecedent. This same rule applies for the words *where, here,* and *there.*

> What **is** the **condition** of the patient in Room 202?
> What **are** your **reasons** for rejecting our offer?
> Who **is** the **president** of that company?
> Who **are** the new **members** of the committee?
> Here **are** the **invoices** we thought were lost.
> Here **is** the **report** about which you asked.
> There **are** two **sides** to every story.
> There **is** only **one** right answer to the question.

An *expletive* is a word such as *it* or *there* that introduces the verb and stands for the real subject. The expletive *it* is singular and requires a singular verb even though the real subject is plural. The expletive *there* is singular or plural according to the subject that follows.

> It is arguments like those that are destroying our morale.
> It is his choice to wait until next month for the vacation.
> There are five people waiting outside to see you.
> There is a letter in the mailbox.

Avoiding the use of these expletives will usually improve your writing style. Notice the smoother construction that results when the above sentences are rewritten without the expletive.

Arguments like those are destroying our morale.
His choice is to wait until next month for the vacation.

or

He chose to wait until next month for the vacation.
Five people are waiting outside to see you.
A letter is in the mailbox.

The *indefinite pronouns* were described in chapter 5. You should remember that most indefinite pronouns are singular in meaning; therefore, they take singular verbs.

Another person is . . . .
Anyone has the ability to . . . .
Each mother will present her son . . . .
No one has said anything to her . . . .

Demonstrative pronouns refer to antecedents that have been expressed or clearly implied. They may serve either as pronouns or as adjectives.

These are the runners who finished the race.   (Pronoun)
Please bring me **those** reports.   (Adjective)

The personal pronoun *them* should never be used as an adjective. Use the demonstratives instead.

Not: Tell them people the hearing will be at 3 P.M.
But: Tell those people the hearing will be at 3 P.M.
Or: Tell them the hearing will be at 3 P.M.

Intensive and *reflexive pronouns* are compound personal pronouns. This means that they are formed by combining two words into a single word. These words as intensive pronouns are used to intensify or emphasize a meaning. Although they are similar to appositives in their function, they are not set off by commas.

The president **himself** gave the order.
I **myself** took the report to the supervisor.
"I will do it **myself**," said the frustrated supervisor.

The reflexive pronoun may appear as the direct object of a verb, the object of a preposition, the indirect object of a verb, or as a predicate nominative.

He taught himself how to ski.	(Direct object)
She did all of the research by herself.	(Object of the preposition)
They bought themselves a new car.	(Indirect object)
She is just not herself since the accident.	(Predicate nominative)

One of the common errors in the use of the reflexive pronouns is the incorrect substitution of these words for the shorter personal pronouns.

Not: Myself and five friends are going to Las Vegas.
But: Five friends and I are going to Las Vegas.
Not: When you finish, give copies of the balance sheet to Linda Rogers and myself.
But: When you finish, give copies of the balance sheet to Linda Rogers and me.

One reason for this kind of mistake seems to be the writer's uncertainty as to whether to choose the objective or the nominative case for the personal pronoun. This kind of writer seems to think that the problem is settled using the reflexive pronoun, *myself,* which seems to fit both the nominative and the objective case.

Another problem you should guard against is the careless use of certain incorrect forms of these pronouns. These include:

The use of hisself instead of himself.
The use of theirselves instead of themselves.

This additional background in pronouns should help you to apply the proper word in most of your writing.

Mood

An additional property of verbs that deserves attention is *mood.* An understanding of this property will help you to achieve subtle but rather important shades of meaning in communication.

Mood is, in many ways, a form of paralanguage. Here the emphasis is on *how* something is said rather than on *what* is said. By understanding the uses of mood, we can determine how the writer regards the thought he is expressing—in other words, *how* he is saying it. The three moods are *indicative, imperative,* and *subjunctive.*

The *indicative mood* is used to make statements or to ask questions. It is the one most commonly used since most of our communications seem to require the expression of thought in this manner. Because it is so frequently used, we have little or no difficulty with it.

The game was played on Astroturf.
When will classes begin next term?
Classes will begin on January 4.
The weather is unpredictable in the spring.

The *imperative mood* is used to express commands, requests, and suggestions. Since some one or some thing is to receive the imperative (the command, for example), the subject of the sentence is often understood rather than expressed. Some examples of the imperative mood are:

Put the books on the desk.　　　(*You,* the subject of the sentence, is understood.)

Go to the meeting in my place.　　(*You* go to the . . .)

Return the folders to the file　　(*You* return . . .)
cabinets.

Often, writers or speakers will use the indicative mood to communicate an idea that would be best expressed in the imperative mood.

Indicative:　　　　I would like to have you submit the report by the end of the month.

Imperative:　　　　Submit the report by the end of the month.

Perhaps the writer or speaker uses the indicative mood to be polite or diplomatic. In some instances this may be the best attitude to reflect; the more direct approach, however, may communicate better. Use of the imperative mood helps the reader, too. Using it results in writing that is shorter, crisper, and easier to understand than that written in the indicative mood. Compare the instructions given in the following paragraphs:

Indicative mood predominates:

The address should be typed in block form, and should be even with the left margin. Single-spaced typing and open punctuation should be used. The address should be started five to eight lines below the date. The typist should proofread carefully.

Imperative mood:

> Type the address in block form, even with the left margin. Use single-spacing and open punctuation. Start the address five to eight lines below the date.

The *subjunctive mood* is used to express a supposition implying the contrary (contrary to fact), a mere supposition, or a wish.

> If I **were** going to town, you could ride with me.

> (The writer is saying that he is not going to town—the idea is contrary to fact.)

> If I **were** he, I would suggest an alternative plan.
> **Had** you made reservations earlier, your accommodations would have been satisfactory.
> He acted as if he **were** the president.

While it may not be critical to remember the exact definition of each of these moods, a knowledge of their significant differences will help you to communicate your ideas more clearly and more precisely. The careful writer will achieve this clarity and precision by refraining from writing any sentences that reflect a shift in the mood of the sentences. A shift in mood is confusing to the reader because the writer shows an inconsistent point of view.

> Stack the morning mail on my desk, then the filing from the previous day should be completed.

> (This construction shows a shift from the imperative mood to the indicative mood.)

> Stack the morning mail on my desk, then complete the filing from the previous day.

> (This sentence uses the imperative mood consistently.)

Appendix B

The spelling of words in the English language varies so greatly that it would be a misnomer to refer to spelling *rules*. Too many variations of rules exist for us to depend solely upon a rigid spelling procedure. However, we will not have to depend totally upon memory to spell our words if we adhere to certain helpful *guidelines*. The guidelines presented in this unit are included for your assistance in determining the correct spelling of selected groups of words. Learn these guidelines, memorize the spelling of various other troublesome words, and you will have overcome a very significant obstacle to correctness in writing.

Guideline No. 1 Use *i* before *e* except after *c*. Exceptions to this include beige, deity, height, heist, heir, leisure, neighbor, veil, either/neither, feign, feint, feisty. (Note that most of these exceptions contain the "ay" sound.)

Guideline No. 2 Merely add the suffix (ing, able, ible, etc.) if the word ends in a consonant that is preceded by a combination of two vowels.

ail	plus	ing	equals	ailing
veil	plus	ing	equals	veiling
sail	plus	ed	equals	sailed
foul	plus	ed	equals	fouled

We can add only the suffix if the word ends in two or more consonants.

act	plus	ing	equals	acting
add	plus	ing	equals	adding
calm	plus	ed	equals	calmed
dress	plus	ed	equals	dressed
howl	plus	ing	equals	howling

Guideline No. 3 The final *e* of a word should be dropped if the suffix begins with a vowel.

abuse	abusing
bake	baking
hate	hating
move	moving
ice	iced
tape	taping
wince	wincing
write	writing

Guideline No. 4 Do not drop the final *e* if the suffix begins with a consonant.

abate	abatement
choice	choiceness
correlative	correlatively
descriptive	descriptiveness

Guideline No. 5 If a word ends with a consonant and the suffix begins with a vowel, add another consonant if

a) the word is one syllable and the last consonant follows a single vowel.

brag	bragging
drop	dropping
got	gotten
plan	planning

b) it is a two-syllable word ending with a consonant that follows a single vowel, and if the accent is on the last syllable.

admit	admitting
begin	beginning
submit	submitting
occur	occurred

Guideline No. 6 If a word ends with double consonants, do not change the spelling of the root word—merely add the suffix.

add	adding
bill	billing
call	calling
class	classing
fill	filling
sell	selling

Guideline No. 7 Change the *y* to *i* and add *es* if a common noun ends in a *y* that is preceded by a consonant.

anthology	anthologies
company	companies
bibliography	bibliographies

Note: If the *y* is preceded by a vowel, add only an *s*.

attorney	attorneys
valley	valleys

These guidelines represent only a few of the many that are available to help you achieve accuracy in spelling. The more you concentrate on correct spelling, the fewer costly mistakes you will make.

Some "Hard-to-Spell" Words

1. absence
2. accidentally
3. accumulate
4. acquaintance
5. address
6. adherent
7. advice, advise
8. analysis
9. anticipation
10. appropriate
11. assimilate
12. assistance
13. assistant
14. belief
15. believe
16. benefited
17. bibliography
18. canceled
19. capsule
20. chronological
21. column
22. coming
23. commitment
24. competent
25. complementary
    complimentary
26. conscious
27. convenient
28. correspondent
29. counsel, council
30. credibility
31. desirable
32. dimension
33. develop
34. discipline

35. embarrass
36. eminent
37. exhilarate
38. existence
39. explanation
40. facilitate
41. familiar
42. fiery
43. forty
44. grammar
45. guarantee,
    guaranty
46. harass
47. height
48. inoculate
49. intangible
50. interpretation
51. intramural
52. judgment
53. kidnaped
54. language
55. liaison
56. license
57. likable
58. maintenance
59. manufacturer
60. marriage
61. miscellaneous
62. mortgage
63. naive
64. ninety
65. occasion
66. occurrence
67. optimistic
68. orientation

69. parallel
70. persistent
71. personal, personnel
72. physiology
73. potential
74. preceding
75. preempt
76. premise
77. prerogative
78. prevalent
79. principal, principle
80. privilege
81. psychology
82. pursue
83. questionnaire
84. rational, rationale
85. responsible
86. restaurant
87. sizable
88. sparse
89. stationary,
    stationery
90. stereophonic
91. supersede
92. technique
93. tentative
94. thoroughly
95. transition
96. vacuum
97. verbatim
98. volunteer
99. weird
100. writing

Note: Where a dictionary may list more than one accepted spelling for some of these words, this list shows the preferred spelling in each case.

Appendix C

1.	⊓	Raise	11.	⁻/	Hyphen	
2.	⊔	Lower	12.	⬭	Spell out	
3.	[	Move left	13.	] [	Center	
4.	]	Move right	14.	(?)	Query	
5.	⊙	Period	15.	¶	Paragraph	
6.	ʌ or ,/	Comma	16.	no ¶	No paragraph	
7.	⊙ or :/	Colon	17.	stet	Let it stand	
8.	;/	Semicolon	18.	≡ (english)	Capitalize	
9.	˅	Apostrophe	19.	lc	Lower case	
10.	˅	Quotation	20.	ℓ	Delete	

Proofreader Marks

21.	Ref.	Pronoun-antecedent reference not clear to reader
22.	Dir or Ind	Wrong psychological approach (Direct-Indirect)
23.	◠	Close up space
24.	#	Insert space
25.	d m	Dangling modifier
26.	m m	Misplaced modifier
27.	Eup.	Inappropriate euphemism
28.	Jargon	Specialized language that may not be understood by reader
29.	KWR	Key word repetition in the same sentence or paragraph may not be appropriate
30.	Trans.	Linking word or phrase needed for transition between ideas

387

31.	*Clarity*	Message may not be clear to the reader
32.	*N. P.*	Ideas expressed are not parallel grammatically
33.	*Neg.*	Negative wording may be offensive to reader
34.	∪ (re c(i)eve)	Transpose (May use *tr*)
35.	*Red.*	Redundancy
36.	*Sin.*	Sincerity may be questioned by reader
37.	*S. I.*	Awkward split infinitive
38.	*Unity*	Sentence or message lacks unity
39.	*Vague*	Ideas not clearly stated
40.	*Viewpoint*	The message has writer viewpoint
41.	*W. C.*	Word choice can be improved for better effect
42.	*Sp.*	Spelling error (May be circled)
43.	*Proof*	Proofreading error (May be circled)

Abbreviations

States & Territories	ZIP	Common	Business Terms	
Alabama	AL	Ala.	a/c, acct.	account
Alaska	AK	Alas.	a.m.	before noon
Arizona	AZ	Ariz.	amt.	amount
Arkansas	AR	Ark.	assn., assoc.	association
California	CA	Calif.	asst.	assistant
Canal Zone	CZ	C. S.	c/o	care of
Colorado	CO	Colo.	Co.	company
Connecticut	CT	Conn.	c.o.d.	collect on delivery
Delaware	DE	Del.	Corp.	corporation
District of Columbia	DC	D. C.	dis., disc.	discount
Florida	FL	Fla.	doz.	dozen
Georgia	GA	Ga.	ea.	each
Hawaii	HI		enc., encl.	enclosure
Idaho	ID		etc.	and so forth
Illinois	IL	Ill.	f.o.b.	free on board
Indiana	IN	Ind.	frt.	freight
Iowa	IA		ft.	foot, feet
Kansas	KS	Kans.	Inc.	Incorporated
Kentucky	KY	Ky.	Ltd.	Limited
Louisiana	LA	La.	mdse.	merchandise
Maine	ME		memo	memorandum
Maryland	MD	Md.	Messrs.	Misters
Massachusetts	MA	Mass.	mo.	month
Michigan	MI	Mich.	mfg.	manufacturing
Minnesota	MN	Minn.	no.	number
Mississippi	MS	Miss.	pd.	paid

States & Territories	ZIP	Common		Business Terms	
Missouri	MO	Mo.		P.O.	post office
Montana	MT	Mont.		p.o.	purchase order
Nebraska	NE	Nebr.		p.m.	afternoon
Nevada	NV	Nev.		P.P.	parcel post
				R.R.	rural route
New Hampshire	NH	N. H.			Railroad
New Jersey	NJ	N. J.		sec., secy.	secretary
New Mexico	NM	N. Mex.		treas.	treasurer
New York	NY	N. Y.		wk.	week
North Carolina	NC	N. C.		wt.	weight
North Dakota	ND	N. Dak.		yd.	yard
Ohio	OH			yr.	year
Oklahoma	OK	Okla.		mm	millimeter
Oregon	OR	Oreg.		cm	centimeter
Pennsylvania	PA	Ps.,		m	meter
		Penna.		km	kilometer
Puerto Rico	PR	P. R.			
Rhode Island	RI	R. I.		mg	milligram
South Carolina	SC	S. C.		cg	centigram
South Dakota	SD	S. Dak.		g	gram
Tennessee	TN	Tenn.		kg	kilogram
Texas	TX	Tex.		l	liter
Utah	UT				
Vermont	VT	Vt.			
Virgin Islands	VI	V. I.			
Virginia	VA	Va.			
Washington	WA	Wash.			
West Virginia	WV	W. Va.			
Wisconsin	WI	Wis.			
Wyoming	WY	Wyo.			

A Special Note to Teachers and Students

A recent study conducted by the authors of this text attempted to determine *what specific factors contributed to writing problems of lay people.* The responses are presented below in random order. By studying these items, you may be able to develop a sensitivity to writing problems experienced by the nontechnical person. Understanding the real barriers to and concerns about writing will allow us to direct our efforts to the solution of the problems.

1. I don't know anything about grammar. I never did learn it.
2. Not being able to get started. How do you begin a letter?
3. Failure to look at a situation from the other person's point of view.
4. Not being able to present ideas in a logical, easy-to-follow format.
5. Lack of cohesiveness.
6. Not taking enough time to do it.
7. Lack of continuity—don't use transitions when I should.

8. Forgetting what I wanted to tell the other person.
9. Omitting important facts.
10. Too long and too wordy.
11. Poor spelling and proofreading.
12. Incompleteness.
13. Bored with having to write.
14. Not a good enough vocabulary.
15. I don't paragraph right.
16. I don't know how to be very creative.
17. I always seem to write too much.
18. Poor sentence structure. (—I think that's what you call it.)
19. Dealing with ideas.
20. My hand can't keep up with my mind.
21. No tact. Too often, I seem to be too abrasive.
22. Too vague.
23. I include too much extraneous information.
24. I don't know how to emphasize certain points in writing.
25. Because of the structured way you have to write, you can't just put the words down the way you would speak them.
26. I have become very self-conscious anymore [sic] when I try to write. At school I would get excited about a paper, and when I got it back from the teacher it would be chopped all to hell. I don't enjoy writing much now.

Appendix D

In the good old days, when your neighbor locked up his castle in an inhospitable manner, you cut down a good, stout tree, trimmed the limbs, turned it into a battering ram, and went calling. But if you have ever swung a battering ram, you know that problems abound—where to catch hold of it, how to keep your toes out from under when your fellow workers decide without warning to knock off for the day and retire to the nearest pub; but most of all, how to get everybody swinging the thing in unison. It is the last problem which takes us to the topic of this text, which, in essence, treats of teamwork within a sentence.

The basic fact is this: Time after time we find that our thoughts include elements which are going in *exactly the same* or in *exactly the opposite* direction. Whenever this happens, we need syntactical teamwork. Not to demand it and use it is as foolish as for one man to try to swing that battering ram all by himself. The analogy goes even further; for just as the battering-ram virtuoso must assemble his assistants, sometimes searching the woods and fields to do so, so must the writer hunt for elements which are parallel and which will gain weight from parallel expression. And just as the battering-ram crew must be sorted out, with persons of equal strength put on each side and adjusted to rhythm, so must parallel elements in a sentence be put into equal grammatical, syntactical and stylistic form. And finally (we may as well squeeze this thing dry), just as so much of the success of a battering-ram party depends on that final whoosh, that culminating followthrough, so the elements in a parallel series should end up with the longest, strongest unit of them all, breaking through the reader's resistance like a fiery part of Apollyon.

Rhetorical flourishes aside, few devices available to the writer of expository prose are so helpful, so frequently applicable, so strengthening to style as parallelism. And one of the pleasant things about it is that we are on our own; we are in the driver's seat. The mere maintenance of order in the parallel structure which we accidentally

Parallelism*

*Source: Linton, Calvin D., *Effective Revenue Writing* (Washington, D.C.: Superintendent of Documents, U.S. Government Printing Office, 1962), pp. 117-29.

compose is drudgery, like the drudgery of keeping all the other aspects of our writing obedient to the rules of correctness; but to seek out opportunities for using parallelism, to juggle the elements until something clicks, then to put the words down and know that we have a living, moving, climactic sentence—this is fun. It gives the same sort of pleasure which we get from operating any other complicated, powerful contrivance. Reader resistance crumbles, ideas which have been skittering about like hysterical puppies come up peacefully and are put on a tandem leash; sentences which have been hiding their meanings like suspicious bookies counting their day's receipts suddenly cast their arms abroad and tell all, conflicting grammatical units kiss and make up—all because of parallelism. I dare hazard the conjecture that at least 75 percent of the most memorable and most quoted passages of literature include parallelism as an important stylistic device.

Parallelism is like something else: It is like a comb drawn through tangled locks. Paragraphs which look hopeless, which suggest that their ideas are so complicated that they must be intuited, not comprehended, can be transformed into neat separate strands and into comely form by drawing through them the ordering comb of parallelism. One of the quickest ways to tell the writing of a man who writes for a living from that of a man who merely makes a living while he writes is to see how much parallelism he uses. Parallelism is basic, for it builds rhythm, and rhythm is basic; it demands order, and order is another word for reason; it adds up to wholeness, and wholeness is the opposite of fragmented dissociation.

If you can stand it, consider parallelism in one last analogical relationship, that of a military review. Bring before your mind's eye the orderly ranks, the similarity of uniforms, the total coordination of a marching army, and compare them to the chaotic confusion of a mob. Many paragraphs are mob scenes when they should be military reviews. Sentences which are all related to one topic are separated from each other; one is dressed in a "loose" uniform, one in a "periodic"; one is simple, the other complex. They belong in the same service; they have the same rank. They should be lined up side by side, but they are scattered like a bunch of recruits in civilian clothes on their first day at camp.

We have said that one does not deal with parallelism successfully simply by correcting all the faulty parallel constructions which grow up like weeds in any first draft. To do so is necessary and honorable, but the writer's real job is to hunt out diligently all the ideas which might profit from parallel expression and line them up. At first, this search will constitute a separate task within the process of revising, for few of us are accustomed to keeping a sharp eye out for potentially parallel units. The task may be done with considerable promise of superficial success if we just keep parallelism in mind as we write, but the full force of parallelism should reach the larger elements. This paragraph should be balanced against that, this interpretation and its implications against the pattern of another interpretation. This means that parallelism which properly permeates an entire report must be planned at the organization stage. The person who begins a long report by grabbing a pencil and sitting down to write the first paragraph cannot expect to make parallelism work for him. It is at the time we are marshaling our facts, making our outline, determining our exact aims, ordering our parts, that ideas which belong side by side show themselves.

The value of parallelism on the surface and in depth is sometimes hard to prove to the skeptical amateur writer. Its absence does not obviously weaken writing which gets its idea across pretty well anyway, and it is sometimes not convincing to insist that the job would be done twice as effectively if parallelism were used. So let's try an experiment.

Just about 200 years ago, Dr. Samuel Johnson produced a dictionary. He did it singlehanded, an incredible feat and one which properly gave him worldwide fame. A few years before, as a poor, unprepossessing scholar, awkward, tic-ridden, and scrofulous, he had turned up in the anterooms of the brilliant, urbane, wealthy Earl of Chesterfield. It was the custom to seek the support of a patron when a literary work was to be undertaken, and the Earl was known to be a man of letters. Johnson, not surprisingly, was not admitted into the Earl's presence, although he returned day after day.

The years went by. The incredible dictionary was on the verge of production. People were starting to praise this astonishing, uncouth, learned, strongminded man. Even the Earl of Chesterfield chimed in. His purpose was obvious: By referring to Johnson's earlier solicitation of him, the Earl hoped to bask in reflected glory. So Johnson wrote a letter to the Earl, one of the most famous in literary history. By its sheer strength of expression it is sometimes said to have dealt the death blow to literary patronage. Whether this is true or not, it is an illustration of what a professional man of letters can do with exposition.

Now to our experiment. In something close to modern jargon, I will compose a paraphrase of the ideas of that letter, carefully avoiding all effective parallelism. Then I will quote the letter as Johnson wrote it. I think you will agree that a large measure of the improvement is due to his deadly use of parallelism.

My Lord,

It has recently been brought to the attention of the undersigned by a representative of the **World** magazine that they are in receipt of two articles of which you are the author in which certain references of an approbationary nature relative to my dictionary are included. It was not anticipated by me that any such communication might be forthcoming, and it is a matter of considerable dubiety as to how to acknowledge such praise, particularly since it has not been my experience to receive such recognition from persons of note.

Some amount of recapitulation might be of service in avoiding undue confusion in this matter. It is a matter of record that the undersigned visited the office of your Lordship, and that it was noticed at that time why your Lordship is so prominent in the better circles. There was, however, so noticeable a lack of encouragement for the undersigned to continue his efforts to secure a personal interview with you that he felt it incompatible with modesty to manifest greater desire than was commensurate with the likelihood of a favorable reception.

There has now elapsed a period totaling seven years since the undersigned undertook to secure an interview with you, and during this period of time he has been continuously engaged in work relative to the dictionary, and he has overcome difficulties so numerous that it would be impossible to catalog them without unduly extending this communication. Suffice it to say, that completion of the dictionary has been accomplished despite the absence of assistance in any area, whether personal, practical, or financial. Such negative response to request for assistance was not anticipated in view of the fact that the undersigned had never had a patron before.

The suspicion not unnaturally arises that a patron is one who habitually extends assistance only at such time as said assistance may no longer be needed. Briefly, acceptability of help such as you at this time offer is contingent upon its being extended at such time as might make it useful, and only under these circumstances may help be considered to be of a kindly nature. In the present case, the help offered by you comes after such a period of delay that it is no longer needed and the undersigned does not desire it. He prefers that the public should realize that he has accomplished his dictionary without help of any kind.

There is still much to be done in the final polishing and publishing of my dictionary, but no disappointment will be felt if, during this period of final work, even less assistance than has already been proffered is extended.
Yours sincerely,

Now hear the original:

My Lord

I have been lately informed by the proprietor of the **World** that two papers in which my **Dictionary** is recommended to the public were written by your Lordship. To be so distinguished is an honor which, being very little accustomed to favors from the great, I know not well how to receive, or in what terms to acknowledge.

When upon some slight encouragement I first visited your Lordship, I was overpowered like the rest of mankind by the enchantment of your address . . .; but I found my attendance so little encouraged that neither pride nor modesty would suffer me to continue it . . .

Seven years, my Lord, have now passed since I waited in your outward rooms or was repulsed from your door, during which time I have been pushing on my work through difficulties of which it is useless to complain, and have brought it at last to the verge of publication without one act of assistance, one word of encouragement, or one smile of favor. Such treatment I did not expect, for I never had a patron before.

Is not a patron, my Lord, one who looks with unconcern on a man struggling for life in the water and, when he has reached ground, encumbers him with help? The notice which you have been pleased to take of my labors, had it been early, had been kind; but it has been delayed till I am indifferent and cannot enjoy it; till I am solitary and cannot impart it; till I am known and do not want it. I hope it is no very cynical asperity not to confess obligations where no benefit has been received, or to be unwilling that the public should consider me as owing that to a patron which Providence has enabled me to do for myself.

Having carried on my work thus far with so little obligation to any favorer of learning, I shall not be disappointed though I should conclude it, if less be possible, with less; for I have long awakened from that dream of hope in which I once boasted myself with so much exultation, my Lord.

Your Lordship's most humble, most obedient servant,

Sam: Johnson.

Incidentally, it might be good practice to go through Johnson's version and underline all parallel constructions. The most deadly, of course, is the second sentence of the fourth paragraph. "The notice which you have been pleased to take . . . ," etc. Notice, too, the sense of rhythm, the smooth flow of the sentence ending ". . . or to be unwilling that the public should consider me as owing that to a patron which Providence has enabled me to do for myself." Note the climactic order of the elements in ". . . delayed till I am indifferent and cannot enjoy it; till I am solitary and cannot impart it; till I am known and do not want it." The last unit speaks softly, but it snaps like a whip.

This particular illustration is 200 years old and the style is formal, but we should not think of parallelism as a device for literary artists only. It is a tool constantly in the hands of the professional writers of exposition—columnists like Walter Lippmann, journalists and essayists like Edmund Wilson, established reporters like John Hightower, writers in special areas like Hanson Baldwin.

The Structure of Parallelism

After our flight into literature, we must return to the workshop. Like all other devices for achieving effectiveness in writing, parallelism operates within rather rigid technical rules. (How nice if we could make our writing good by sheer enthusiasm, by buying a huge pen and writing in one-foot strokes, instead of by learning and practicing and polishing.) The rules emerge from the definition: Elements are parallel when they have the same grammatical and syntactical form, and when they stand side by side within a sentence. Most of the trouble at the mechanical level arises when units which are parallel in meaning are not parallel in form. The simplest way to approach the matter is to list the most common constructions which demand parallelism.

1. Coordinate Conjunctions By their very nature, coordinate conjunctions must unite elements which are parallel in grammar, syntax, logic, and position. The demand is so strident that one rarely sees violation at the simple grammatical and syntactical level, but often at the logical one. We listed several illustrations in Text 3—sentences which join units which are shown, on careful reading, to be logically unrelated.

Let us now note a few purely mechanical defects:

1. The Director told the staff to collect the material and get to work and that the original provisions would apply.
2. Finding the answers to his questions was not difficult, but to convince him of the rightness of them was a superhuman task.

3. All of them were given training in handling investigative reports and how to interpret the conclusions.
4. The careful writer must always plan beforehand, revise carefully, and most important of all, not forget the reader's need.
5. Every statement or conclusion which the investigator makes or reaches is grist for the legal mill.
6. Five of the petitions were approved and denials were handed down in the other three cases.

Here are enough to work on for a moment, and we should begin by observing the usefulness of a visual diagnosis. Sentence No. 1 above, for example, really looks like this:

The Director told the staff:

    a. to collect the material
    b. (to) get to work
    c. that the original provisions would apply.

When exploded like this, the error of the third unit is apparent. Incidentally, the second unit is satisfactory, since the infinitive form does not actually demand that the "*to*" prefix be used. Stylistically, however, it would be smoother to say "to get to work." Correctly, the sentence should run:

The Director told the staff:

    a. **to collect** the material
    b. **to get** to work
    c. **to apply** the original provisions.

This sentence, with its elements in series, illustrates a common and much-sinning form. When a sentence gets quite long, the fact that it consists of units in series is often obscured, particularly if subordinate modifiers are inserted within each unit and if the units are of clause complexity. For example: "Economic facts are much more widely known today than in the past and most people know inflation to be the result of rapidly rising prices and that the supply of goods decreases while pressures to buy build increasing stresses and the value of money is reduced." The comb of parallelism is urgently needed!

Sentence No. 2, above, presents a simpler pattern. The coordinating conjunction "*but*" is trying to join "*finding*" with "*to convince*," and participles won't speak to infinitives. It should read, of course, "*Finding* the answers to his questions was not difficult, but *convincing* him of the rightness of them was a superhuman task."

Sentence No. 3 is similar:

All of them were given training:

    a. in handling . . . and
    b. in interpreting . . . .

This sentence also illustrates a general principle governing the use of parallel construction: It is usually well to repeat the "tag" word (in this sentence, the preposition "*in*") before each parallel unit. No rule can be applied here, since style and rhythm are also affected by such a repetition.

Sentence No. 4 illustrates an error of some refinement. The three elements in parallel form are all in proper grammatical dress, but the third item is negative, with some injury to smoothness. It would be more effective if it read:

The careful writer must always:

    a. **plan** beforehand
    b. **revise** carefully
    c. **remember** the reader's need.

Sentence No. 5 exhibits the ineffectiveness of the "respectively" construction. That is, parallel elements which demand separate idiomatic prepositions or separate verbs should not be lumped together in one place, their respective completions in another. For example: "Every *advance* and *retreat toward* and *from* the goal" should be changed to read "Every *advance toward* and *retreat from* the goal." Even when the complete units are kept together, the style is sometimes awkward: "Every fact *bearing on, significant in,* and *related to* the problem must be kept in mind." (These propositions are idiomatic—their correctness is determined not by logic or grammatical principle but by usage.) But this is better than writing "Every fact bearing, significant, and related on, in, and to the problem . . ."! This is, in effect, what Sentence No. 5 does. To run smoothly, it would have to be rewritten: "Every statement which the investigator makes, and every conclusion which he reaches, is grist for the legal mill."

Sentence No. 6, by changing the subject in the middle of the sentence, violates the unity which "*and*" promises. The coordinator is really trying to join two clauses: "Five of the petitions were approved and three were denied."

We use one or another of the six coordinating conjunctions so casually and frequently that we often fail to check the units joined. Usually our ear catches any gross unbalance, but it is good practice to spend some time just noting exactly what is joined by every coordinating conjunction we use. And we must always be careful to avoid using "*and*" as a sort of glue to hold sentence parts together. The act of coordinating demands both strict logical justification and careful grammar and syntax.

2. Linking Verbs Elementary grammar teaches us that linking verbs demand exact equality between the two units they join. They do not like to join a nominative-case subject to an objective-case predicate noun, although they have often been forced to do so in recent years. They hold the line firmly, however, as they should, except in the common "it is me" situation. Most of the violations of linking-verb parallelism occur in the realm of logic, not grammar. We noted in Text 3 the illogic of declaring that "the performance specification is a question we have not considered" or that "the communications system is a problem which management must solve," since the performance specification is a declarative sentence, not a question, and the communications system may be "large" or "electrical" or "cumbersome" or "efficient," but it is not, by copulative verb definition, a *problem*.

Here is a sentence which balances two substantives, a gerund and an infinitive, but the effect is awkward: "Learning to reel off a rule by heart is not necessarily to master it." Here the units joined by "is" are "learning" and "to master." The writer means this: "*To learn . . .* is not necessarily *to master*." "Merely *to read* the minutes of the meeting is much less effective than *attending* the meeting itself." Should be: "Merely *reading* the minutes. . . ."

3. "Not only . . . but also" The phrase "not only" is a promise which must be fulfilled, and it promises that the idea which follows it will be matched with another idea, equivalent in logic, grammar, and syntax, immediately after the "but also" (sometimes just "but"). As a practical matter, therefore, we should give a glance at every "not only" we write and make sure it is completed in coordinate form.

Here are some examples of violation of the rule.

1. Actually it was not only a matter of excessive expenditure of money and poor planning, because no one had ever attempted to plan the program within available resources.
2. The disadvantages of the reduction were seen not only in the extent to which restrictions were imposed on the use of outside consultants but also it became difficult to maintain the advisory service by mail.
3. This office is in a position not only to provide guidance

and suggestions in the setting up of similar programs but it will also be glad to mail its monthly bulletin to any agency which requests it.

4. The questioning was intended not only to elicit information relevant to the case in point but it was also aimed at securing background material on three other suits which were pending.

5. Not only is he concerned with the moral effect of such decisions but also with the influence of such decisions on future hearings.

6. The new system has not only saved a great deal of duplication; security consciousness has rapidly improved at the same time.

Sentence No. 1 does not really violate parallel structure; it simply fails to make delivery on the second element. After beginning the "not only" form, it concludes by switching to a "because" clause. Moreover, the two main thoughts of the sentence are not parallel in logic. They need an entirely different syntactical package. Perhaps the writer means something like this: "We cannot be said to have spent too much money, because no one had ever figured out what it would cost; nor can we be accused of violating the plan, because we were not given one." That employs parallelism, but not between the two ideas un-equally yoked in the first version.

Sentence No. 2 follows "not only" with a prepositional phrase, "in the extent"; the "but also" is followed by a clause in the passive voice. The matter can be adjusted either way, of course—either by turning the last half into a prepositional phrase or the first into a clause. This would be correct, but perhaps a bit too elaborate: "The disadvantages of the reduction were seen not only *in the extent* to which restrictions were imposed on the use of outside consultants but also *to the degree* that it became difficult to keep up the advisory mail service." (Such a complicated package to communicate a fairly simple thought is un-necessary. As we revise, we should "listen" for such wasteful elaboration and be willing to throw the sentence out and begin from scratch.)

Sentence No. 3 uses the "not only . . . but" construction to perform a function of almost straight coordination. A coordinating conjunction might do the job better—"This office can give guidance and make suggestions in the setting up of similar programs, *and* it is glad to mail its monthly bulletins to any agency which requests them." If the sense of the "not only . . . but" is felt to be important, the construction can be used to join entire clauses when it introduces the sentence: "*Not only* is this office in a position to . . . *but also* it will . . . ."

Sentence No. 4 is easily corrected: "The questioning was intended not only *to elicit* . . . but also *to secure* background material. . . ."

Sentence No. 5 technically violates parallelism in the fact that the "not only" introduces a clause, the "but also" only a prepositional phrase. The purist would insist on this: "He is concerned not only *with the moral effect* but also *with the influence* of such decisions on future hearings." The original version, however, is quite satisfactory for ordinary, weekday work.

Sentence No. 6 is a fraud. We make our down payment on the strength of the preliminary "not only," but we get only a semicolon in return. It is another case of an abandoned parallelism, this time a badly needed parallelism. The sentence cannot, however, be cured by the mere insertion of "but also" in front of "security consciousness." That would make it sound as if "duplication" and "security consciousness" were being joined. It was probably because of this problem that the writer threw in the semicolon and the clause. He meant to say: "Not only has the new system prevented much duplication but it has at the same time also rapidly improved security consciousness."

4. "The reason . . . is because" Perhaps this construction does not deserve listing as a separate item, but errors occur frequently enough to demand a special warning. The principle governing the form is that of the linking verb. "Reason" is a substantive; it will not mix on equal terms with a "because" clause. Consequently, a sentence like this: "The reason for his inadequacy is because his legal training was interrupted for 3 years" should be changed to read: "*The reason* for his inadequacy is *the fact* that his legal training was interrupted for 3 years." Or: *The reason* for his inadequacy *is the interruption* of . . . ."

5. "Rather than" By logic and long habit, "rather than" yearns for parallelism as the hart pants for the waterbrook, but it is often frustrated. Only when a sentence is short and simple can the phrase be fairly confident that all will work out well. We would not be likely to write, "He was inclined to act rather than talking." But we often see constructions like this: "He should have accepted the post promptly and without comment rather than complaining about the manner in which it was offered to him." The second part should, of course, read ". . . rather than complained . . . ." This construction can sound awkward even when correct if the separation between the two parallel elements is too great, particularly if the verb is compound and if the auxiliary part of the verb is not repeated. In the sentence just quoted, for example, the "have" must be carried over in our minds to "complained," and it is a pretty long portage. A blanket principle of good writing is that a construction which *sounds* incorrect must be revised even if it disobeys no rule of grammar.

Here are some examples of violation of the "rather than" rule:

1. This office wished to assist in the movement rather than acting as a drag upon it.
2. Under our normal rules of procedure, the question should have been postponed until approval had been received from the Planning Section rather than being acted on at the first meeting.
3. Rather than turning our backs on the need for expansion, we should confront the issue squarely and begin to plan for its solution.

Sentence No. 1 tries to balance "to assist" with "acting." It should read, "This office wished *to assist* in the movement rather than *to act* as a drag upon it." This corrects the mistake, but it slightly tampers with logic. The antithesis is not exact. The desire to assist is not balanced over against any desire to be a drag. In other words, the "rather than" construction is not well adapted to the thought; an entirely different sentence is needed.

In sentence No. 2, "been postponed" is balanced over against "being acted," with some violence to style and exactness. Again, the "rather than" form is probably not the best. "Under our rules of procedure, the question should have been postponed pending approval by the Planning Section, not acted on at the first meeting."

Sentence No. 3 indirectly introduces us to a phenomenon: "instead of" appears to carry much the same meaning as "rather than," but it does not demand parallelism. It functions as a preposition and should be substituted for "rather than" whenever the situation demands it. Sentence 3 would then read: "*Instead of turning* our backs on the need for expansion, *we should confront* . . . ." The force of "rather than" is *comparison;* the force of "instead of" is *exception.*

"As well as" follows the same general rules as "rather than." "He directs the statistics branch as well as advises (not advising) the new employees."

6. Unannounced "and which" constructions   The phrase "and which" demands a previous "which" construction as its parallel companion. We cannot correctly say, "The second question in this case, much more important and much more difficult to decide, and which we had previously met to discuss, may now be bypassed." This construction often signals a sentence which is trying to say too much. There are probably two full statements here. "The second question which we met to discuss is much more important and more difficult to decide. Now, however, it may be bypassed."

The same principle applies to "but which" clauses. "It is a group established only 3 months, but which has already done much to justify our confidence in it." Such a construction may be corrected by repeating the subject or by using a pronoun in place of it: (". . . but it had . . ."). To avoid falling into the error, we should check every coordinating conjunction which appears before "who" or "which" to make sure that there is a preceding *who-* or *which-*clause.

The Rhetorical Effect of Parallelism

Structurally and logically, parallelism groups ideas which belong together and displays their unity and relevance. Elaborate parallelism, however, is not appropriate to expository writing. Lincoln did well to pack his short address at Gettysburg with parallelism, but the same quality which makes that speech memorable might make ordinary prose objectionably artificial. "But, in a larger sense, we cannot dedicate, we cannot consecrate, we cannot hallow this ground . . . . The world will little note nor long remember what we say here; but it can never forget what they did here." Simple, natural parallelism, however, is always beneficial, and against such there is no law. "Too little too late" did yeoman service during World War II, and continues to come out of retirement occasionally. And how simple and pleasant is this little line from a worthy of the 17th century who had just suffered through an overlong sermon: "It is a wonder to me how men can preach so little and so long, so long a time and so little matter." (Actually, this is a refined form of parallelism called "chiasmus," in which the order of the first element is inverted in the second, "so little . . . so long, so long . . . so little . . . .")

Two elementary considerations determine the order in which parallel elements should be expressed: logic and rhetorical effect. If the elements involve a logical progression or a time sequence ("The suggestion will be carefully studied by the supervisor, by the local committee, and finally by the Director himself") or a sequence of climactic development ("His statements show him to be inexact, careless, and perhaps even untruthful"), these considerations will determine their order. Apart from these two overruling conditions, sentence smoothness will help decide the issue. As a general rule, the longest of a series of parallel units should come last. "I am not sure where we can get *the space, the instructors,* or any of *the essential training aids.*" A sharp, short final element can be used for emphasis or irony: "From his own explanation of his job, it is not clear whether he should be put in charge of a research project, made the chief editor of the section, or fired."

But apart from making some comment on the nature and structure of parallelism, we can be of only slight help to the writer. Everyone must experiment for himself and decide where and how to use it. Beyond the matter of mere correctness, parallelism is a stylistic device, and it expresses our personality as much as it does our craftsmanship. It must not be permitted to defeat itself by being overused. "He that speaks must not look to speak thus every day," wrote Owen Felltham in 1628. And the same worthy also notes: "A combed writing will cost both sweat and the rubbing of the brain. And combed I wish it, not frizzled nor curled."

Appendix E

Examples of Report Parts

A STUDY OF THE EFFECT OF THREE DIFFERENT METHODS

OF PRESENTING

A REVIEW OF WRITING PRINCIPLES AND GRAMMAR TO

BUSINESS COMMUNICATION STUDENTS

A Term Paper

Presented to
Dr. Omar C. Bridges
University of Tallahassee

In Partial Fulfillment of the
Requirements for
OA-451

by
Richard C. Corlett

August 1977

Figure E.1 Example of title page with four-part arrangement

TABLE OF CONTENTS

iii

Figure E.2 Example of table of contents—Style A arrangement and organization

TABLE OF CONTENTS

iii

Figure E.3   Example of
table of contents—Style B
arrangement and organiza-
tion

The students enrolled in the business letter writing classes at the University of Florida and the University of Washington were surveyed to determine the extent of their preparation for writing as a result of their English classes. The study showed that 50 percent of the students at the University of Florida and 40 percent of the students at the University of Washington felt that the freshman English courses gave students "little or insufficient training and constructive help in actual composition."[34] Many of the students wished that more emphasis had been given to grammar and organization rather than mere exposure to these elements through assigned readings.[35] In spite of the recognition that graduates should have the ability to use the fundamentals of English, this ability is often not acquired in the English composition courses.

When students enroll in a business communications course, the question of what to do about their obvious grammar deficiencies is handled in a variety of ways. One method is to assume that the problem does not really exist:

> Since business communications should be one of the final courses the student takes, the emphasis should be on more effective means of communicating. Although the course normally includes some spelling, grammar, and mechanics, it must be assumed that the student has had several years of instruction in English and should know these basics.[36]

---

[34] Herta Murphy and C.W. Wilkinson, "Surveys Within Our Business Writing Courses," *The ABWA Bulletin*, XXV (March, 1961), 24.

[35] Ibid.

[36] John D. Hall, "What's In a Course In Business Communications?" *The Balance Sheet*, LIV (February, 1973), 199.

Figure E.4 Example of report page with footnote sample

A problem which many business communications teachers face is that of adding any new content to a course which is already filled with other elements of business communication topics. The average enrollment in a business communications class ranges from 20-29 students.[40] Because of the large amount of writing which should be included in a class of this nature, the recommended size is 18.[41] Gerfen states that the question is not whether it is worthwhile to teach students the fundamentals of writing, but rather, "how to accomplish this task, and who is to do it."[42]

Harder observes that there is not sufficient time in a semester course to cover all the important aspects of business communications. He looks forward to the development of programmed learning texts which will teach the English fundamentals to students enrolled in the business communications course.[43]

The importance of good English usage is expressed by a number of writers of textbooks. Shurter writes:

> To the letter writer, a knowledge of correct English usage is a basic and minimum skill. Not only do grammatical errors distract his reader, but ignorance of correct usage interferes constantly with the task of writing.[44]

---

[40]Murphy and Peck, "Trends of Business Writing Courses," p. 11.

[41]Lord, "Business Writing Courses in U.S. Colleges and Universities," p. 21.

[42]Gerfen, "The Status of Business Writing," p. 4.

[43]Virgil E. Harder, "Communication Theory: Should It Be In a Business Writing Course?" _The Journal of Business Communication_, VII (Winter, 1969), 42.

[44]Robert L. Shurter, _Effective Letters in Business_, 2nd ed. (New York: McGraw-Hill Book Company, Inc., 1954), p. 36.

Figure E.5 Example of report page showing abbreviated references for previously listed footnotes

Chapter 4

SUMMARY, FINDINGS, CONCLUSIONS, AND RECOMMENDATIONS

The purpose of this study was to determine the effects of a course in writing principles and grammar presented by three different methods to business communication students. The effects studied included an attempt to determine whether a practical understanding of writing principles and grammar can be assimilated as part of the traditional work of a one-semester business communications course without sacrificing the learning to be gained in the traditional course.

This chapter includes a summary of the steps involved in the development and execution of this study, a listing of the findings of the study, conclusions resulting from the findings of this study, and some recommendations for implementing classroom procedure, additional testing, and research in these areas of business communication.

SUMMARY

A review of literature on the relationship between business communication and effective writing principles indicated that educators and businessmen recognize the need for understanding and using good grammar skills. Businessmen stated that employees who lack these skills are not as likely to be promoted as those who have the ability to speak and write effectively. Educators recognize the importance of these skills and acknowledge that students are generally deficient in their understanding and use of grammar and punctuation. The courses only. These students also achieved significantly higher scores than did those

Figure E.6   Example of
report page showing
sample of summary begin-
ning for chapter

students who had access to the effective writing principles text but were not required to study it.

    3. There will be no significant difference in the standard of performance in grammar proficiency achieved by business communication students who have taken the traditional course when compared with students who have studied the effective writing principles text and received reinforcement along with the traditional course.

    This hypothesis was rejected. The study showed that there was a significant difference in the standard of performance in grammar proficiency achieved by business communication students who took the traditional course when compared with students who studied and received reinforcement of the effective writing principles along with the traditional course. The students who studied and received this reinforcement of the effective writing principles achieved significantly higher scores on the measurement of grammar proficiency than did the students of any other group.

    4. There will be no significant difference in the standard of performance in the traditional course work achieved by business communication students in the traditional course class when compared with students who have

        a. had access to the effective writing principles text but followed the traditional course.

        b. studied the effective writing principles text along with the traditional course.

        c. studied the effective writing principles text and received reinforcement along with the traditional course.

Figure E.7   Example of report page showing reference to consideration of hypotheses

Glossary

The following list of terms and definitions provides a quick and easy reference to key words used throughout the text. Each term is accompanied with a brief definition that is expanded upon in its appropriate chapter.

Abstract Words Those words relatively high on the abstraction ladder—those words that are generally harder to "visualize" and harder to understand than concrete words

Abstraction Ladder The device for categorizing and classifying words according to their level of difficulty

Acting The overt or covert action in response to a message

Active Voice The word order showing the subject of the clause performing the action (for example, *He told her . . . .*)

Adjective A word that modifies nouns and pronouns

Adverb A word that modifies verbs, adjectives, and other adverbs

Appositive A word or phrase which is placed beside another word or phrase to rename or explain the first

Attention Line A part of the letter format which serves to direct the correspondence to a particular individual or unit within the organization

Business Jargon Specialized language known only to those who are familiar with practices, procedures, or situations in business

Case

The property or characteristic of nouns and pronouns which shows their relationship to other parts of the sentence

Circumlocution

The act of using a particularly confusing combination of words with the intent of "writing around" a situation or of avoiding it entirely

Clause

A group of related words having both a subject and a verb

Communication

The transfer of meaning and understanding from one person to another

Communication Process

The steps involved in communicating with others—the basic steps include *ideating, encoding, transmitting, receiving, decoding,* and *acting*

Complex Sentence

A sentence that contains one independent clause and one or more dependent clauses

Complimentary Close

The courteous word or phrase that closes the letter

Compound Adjective

A modifier composed of two or more adjectives that collectively modify a given word

Compound-Complex Sentence

A sentence that contains at least two independent clauses and one or more dependent clauses

Compound Sentence

A sentence that contains two or more independent clauses and any number of phrases

Compromise

The method of resolving conflict by seeking an attitude of "give and take" from the conflict participants

Concrete Words	Those words relatively low on the abstraction ladder; those that are generally easier to "visualize" and, therefore, easier to understand
Conflict Resolution	The settling of a conflict which arises because of differences in perception
Confrontation	The method of resolving conflict by using the problem-solving technique—a consideration of the facts of the conflict and a collective effort to choose the best alternatives available
Conjunction	A word that connects other words, phrases, or clauses in a sentence
Conjunctive Adverb	A modifier that serves to connect two related independent clauses
Coordinate Conjunction	A word that serves to connect two ideas of equal rank
Dangling Modifier	A modifying phrase that cannot logically modify the subject of the main clause in the sentence
Dateline	Refers to the line on which the letter date is typed
Decoding	The receiver process of assigning meaning to symbols
Deductive Approach	The psychology of a letter that presents the essence of the message at the beginning and follows with explanatory information; also known as the direct approach
Dependent Clause	A group of related words that contain a subject and verb but relies on another clause to complete its meaning
Dependent Variable	The characteristic which is being measured as a part of the study

Dewey Decimal System	A system of classification used by some libraries in recording and shelving publications; a system based on "first-digit" format
Dynamic	The characteristic of reality that implies the changing nature of all animate and inanimate things
Elite Type	Refers to the size of the type keys—elite type uses twelve spaces to the horizontal inch
Empathy	The feeling of understanding that is obtained by projecting one's self into the role of the other person
Emphatic Form	A companion form of the verb *do* used to add emphasis
Encoding	The sender process of assigning meaning to symbols
Euphemism	A word or group of words used to make an idea or situation less objectionable than it really is
First-Phase Collection Letter	The collection letter written to a debtor reminding him or her that the account is overdue
Forcing	The method of resolving conflict by imposing authority upon the participants in the conflict; a unilateral decision
Future Perfect Tense	Refers to an action or condition that will be completed by some specific time in the future
Future Tense	Indicates the time of the action or condition to be in the future
Gerund	A verbal ending in *ing* which functions as a noun; a gerund phrase that functions as the object of a preposition may serve as an

adjective or adverb; the gerund or gerund phrase may also serve as the subject of a clause

Hypothesis	A tentative explanation or a solution to the problem which is being studied
Ideating	The development of the idea (message) that is to be transmitted
Independent Clause	A group of related words that expresses a complete thought and could, by itself, function as a complete sentence
Independent Variable	Also known as the experimental variable; a variable which is fixed by the limits of the study or experiment
Inductive Approach	The psychology of a letter that presents the essence of the message after the necessary explanation has been provided; also known as the indirect approach
Infiniteness	The characteristic of reality that refers to the unlimited nature of that which exists
Infinitive	A verbal which is a simple, unchanged form of a verb that expresses action or a state of being; does not function as a verb, but rather as a noun, adjective, or adverb
Inside Address	Refers to the name and mailing address of the addressee and appears on the letter itself
Interjection	A word used to express or make an exclamation
Intermediate-Phase Collection Letter	The letter written to debtors after they have not responded favorably to the first-phase collection letter
Interoffice Memorandum	A written communication developed by and for workers within the same organization

Kinesics	The classification of nonverbal communication that pertains to how we use "body language" to communicate
Knowledge of Results	The information one has regarding the results of expended effort
Last-Phase Collection Letter	Those letters written to debtors as a last resort and after they have failed to respond favorably to the previous communications
Letter Format	Refers to the actual placement of the typewritten word; most familiar formats include the *full-blocked, modified block,* and the *AMS simplified*
Letter Placement	Refers to the actual physical location of the printed matter in relation to established margins
Letter Tone	The "attitude" reflected in the message and determined by the specific words chosen by the writer
Library of Congress	A system of classifying written documents; uses letters of the alphabet rather than numbers for the main classification
MBO	Management by Objectives; refers to managing an organization by sharing goal-setting activities with subordinates
Mean	The arithmetic average
Measures of Central Tendency	The three kinds of "averages" about which the scores or observations in a test may be grouped
Median	The midpoint of all the scores when they are arranged in ascending or descending order
Message Unity	See "Unity"

Misplaced Modifier	A modifier that is placed in such a way that it actually modifies the wrong word or phrase in the sentence
Mode	The score that occurs with the greatest frequency in a group of scores
Modifier	A word or group of words that in some way changes, clarifies, or limits another word or group of words
Nominative Case	The case used primarily to name subjects of verbs or as a predicate complement after a linking verb
Nonrestrictive Modifier	The group of modifying words considered not essential to the meaning of the sentence; these words are set off from the rest of the sentence by commas
Nonverbal Communication	The communication of messages without the use of verbal symbols
Noun	A word that names a person, place, thing, or quality
Number	The characteristic of a word that tells whether it is singular or plural
Objective Case	The case used to name words that function as objects; these words may be the objects of verbs, verbals, or prepositions
Paralanguage	The classification of nonverbal communication that pertains to *how* we say something rather than to *what* we say
Parallel Structure	Sentence structure designed to present ideas of equal rank and importance in similar grammatical form
Parenthetical Expression	An expression that gives additional or qualifying information about some other element in the sentence

Participle	A verb form which functions as an adjective; this element, like infinitives and gerunds, is a member of the larger classification known as verbals
Passive Voice	The word order showing the subject being acted upon (for example, *He was told by her . . . .*)
Past Perfect Tense	Refers to an action in the past that occurred prior to another past action
Past Tense	Indicates the time of the action or condition to be in the past
Personal Distractions	Those physical and psychological distractions that inhibit effective listening
Phrase	A group of related words not having a subject or verb
Pica Type	Refers to the size of the type keys—pica type uses ten spaces to the horizontal inch
Population	The complete set of individuals or measurements which have some common characteristic
Possessive Case	The case used to show possession
Present Perfect Tense	Refers to some action just completed or to some action which started in the past and continues into the present
Present Tense	Indicates the time of the action or condition to be the present
Preposition	A word used to connect or show relationship between nouns or pronouns and some other word or words in a sentence
Presets	Predispositions we have about a particular topic which result in closed minds and an

unwillingness to consider matters contrary to our immediate beliefs

Primary Objective The specific reason for a particular communication; to convey a specific message

Primary Research The data-gathering method of obtaining information directly from the original source; usually accomplished through interviews, questionnaires, direct observation, or from experiments

Progressive Form The form used to tell the reader that action referred to is, has been, or will be moving forward, or progressing, through the time indicated; this verb tense formed by adding *ing* to the verb of the sentence

Pronoun A word that takes the place of a noun

Pronoun-Antecedent Agreement The agreement (harmony) between the pronoun and its antecedent (the word it is referring to) in number and person

Proxemics The classification of nonverbal communication that pertains to how we use space to communicate attitudes

Random Sample Refers to a selection process by which every individual in the population has an equal opportunity of selection

Ratio An expression of the relationship between two values; is shown as the quotient of one value being divided by the other

Readability Level The intellectual level at which the communication is written (a measure of difficulty)

Reader Viewpoint The orientation of the writing that puts interests and/or concerns of the reader before those of the writer

Reality That which exists in the real world

Receiving	The actual perception of the message that has been transmitted
Redundancy	The unnecessary repetition of an idea in a message
Reliability	Refers to the quality of a test to measure consistently what it does measure
Restrictive Modifier	The group of modifying words considered essential to the meaning of the clause
Salutation	Letter part which addresses a particular reader or group within the organization; also serves to introduce the element of courtesy
Sample	A subset of the research population
Secondary Objective	The "other" message inherent in all good business communications—the goodwill factor
Secondary Research	The data-gathering method of obtaining information from any source which did not originate with the researcher
Self-Interest	Refers to the tendency for individuals to perceive things in relation to their own needs—a barrier to effective listening
Sentence	A word or group of words expressing a complete thought
Silent Message	The communication which is achieved without the use of verbal symbols
Simple Sentence	A complete thought that contains only one independent clause, but may contain many phrases, a compound subject or verb, and/ or many modifiers
Sincerity	The quality of writing that encourages believability

Smoothing	The method of resolving conflict by playing down the differences between participants
Speaker Delivery	The various techniques a speaker uses when delivering a message in oral form
Subject Line	This notation indicates the subject of the message in abbreviated form
Subject-Verb Agreement	The agreement (harmony) between the subject and verb of a sentence in number and person
Synopsis	A summary or "thumbnail" sketch of the larger report
Techniques of De-emphasis	Those devices used to subordinate ideas to others in a given context
Techniques of Emphasis	Those devices used to make ideas stand out above other information within a given context
Title Fly	A page of a report containing only the title
Transmitting	The sending of the message (speaking, writing, gesturing)
Tendency to Evaluate	The barrier to effective listening that involves listeners who evaluate a message prematurely—before the entire message has been transmitted
Trite Expressions	Worn-out words and phrases which have long since lost their meaning and sincerity
Uniqueness	The characteristic of reality that refers to the individual nature of things; implies that no two or more things in the real world are exactly alike

Unity	Refers to a single purpose; sentences, paragraphs, and entire letters should contain this quality of good writing; unity implies the absence of nonrelated material
Universe	The complete set of individuals or measurements which have some common characteristic
Validity	Refers to the quality of a test to measure what it claims to measure
Variable	A property or characteristic which is subject to change
Verb	A word used to express action or a condition of being
Verb Tense	The property of a verb which indicates the time of the event or condition being referred to
Verbal	A verb form which functions as a modifier or subject rather than as a verb
Withdrawing	The act of noninvolvement as it pertains to the techniques of resolving conflict
Writer Viewpoint	The orientation of the writing that puts the interests and/or concerns of the writer before those of the reader

Index